COME As You Are

BETWEEN MEN ~ BETWEEN WOMEN
LESBIAN AND GAY STUDIES

LILLIAN FADERMAN AND LARRY GROSS, EDITORS

Edward Alwood, *Straight News: Gays, Lesbians, and the News Media*

Corinne E. Blackmer and Patricia Juliana Smith, editors, *En Travesti: Women, Gender Subversion, Opera*

Alan Bray, *Homosexuality in Renaissance England*

Joseph Bristow, *Effeminate England: Homoerotic Writing After 1885*

Claudia Card, *Lesbian Choices*

Joseph Carrier, *De Los Otros: Intimacy and Homosexuality Among Mexican Men*

John Clum, *Acting Gay: Male Homosexuality in Modern Drama*

Gary David Comstock, *Violence Against Lesbians and Gay Men*

Laura Doan, editor, *The Lesbian Postmodern*

Allen Ellenzweig, *The Homoerotic Photograph: Male Images from Durieu/Delacroix to Mapplethorpe*

Lillian Faderman, *Odd Girls and Twilight Lovers: A History of Lesbian Life in Twentieth-Century America*

Linda D. Garnets and Douglas C. Kimmel, editors, *Psychological Perspectives on Lesbian and Gay Male Experiences*

Richard D. Mohr, *Gays/Justice: A Study of Ethics, Society, and Law*

Sally Munt, editor, *New Lesbian Criticism: Literary and Cultural Readings*

Timothy F. Murphy and Suzanne Poirier, editors, *Writing AIDS: Gay Literature, Language, and Analysis*

Noreen O'Connor and Joanna Ryan, *Wild Desires and Mistaken Identities: Lesbianism and Psychoanalysis*

Don Paulson with Roger Simpson, *An Evening in the Garden of Allah: A Gay Cabaret in Seattle*

Judith Roof, *A Lure of Knowledge: Lesbian Sexuality and Theory*

Alan Sinfield, *The Wilde Century: Effeminacy, Oscar Wilde, and the Queer Moment*

Thomas Waugh, *Hard to Imagine: Gay Male Eroticism in Photography and Film from Their Beginnings to Stonewall*

Kath Weston, *Families We Choose: Lesbians, Gays, Kinship*

Carter Wilson, *Hidden in the Blood: A Personal Investigation of AIDS in the Yucatán*

COME As You Are

SEXUALITY AND NARRATIVE

Judith Roof

COLUMBIA UNIVERSITY PRESS
New York

Columbia University Press
New York Chichester, West Sussex

Copyright © 1996 Columbia University Press

Library of Congress Cataloging-in-Publication Data
Roof, Judith
  Come as you are : sexuality and narrative / Judith Roof.
    p. cm.
  Includes bibliographical references and index.
  ISBN 0–231–10436–7 (cloth : alk. paper). — ISBN 0–231–10437–5
  (pbk. : alk. paper)
    1. Sex in literature. 2. Homosexuality in literature.   I. Title.
  PN56.S5R58   1996
  809'.933538—dc20   96–10159

Printed in the United States of America

c 10 9 8 7 6 5 4 3 2 1
p 10 9 8 7 6 5 4 3 2 1

For AN

CONTENTS

ACKNOWLEDGMENTS

This book is an attempt to treat some of the unanswered questions from *A Lure of Knowledge: Lesbian Sexuality and Theory*, particularly those having to do with narrative and identity. For this reason, I still owe thanks to Richard Mohr who supported the initial project, and particularly to Ann Miller whose astute readings, sense of humor, and calming influence have made publishing these books much more a delight than a pain. Many portions of this project were first presented as lectures during 1992–1993 and I thank the sponsors of those lectures for enticing me to generate much of the book: the University of Wisconsin-Madison, the Ten Percent Society, and Dale Bauer; CUNY Graduate School, CLAGS, and Judith Butler; Tulane University, GALA, Rebecca Mark, and Dan Balderston; Swarthmore College, the Sager Fund, and Dan Smartt; the University of London, Theresa Brennan, and Paul Julian Smith; the University of Amsterdam and Renée Hoogland. I would like to thank Carl Dawson for providing research and collegial support and also those—Dennis Allen, Eva Cherniavsky, Renée Hoogland, Eric John Martin, Maaike Meijer, Melissa Mowry, Frank Smigiel, Michele Shauf, and Paula Jayne White—who helped with discussion, research, preparation, and/or insightful reading of this manuscript. Finally thanks to Thomas B. Byers, Andrea K. Newlyn, Patrick O'Donnell, Dianne Sadoff, Robyn Wiegman, and Lynda Zwinger, whose friendship and intellectual stimulus made me want to finish this project.

INTRODUCTION

COMING TO

I have never begun a novel with such misgiving. If I call it a novel it is only because I
don't know what else to call it. I have a little story to tell and I end neither with a
death nor a marriage. Death ends all things and so is the comprehensive conclusion
of a story, but marriage finishes it very properly too and the sophisticated are ill-
advised to sneer at what is by convention termed a happy ending. It is a sound
instinct of the common people which persuades them that with this all that needs to
be said is said. When male and female, after whatever vicissitudes you like, are at last
brought together they have fulfilled their biological function and interest passes to
the generation that is to come.
—W. Somerset Maugham, *The Razor's Edge*, p. 1

I have never begun a book with such misgiving. If I call it a book it is
only because I don't know what else to call it. I have a little theory to
propose and I end neither with an answer nor a proposal. The answer
ends all things and so is the comprehensive conclusion to a theory, but

a proposal finishes it very properly too and the sophisticated are ill-advised to sneer at what is by convention termed a satisfying ending. It is a sound instinct of the common people which persuades them that with this all that needs to be said is said. When question and answer, after whatever vicissitudes you like, are at last brought together they have fulfilled their philosophical function and interest passes to the issues that are to come.

This book's question is how ideas of narrative and sexuality inform one another. How do twentieth-century Western cultural understandings of narrative inflect, mold, determine, and/or reproduce understandings of sexuality and how do understandings of sexuality influence, define, configure, and/or reproduce narrative? Since I surmise from the start that narrative and sexuality somehow jointly engender and reproduce a heterosexual ideology, I have already brought them together to fulfill their figuratively "biological" or in any case (re)productive function. But my interest does not pass to the "generation" to come, it sticks obsessively to how I might undo the story I have concocted.

As I trace the stubborn pairing of narrative and sexuality through the lengthy vicissitudes of psychoanalysis and structuralist theories of narrative, through analyses of short stories, novels, films, and television shows, and finally through a critique of the politics of identity and identification, I cannot disengage them. My failure does not leave the thankfully surviving couple together for a conventionally satisfying ending; there seems to be no chance for a happier, less oppressive confederation between the two nor can I find a way to finagle their opportune divorce. Like Maugham's indeterminate novel, this book terminates uncertainly with the question of how to break narrative and sexuality apart, entwined as they are (and we with them) like tragically doomed lovers whirling around Dante's third circle.

If Maugham's novel recipe begets a good story, then this book may not be a good story. But perhaps Maugham is not quite right; perhaps the end is always in the beginning and a story's satisfaction consists in going on anyway. In any case, we cannot escape narrative, even imperfect narratives, since narrative is the inevitable register through which we define, reason, analyze, criticize, and comprehend the protagonists—narrative and sexuality—in this story. Let me therefore introduce the players so they can fulfill whatever function scholarly inquiry decrees.

THE NARRATIVE OF NARRATIVE

"To raise the question of the nature of narrative," Hayden White observes, "is to invite reflection on the very nature of culture and, possibly, even on the nature of humanity itself."[1] Linking narrative to culture and humanity, White sketches narrative's pivotal operation not as the mere proliferation of stories but rather as a complete and definitive engagement with our concepts of culture. Declaring narrative's total omnipresence, Roland Barthes asserts that "narrative is international, transhistorical, transcultural: it is simply there, like life itself."[2] Of course, narrative is not "simply there"; its shapes, assumptions, and operations manifest a complex, naturalized process of organization, relation, and connection. Narrative is so subtly and ubiquitously operative that I cannot even define it except through narrative—a narrative of narrative where parts come together to make a sensible whole. And you would not be able to comprehend my observations about narrative unless I cast them in a narrative form.[3]

Narrative constantly reproduces the phantom of a whole, articulated system, where even the concept of a system is a product of narrative, where the idea that there are such things as parts and wholes is already an effect of a narrative organizing. As a pervasive sense of the necessary shape of events and their perception and as the process by which characters, causes, and effects combine into patterns recognized as sensical, narrative is the informing logic by which individuality, identity, and ideology merge into a cooperative and apparently unified vision of the truths of existence. As a set of ordering presumptions by which we make sense of perceptions, events, cause/effect relations (and even the idea that sense can be produced by a notion of cause/effect), and life, narrative permeates and orders any representation we make to ourselves or to others. As a cultural, psychological, ideological dynamic, narrative aligns disparate forces and elements into productive configurations of difference and opposition. These configurations produce the perpetual opportunity for synthesis, for totalizing, cathartic gestures linked to insight, knowledge, reproduction, and temporary stability.

Narrative's pervasiveness makes it difficult to locate. One discourse among many, narrative appears to organize our understandings of discourse and its divisions. Its omnipresence, ranging from the local and idiosyncratic to the cultural and philosophical, makes narrative seem both artifact and organizing principle, text and the embodiment of ideology itself. This sense of narrative ubiquity is further bolstered by the fact that narrative does not exist or operate separately from other modes—identity, ideology, subjectivity, and sexuality—by which we organize existence and experience. The significant categories of life are already narrative both in our apprehension of them as significant and in our understanding of that significance. While narrative's organizing function seems to situate it as a powerful ur-force, its ubiquity is probably more an effect of its representational capabilities. Narrative's intersection of language, psychology, and ideology makes it an appropriate and compelling construct for the negotiation and containment of the contradictions and anxieties that inevitably attend the focal and delusively stable organizations of existence.

Its myriad loci suggest that narrative both operates like ideology and is shaped by ideology. Generally speaking, "ideology is the system of ideas and representations which dominate the mind of a man [sic] or a social group."[4] While this is Louis Althusser's reading of Marx's concept of ideology in a context quite different from any analysis of narrative, it has the virtue of proposing ideology as a system that operates in some relation to representations. For Althusser, ideology operates as a part of dominant apparatus, representing "the imaginary relationship of individuals to their real conditions of existence" (153). The material conditions of production comprise the context for this rendering of ideology; ideology is one way the relations of production are reproduced. While narrative undoubtedly participates in constructing, managing, and reproducing this "imaginary relationship," narrative's far-reaching and diverse operation suggests that a less focused framework might better capture narrative's aegis.

Roland Barthes' rendering of ideology is probably more descriptive of an ideology coextensive with narrative's broad context. In his examination of the cultural operation of myth, Barthes sees bourgeois ideology as a particular confusion of nature and history, where the historical is rendered natural.[5] While this confusion explains specific ways the bourgeoisie has rendered its interests universal, the model of an ideology that works through "signs which pass themselves off as natural, which offer themselves as the only conceivable way of viewing the world," which "convert culture into nature," which " 'naturalize' social reality" and "make it seem as innocent and unchangeable as Nature itself," resonates with both narrative's ubiquity and its seemingly mimetic logic.[6]

Narrative appears, thus, to reproduce natural experience, but the logic of its representation recalls Althusser's concern about how the relations of production are reproduced. While the "natural" events that seem to account for narrative's shape—the events Maugham so nicely summarizes—appear to be natural, they are in fact not only reproductions of the quintessentially naturalized "biological function" of human reproduction, they are also metaphors of capitalist relations of production. The connection between reproduction and production occurs in their common appeal to a productive joinder. Where in human reproduction male and female come together to produce offspring, in capitalist production capital and labor come together to generate products. Reiterating a similar dynamic—the same dynamic Maugham identifies as the model of a good novel—reproduction, production, and the ways that we understand and represent them are the very processes and institutions naturalized in and by ideology. The connection between human heterosexual reproduction and capitalist production provides an irresistible merger of family and state, life and livelihood, heterosexual order and profit whose formative presence and naturalized reiterations govern the conceptions, forms, logic, and operation of narrative. As ideology, this pattern of joinder to product also accounts for the countless analogies to child/product—knowledge, mastery, victory, another narrative, identity, and even death—that occupy the satisfying end of the story.

Narrative's apparent rendition of life experience, then, is already an ideological version of (re)production produced by the figurative cooperation of a naturalized capitalism and heterosexuality. Narrative's dynamic enacts ideology and narrative's constant production proliferates that ideology continually and naturally, as if it were simply a fact of life and sense itself.

Like trying to define narrative without narrative, how can we determine narrative's ideologies without somehow reiterating them? Looking for ideology as a defining characteristic means already acquiescing to an understanding of narrative that assumes that narrative has an ideology, that such an ideology might be discerned through reading narratives or theories of narrative, and that discovering such an ideology, like discovering an origin, would account for narrative's complex dynamic. But even the search for narrative's origin—for some primitive narrative that provides the pattern for all narratives—assumes narrative's conventional logic and assumptions. Refinding these assumptions in the place of an originary but fictive protonarrative means defining narrative and its ideology through narrative and its ideology. In other words, if positing an originary narrative risks an unwilling tautology— defining the conclusion by projecting it into the premises—such tautology is inevitable. The only way to combat it is to be aware of it, as long as that awareness is not itself already a narrative convention.

Since deducing an ideology cannot be accomplished except through ideology, perhaps I should look to those places where narrative asserts its own ideology "with a vengeance," as Teresa de Lauretis might characterize such excess, in those narratives openly about narrative.[7] At least these cases offer the illusion that narrative speaks openly about itself. Privileging self-conscious narrative, however, still reflects the operation of an ideology (that consciousness and recognition of one's ideology exempts one from its operations), though self-reflectivity implies a more conscious, hence supposedly less self-interested site of analysis. The tendency to tautology is further deferred when several apparently self-reflective processes intersect; where, for example, self-conscious processes of narrative coalesce with the self-reflective analysis of human development as sometimes happens in Sigmund Freud's writings. Here the circular paradox of narrative ideology becomes visible at least on one level, since the coexistence and comparison of narrative's narrative and narratives of development bring their premises and interrelation into starker relief. This is not, however, to recommend a genre such as autobiography as an ideal specimen text, since what is crucial is not the self-reflectivity of the process of narrating "self" but rather the sense that there is no subject, no "self" to narrate, that self, like narration, cannot exist except through narrative. And even this connection does not escape the furtive cast of some preexistent narrative of narrative, some notion of the story's ending and how we get there.

THE NARRATIVE OF SEXUALITY

In the concluding "Summary" to his 1905 "Three Essays on the Theory of Sexuality," Sigmund Freud simultaneously narrates a brief history of human sexual development and his theory of it. It is not surprising that history and theory are entangled, since Freud's theory of sexuality in 1905 is already narrative, performing a politic of sexualities in narrative terms and a narrative dynamic in sexual terms. Freud's pervasive liquid metaphors of sexuality simultaneously serve as the fluid figures of narrative progress. Characterizing libido as a current of water whose physical demand is simply to flow freely to its destined end, Freud envisions both story and sexuality as a single strong stream gushing gleefully into the wide sea of human generation. This oceanic finale exalts both healthy heterosexuality and *the* satisfying story. Any impediments to an unobstructed flow force the current away from its appointed end into tiny, doomed side streams, their deviance spawning a degenerate or perverted story in place of the felicitous convergence of river and sea.

Freud begins his exposition of sexuality with an essay on the "Sexual Aberrations." He begins this way not only because such aberrations contrast with the mechanisms of normative sexuality but also because the sheer ubiquity of aberrations represents an all-important rebuttal to what Freud summarizes as the existing mainstream, but incorrect narrative of sexuality:

> Popular opinion has quite definite ideas about the nature and characteristics of this sexual instinct. It is generally understood to be absent in childhood, to set in at the time of puberty in connection to the process of coming to maturity and to be revealed in the manifestations of an irresistible attraction exercised by one sex upon the other; while its aim is presumed to be sexual union, or at all events actions leading in that direction.   *(1)*

Outlining a linear chronological trajectory from absence to presence, Freud characterizes this narrative as a "false picture" containing "a number of errors, inaccuracies and hasty conclusions" (1). One hasty conclusion is the narrative's conclusion, hasty because there have not been enough impediments in the way of its realization. One inaccuracy is infantile sexuality's absence from the beginning. But the real problem with the story is that it is a completely unsatisfying narrative, going from nothing to something without threat, risk, conflict, impediment, or motive. Without the possibility that something might go wrong, the saving force of heterosexual attraction means nothing.

Freud's own narrative of sexuality begins with the aberrations that provide the damming stuff against which the hero of normative heterosexuality must struggle. It is as if Freud takes the narrative of sexuality apart, initially enacting aberrations' deviance to prove that they are necessary to the story, highlighting their presence to underline his understanding of the sexual narrative as complex, ambivalent, and suspenseful. Tracing aberrations in the first essay and infantile sexuality in the second, Freud connects the two in the third as necessary parts of the sexuality's narrative:

> We were thus led to regard any established aberration from normal sexuality as an instance of developmental inhibition and infantilism. Though it was necessary to place in the foreground the importance of the variations in the original disposition, a cooperative and not an opposing relation was to be assumed as existing between them and the influences of actual life. It appeared, on the other hand, that since the original disposition is necessarily a complex one, the sexual instinct itself must be something put together from various factors, and that in the perversions it falls apart, as it were, into its components. The perversions were thus seen to be on the one hand inhibitions, and on the other hand dissociations, of normal development. Both these aspects were brought together in the supposition that the sexual instinct of adults arises from a combination of a number of impulses of childhood into a unity, an impulsion with a single aim. *(97–98)*

Detailing a chronological narrative that proceeds from risky multiplicity to productive singularity, Freud's story features a struggle and victory instead of the erroneous account's inevitable and unmotivated line of least resistance. In his narrative, Freud situates the perversions as the spot where the story falls apart, a spot that is also a part of the story, serving its function as inhibition or dissociation only in relation to the narrative's ultimate end, "the discharge of the sexual substances" (76). While "the final outcome of sexual development lies in what is known as the normal sexual life of the adult, in which the pursuit of pleasure comes under the sway of the reproductive function and in which the component instincts, under the primacy of a single erotogenic zone, form a firm organization directed towards a sexual aim attached to some extraneous sexual object" (63), perversions, chronologically and analogically linked to infancy and foreplay, threaten to substitute themselves for this normal end pleasure. "The motive for proceeding further with the sexual process then disappears, for the whole path is cut short, and the preparatory act in question takes the place of the normal sexual aim" (77).

Supplanting the proper conclusion, perversions cut the story short, in a sense preventing a story at all by tarrying in its preparations. But this premature abridgment only has significance in relation to the "normal"; we only know the story is cut short because we know what length the story is supposed to be. Perversion, then, acquires its meaning as perversion precisely from its threat to truncate the story; it distorts the narrative, preventing the desirable confluence of sexual aim and object and male and female, precluding the discharge of sexual substances, and hindering reproduction. And yet the aberrations are the foreplay necessary to ever getting to the end at all. Comprised of perversions, foreplay leads to the proper play of confluence and discharge; without perverse foreplay, no discharge would occur. An integral threat, the perversions are absolutely indispensable to the story; their possibility and presence complicate the narrative of sexuality, making Freud's story the right story—right because it is a narrative instead of the simplistic developmental trajectory commonly held to be the truth of sex, right because his narrative of sexuality reenacts sexuality's narrative configuration.[8]

Freud, however, may be far more right about the story and its ideological imperatives than he is about the nature of sexuality. In his account the final leap from perversion to normalcy is accomplished without motive as the effect of an inherent, automatic, naturalized heterosexual desire. "No doubt the strongest force working against a permanent inversion of the sexual object is the attraction which the opposing sexual characters exercise upon one another," he speculates (95). And even if homosexuality, at least between men, might also result in the good end Freud assigns to the story—the desirable discharge of sexual substances—the underlying, satisfying requisite for the real story is not just discharge but discharge in the correct venue, naturally derived from the inevitable attraction between the sexes and leading to reproduction, the only function that can disqualify all but heterosexuality from the main stream.

In Freud's story, the naturalized primacy of heterosexuality constitutes a "normal" that appears without motive, one that is so ideological as to be completely natural. The reproductive demand of the end of the story produces this normalcy rather than reproduction being the logical end to an inevitable—and irresistible—heterosexuality. Reproduction produces heterosexuality instead of heterosexuality necessarily leading to reproduction. This governing reproductive ideology is not any literal command to go forth and multiply; rather, it is the expression of an ideology of value and meaning that resides in the pattern of joiner to product where products parallel such other metaphorically reproductive yields as children, knowledge, and victory. The reproductive imperatives of the story produce heterosexuality as the magical, motiveless mechanism that turns everything right, while homosexuality and other perversions—also necessary elements—make all fail to cohere, exposing the story's parts in a meaningless, short-circuited, truncated, narrative gratification that heterosexuality seals up again. The sexual players have their metaphorical parts and the narrative has its reproductive engine.

THE SEXUALITY OF NARRATIVE

> Two women (instead of a woman and a man) overcoming parental opposition, surviving the wilderness, enjoying domestic bliss together, achieving orgasm with a finger instead of a penis is only Romeo and Juliet again with two differences: happy endings—of both kinds.
> —Bertha Harris, "What We Mean to Say," p. 6

While Freud complicates and to some extent reverses the polarities of the commonly held account of sexual development, his understanding of sexuality is already heavily influenced by narrative, not as the specific shape of a specific story but as a way of organizing cause/effect relations. His narrative is already governed by a heterosexual ideology, or heteroideology, reflected both in the story of the development of literal heterosexuality and in the ways narrative functions to distribute sexualities in metaphorical positions in a narrative dynamic that proceeds from parts to a whole, from little tributaries to the big stream that was there all along. Narrative's sexuality is, thus, not so much the literal heterosexual content of a story as D. A. Miller claims: "the couple is in full and open possession of a story, a story, moreover, that one hardly exaggerates in our culture to call *the* story. Outside the heterosexual themes of marriage and oedipalized family (the former linked to the latter as its means of transmission), the plots of bourgeois life ... would all be pretty much unthinkable."[9] Rather, our very understanding of narrative as a primary means to sense and satisfaction depends upon a metaphorically heterosexual dynamic within a reproductive aegis.

Its reproductive impetus and metaphorically sexualized positions of hetero versus homo do not, however, entirely define the sexuality of narrative. While for the most part Freud's story of sexuality explains rather than captures or expresses the sexualities it describes, when it brings diverse positions together in a coherent and meaningful whole coincident with the appearance of heterosexuality, it enacts heterosexuality through narrative's dynamic. In like fashion, the perverse, as in Freud's theory of sexuality, plays within and against structure. This perverse, as Roland Barthes elaborates it in *The Pleasure of the Text*, performs through the text of pleasure and the text of bliss, both fugitives from narrative, the former produced as the comfort yielded by going with "the text that comes from culture and does not break with it," and the latter generated by the narrative's edges, seductive appearances, in the "seam" between "culture and its destruction."[10]

For Barthes, a text's eroticism is only indirectly linked to a sexuality he locates as an appurtenance of the father. Defining sexuality as an "Oedipal pleasure (to denude, to know, to learn the origin and the end)" (10), the oedipal pattern Barthes delineates is the same as the narrative dynamic I have just described as enacted by Freud's own narrative assumptions. Narrative and sexuality join at the oedipal; therefore neither Barthes's text of pleasure nor bliss has a sexuality insofar as each exists apart from or in playful relation to that oedipal. Instead they are erotic, gaining a sexual cast only when either the bliss of reading or the blissful text directly engages the oedipal that imports the heterosexual, familial, masterful tropes of knowledge, identity, gender, and sexuality. Pleasure comes when the "body pursues its own ideas" (17), protected from oedipal sexuality "by perversion which shields bliss from the finality of reproduction" (24). Eroticism comes from a dynamic produced by a concatenation of edges, gaps, loss, and desire, but is structurally unfixed except as it coexists with and is produced and enjoyed despite cultural imperative.

Structurally, the counterreproductive perverse seems to occupy the space between sexuality and eroticism, between narrative and the body, between structure and an almost unimaginable lack of structure—that site structurally fixed at death or origins as the two loci where structure provides the illusion of the perverse's disappearance. While Freud categorizes homosexualities as perverse, as examples of something gone wrong at the beginning or end of the sexual story, the perverse in turn jeopardizes the sexual system itself, threatening no structure and no narrative in a system dependent upon both. It is tempting to locate Barthes's perverse bliss as a gay text, but to do so is to reinscribe bliss as a discrete category within a still governing narrative heteroideology. Defining the perverse as homosexual threatens to import the entire narrative heterodynamic, arresting textual play in favor of a fixed narrative impetus labeled homosexual.

Thus, one can only enjoy bliss without a structural fix. Its dynamic, vaguely parasitic on the memory of narrative, is textual rather than narrative, that is, is produced by properties of the text as text (language, image, rhetoric) as they play through and around narrative. To have sexuality is to have narrative; to have narrative is to have sexuality. As circular as this relation might seem, what is important is the distinction it suggests between structure as represented both by the desires of narrative and of sexuality and by a different desire, produced by the dynamic intersection of text and reading, narrative and not, and both at the same time.

How then can there be a perverse narrative? Insofar as perversity belongs to narrative as the instance of its potential dissolution, the perverse narrative, like *The Pleasure of the Text* or Djuna Barnes's *Nightwood*, would be a narrative about narrative dissolution, a narrative that continually short-circuits, that both frustrates and winks at the looming demagogue of reproduction. Insofar as lesbian or gay is linked to perversion, the lesbian or gay narrative might be the perverse narrative. But the perverse narrative's perversity is not in its subject matter, for that is squarely planted in the realm of narrative, but in the way any such narrative enacts a perverse relation to narrative itself. *The Pleasure of the Text* flirts, evades, reveals, and conceals its narrative of reading, suggesting, cajoling, and teasing with suggestions of something narrative and not, the quality of an interchange, and a process of profaning the oedipal sanctity of structure and control.

Nightwood aligns the narrative of the Volkbein's misfired generation, a parodistic version of the narrative of productive procreation, against the narrative of the somnambulistic Robin Vote whose complete anaesthesia makes her both an object of desire (for Felix, Nora, and Jenny) and the character who cannot be a character because narrative has no meaning for her. Tracing Robin's perverse lack of narrative cooperation, *Nightwood* reveals how much the other characters are bound into narratives of coupling and reproduction. Guided by the transvestite commentator, Dr. Matthew O'Connor, whose narrative of self-knowledge sustains the perverse narrative to its bestial end, *Nightwood* is the paradoxical narrative of the perverse narrative. Conscious of the perversity it narrates, it is also conscious of that perversity's relation to the reproductive narrative that it installs at the novel's opening birth scene and maintains in the multiple failed couplings of characters who always believe in their fantasy narrative of the other.

Nightwood's narrative perversity is not produced by the presence or activities of transvestite or lesbian characters but rather in the narrative's actual perversion of the reproductive narrative. This occurs not because *Nightwood*'s narrative actively thwarts or frustrates reproduction but because reproduction, brought to the fore as an insistent and visible ideology, is no longer the alibi of the story. Instead *Nightwood* narrates the failure of a reproductive ideology as it traces the weakening of Felix's generation from his strong Teutonic mother to his feeble son, Guido. And while heteroideology still governs in stories where reproduction is prevented, frustrated, or disappointed, in *Nightwood* reproduction is self-consciously reduced to just another pathetic narrative that languishes rather than dies, affording an obviously false structure and motive superseded by the lesbian characters' retreat to the new world (and to their past).

Nightwood is still narrative, still furnishing a beginning and end and sets of cause/effect relationships located in character psychology. But it sustains itself as a narrative by its indirect appeals to narrative—by Dr. Matthew O'Connor's self-conscious reference to the narrative context of his own telling. The middleman between the reproductive and something else, O'Connor's wouldbe wise narrative of a human nature broken loose from its reproductive, oedipal moorings sustains and short-circuits at the same time, producing the reproductive story while putting it in its place.

At the same time, *Nightwood* tells another story, the story narrated by the novel's third-person omniscient narrator, who organizes Dr. O'Connor's perverse excursions as well as the other characters' coupling failures. While those failures might be understood as an effect of their "perversion"—Nora's, Robin's, and Jenny's lesbian attachments; Felix's misguided narrative of Robin's archetype—in most cases the nature of the failure as specifically a failure of the couple prevents any approach to the literally reproductive. Instead *Nightwood* reproduces knowledge—the knowledge of character, of the night, and of the nature of the pathetic reproductive story itself in the literal terms of its vestment. The net result is a narrative that enacts the relation between reproduction and perversity but is not a narrative with a sexuality except in so far as the perversion of the reproductive mainstream is accomplished by mainly homosexual characters. And if the homosexual characters contribute to the perversion of narrative's reproductive aegis, their role demonstrates even more than ever that the sexuality of narrative is straight.

While the sexuality of narrative may be metaphorically heterosexual, perversions, as a structural part of narrative, are not exactly aligned with either lesbian or gay male. Rather, lesbian and gay male characters are synecdoches of the perverse; the slippage between the larger category of the perverse and the specific example of the lesbian and/or gay male points to the operation of a distinctly heterosexual oedipal structure that fixes and defines as opposed to the shifting operations of Barthes' textual erotic. The tendency to locate and name perversity as a necessary part of heterosexual structure contains perversity within a still-Oedipal, still-reproductive domain even as the perverse might, as in *The Pleasure of the Text* and *Nightwood*, illustrate the reproductive's possible lack of hegemony or fool us by offering itself as the whole story.

RECOMMENCING

I began this project with a long list of nagging questions. Why is the story always the same? Why, no matter how sympathetic, clever, radical, or well-meaning the author, the circumstance, the occasion, is the story of the lesbian always really the same old story and her fate the same old, vaguely oppressed fate whether she is the protagonist or a minor character? Why am I rarely happy with any narrative that represents or suggests the presence of lesbian sexuality? There always seems to be something slightly alienating if not definitively wrong about it (assuming there could, possibly, be a "right" story). If culture is defined by or defines the story—if narrative is a means of cultural evaluation and oppression—must we change the story and the role the lesbian plays in it to alter the lesbian's place in culture? If lesbian sexuality is entirely a construction of the discursive fields that define it, is it possible to represent the lesbian differently and still have either a recognizable lesbian or a discernible narrative? Finally, if narrative is epistemologically pervasive, how do I understand narrative without narrative? How do I consider these questions without reiterating the very structures I try to discern and critique?

In this book I focus on narrative and sexuality as organizing epistemes and as expressions of a figuratively heterosexual reproductive ideology in twentieth-century Western culture. Interwound with one another, narrative and sexuality operate within the reproductive and/or productive, metaphorically heterosexual ideology that also underwrites the naturalized understanding of the shape and meaning of life. Narrative and sexuality's intimacy goes beyond the identity of terms they share (*climax*, for example); they are interwoven with one another as interdependent, mutually reflective, reciprocal organizations. The imbrication of narrative and sexuality is a symptom of their common progenesis in a specific, already heterosexual ideology that presents a critical difficulty in even thinking about them outside of that same set of ideologies.

The reciprocal relation between narrative and sexuality produces stories where homosexualities can only occupy certain positions or play certain roles metonymically linked to negative values within a reproductive aegis. This marriage of sexuality and narrative has several consequences: 1) the production of sexual categories whose existence and constitution depend upon a specific reproductive narrative heteroideology; 2) the preservation of literal and metaphorical heterosexuality as (re)productive (and hence valuable); and 3) the constitution of narrative that includes both heterosexuality and homosexuality as categories necessary to its dynamic.

My hypothesis about narrative's heteroideology builds on the insights of three different theorists. Teresa de Lauretis's understandings of the ideological relation of gender and narrative point to a problem Judith Butler also identifies: the tendency of Western cultural discourse to replicate its own, oppressive, founding terms. "The problem," as de Lauretis describes it, is "that most of the available theories of reading, writing, sexuality, ideology, or any other cultural production are built on male narratives of gender, whether oedipal or anti-oedipal, bound by the heterosexual contract; narratives which persistently tend to reproduce themselves in feminist theories."[11] De Lauretis's suggestion that theories and ideologies are narratives and that those narratives are somehow defined by the "heterosexual contract" invites further investigation into this relation as a primary mode of cultural production as well as a site of discursive and ideological operations and limits.

Monique Wittig's observation of the founding alibi of heterosexuality and its relation to representation—"These discourses of heterosexuality oppress us in the sense that they prevent us from speaking unless we speak in their terms"—raises the question of how this policing occurs.[12] Judith Butler, while recognizing the heterosexist tendency of "the matrix of power and discursive relations that effectively produce and regulate the intelligibility of those concepts ['person,' 'sex,' or a 'sexuality']," asks, "what constitutes the possibility of effective inversion, subversion, or displacement within the terms of a constructed identity?"[13] This book takes up de Lauretis's narrative suggestion as a way both to define redundant discursive limitations and to forge a strategy to disrupt the insistent system by which identities are conceived and constructed.[14]

My argument about the interrelation of narrative and sexuality depends upon presumptions about the historical venue of this phenomenon, a particular definition of sexuality, narrative's preeminently structuralist nature and its cultural efficacy as well as the deliberate but reasoned omission of some of the impossibly large number of terms and discourses that might participate in the relation of narrative and sexuality. I concentrate more on discerning narrative/sexuality's heteroideology than on interpreting representations of literal sexualities in specific narratives, except where stories serve as examples. I also stress the metaphorical quality of narrative heteroideology, because it is through the metaphorical rather than the literal that sexuality inflects all that seems not immediately sexual. Metaphor accounts for how it is that narrative can convey and situate a sexual ideology while not appearing to represent sexuality at all. Thus, what is important is not so much literal representations of specific sexualities but rather a more pervasive, structured interrelation among sets of terms and values associated with positions and functions within narrative.

I locate the beginnings of this particular manifestation of narrative and sexuality's interrelation in accord with Michel Foucault's understanding of the emergence of the category of sexuality in the nineteenth century in volume 1 of the *History of Sexuality*.[15] If, however, I am to be suspicious of narrative, history is one narrative to be wary of, especially as it appears to offer a means to an origin that provides both answer and explanation. While the question of the origin of contemporary conceptions of sexuality and homosexuality has rightly compelled many theorists, I am more interested in tracing how the imbri-

cation of narrative and sexuality pervades contemporary culture, working to sustain and (re)produce a particular understanding and relative
valuation of a sexuality that consists of the binary categories hetero-
and homosexual.

For the purposes of this book, the term *sexuality* refers to naturalized, historically located cultural assumptions about identifiable sexual
categories based primarily on the gender of object choice and delim-
ited to the heterosexual and the homosexual (both male and female)—
though the homosexual is a synecdoche of the larger field of "perverse"
object and aim choices that currently comprise our ideas of sexual
desire and behavior. The reduction of a larger field of sexuality to two
categories is partly an effect of narrative's binary operation within a
reproductive logic; in this sense there are really only two sexualities:
reproductive sexuality, which is associated with difference and becomes
metaphorically heterosexual, and nonreproductive sexuality associated
with sameness, which becomes metaphorically homosexual.

Its relation to narrative is only one out of a number of possible ways
sexuality intersects with, informs, and organizes discourses and knowledge and is, in turn, informed and organized by them. While there are
other ways sexuality is deployed across the cultural field—and while the
contemporary critical tendency is to enable the interplay of multiple
possibilities—I want to map the connection between narrative and sexuality as a way of at least partly understanding how sexual ideologies
tend to remain consistent in the face of social change, how they are disseminated and remain in circulation, and how vastly divergent terms
(such as *Nazi* and *lesbian*) are repeatedly associated. This is not to claim
that narrative is necessarily the only or even the most important of
many possible discursive relations, but it is to suggest that as an organizing structure, narrative plays a large part in the stubborn return of a
particularly heterosexual normativity.

Because I focus primarily on the connections between narrative and
sexuality and because of the self-circling nature of those connections,
it may appear as if I am constructing a closed circuit, an impossible
labyrinth whose claustrophobic interreferentiality permits no hope for
escape or change. In the sense that humans tend to employ narrative to
cover over or rearticulate contradictions, gaps, or inconsistencies, narrative is a kind of closed circuit, especially about narrative itself. Insofar
as perceiving the reach and kind of narrative's influence might actually
alert us to narrative's heteroideological uses, this is not a hopeless story

at all but one way to begin to try to dislocate or alter the uses of narrative and its insistent presumptions.

In focusing on the relation between narrative and sexuality, I inevitably underplay other terms—*class, race, nationality*—whose connection to these two would also be informing. It is undoubtedly artificial to focus on two terms when focusing on twenty would still not suffice to account for any complex cultural phenomenon. While my purpose is to understand something about the nature of narrative and the disposition of sexuality in modern Western culture, my focus on these categories and not others is also determined by the incredible complexity of their interrelation. This is not to suggest that their complexity is isolated to narrative and sexuality alone but to acknowledge that these two terms are all this book will consider.

And even those two terms are too much. I often reduce the term *sexuality*, though itself a large dynamic system, to its lesbian example, not because there is an identity between the category of sexuality and the lesbian but because the configurations of the lesbian tend to mark failures of the system.[16] I assume that the category *lesbian* represents both a construction participating in this larger sexual ideology and a name applied to the practices, identities, definitions, or self-definitions of real women. The complex relation among these terms—ideology, representation, and actual women—is a complicated articulation. There is no lesbian who is not affected by ideology nor any ideology that is not in some way inflected by women's lives, but this also means that there is no pure ab quo unmediated lesbian experience—no "authentic" lesbian—and no comprehension of the term *lesbian* outside of a larger ideological system.

For reasons I shall argue, the lesbian position is often indicative of how the sexual ideology in narrative operates and is itself a sufficiently complex example of the interrelation of narrative and sexuality. I am most interested in what the lesbian position can reveal both about narrative and about how *lesbian* gets to be what it is. It is also the case that the categories, including the lesbian, that occupy the metaphorically homosexual position in narrative perform differently in that position; there is a difference, for example, between the narrative disposition of the lesbian and the male homosexual. Suggestions about the ideological positioning of analogous categories, except insofar as they bear directly upon the lesbian example, I leave to others to question, refute, develop, or refine.

While the notion of narrative and sexuality as reciprocal systems suggests a structuralist approach, narrative itself is a structuralist category, its operation depending upon a knowledge of structure. Despite the insights of poststructuralism (or perhaps because of them), narrative is entirely structuralist even when it is postmodern, fragmented, or presumed missing. Even if narrative structure is an illusion that compensates for lack or provides a false mastery of what can never be mastered, these defenses exist because narrative is a structural defense against a chaotic world. And narrative's structuralism, intimately linked to still prevalent structuralist ways of understanding it, may well be necessary to its ideological operation, to its incorporation and replication of the pretentiously "complete" and "true" structures of capitalism, religion, and the nuclear family.[17] If this book seems anachronistically structuralist or perversely interested in structures, then, it is because I have taken as my object of inquiry those structures that persist despite a postmodern failure of what Jean-François Lyotard calls "legitimating metanarratives," and because both narrative and sexuality *as structures*—as finished complete, unified (if delusively so) products—fit readily into commodity culture's systems of exchange and logic of simulation. In this sense, contemporary culture has incited the production of even more narrative—a specifically structuralist understanding of narrative—packaged, produced, and disseminated as life.[18]

My focus on structure also creates the illusion of a totalized or closed system that includes and can account for everything. This sense of systemic totality is a feature of the narrative ideology I try to locate as well as an attribute of cultural understandings of just what narrative, in its largest sense, is. There are other understandings of how ideas, events, and language might be organized, but those organizations—including repetition and/or simple alternation—are not culturally intelligible as narrative. Our failure to credit such other organizations with meaning is due to our sense that a narrative must produce something and/or go somewhere in an analogue to time or space.

Given these suppositions about narrative, it is not sufficient to account for the often negative narrative disposition of lesbian characters by understanding stories as direct expressions of conscious or unconscious homophobia and misogyny. Although there is some relation between the narrative disposition of characters and homophobia, that relation extends beyond personal anxiety. Cultural homophobia does not account for either the reiteration of the same narrative structure in sympathetic stories by or about lesbians or for the consistency of their representation; it is a product of the same ideology that organizes narrative. Something in the way we understand what a story is in the first place or something in the way narrative itself operates produces narrative's "heterosexually friendly" shape. If this is the case, then simply changing people's minds through good public relations would not change the story all that much.

Finally, given its realm of apparent influence, I assume that there is some political agency to narrative—that where narrative underwrites cultural ideology, it might also be used to challenge and change it. My optimistic and perhaps overly idealistic hope is that if we know enough about the mechanisms of culture and their interrelationships we might be able to wield them, or at least influence their shape. This dream of mastery, however, requires that I submit myself to narrative—to the narrative that defines the very dream of knowledge that engenders this project. If even my analysis of narrative complies with ideologies of narrative, am I not sustaining those ideologies even as I try to expose them? And isn't my projected mastery the typical end to the story?

What I hope to demonstrate is both a narrative tendency connected to sexualized ideologies and specific examples of how the ideologies of narrative and sexuality work. Rather than tracking specific contents, plots, or patterns to discern a majority occurrence or its cultural currency, my analysis attempts to discern narrative's dynamic, its impetus to negotiate disparate elements through the sexualized terms by which production and reproduction are conceived in Western culture. It is likely that this dynamic is neither completely static nor entirely structural (though it might appear to be so) but is, rather, flexional and inflective, moving the choice and linear ordering of elements through complex, self-contradictory compromise formations whose provisional effect is the representation of a sense of cause and effect in history and the production of an illusion of meaning and order.

COMING TO

As a narrative, this book can not help but be narrative, but as a critique it might be self-conscious of the ways narrative works to efface its own assumptions. Because I am treating large epistemic categories and because as much as possible I must try to avoid falling into the narra-

tive ideologies I critique, this book proceeds with a structural consciousness of its own narrative. I begin therefore with the end as that
moment of illusory completion that, as I have pointed out in Freud's
narrative of sexuality, defines the story in the first place. Deliberately
keeping the end in mind rather than assuming it makes visible, at least
momentarily, our investment in the whole narrative process.

Beginning, therefore, at the end in chapter 1, "The End Is Coming,"
I examine ideas about narrative's end in narratives, narrative theory, and
psychoanalysis. Tracing narrative's metaphorically reproductive impetus
through the larger historical and cultural relation between ideologies of
narrative and of sexuality, I examine assumptions about narrative shape
and organization and their contemporary currency. Through narratives
of orgasm, Freud's *Beyond the Pleasure Principle*, Peter Brooks's "Freud's
Masterplot," and Michel Foucault's *The History of Sexuality*, I track this
end fixation as it derives from our very sense of narrative itself and as it
appears insidiously to determine narrative's dynamic and our understanding of it.

But the critical tendency to look for a narrative origin suggests
equally that narratives's end always looks for another beginning, the
founding moment or essence of narrative itself. In chapter 2, "Come
Together," I examine understandings of what makes narrative narrative.
Reading through the narratives of structuralist theories of narrative, I try
to determine how theories both understand and depict the quality or
process by which narrative becomes narrative and not something else. In
other words, for a moment I give in to the impetus to discern a narrative origin and actively look for it. Since narrative is still preeminently
structural, structuralist accounts of narrative seem the best arena in which
to examine the ways narrative structure reproduces and reinforces itself.

While these theories offer descriptions of narrative and narrative
process, they are more symptomatic of the same reproductive ideologies I discuss in chapter 1 than they are successful at offering any truth
or essence of narrative. I read the narrative theories of Tsvetan Todorov,
Roland Barthes, Algirdas Greimas, and others against Colette's short
story, "The Secret Woman," not only to emphasize the narrative nature
of structuralist theory but also to reveal narrative's (and its theories')
dependence upon ideologies of gender and sexuality. "The Secret
Woman's" narrative consciousness, its play on the characters' and readers' narrative assumptions, and its commentary on the nature of narrative's investment in mastery illustrates on the level of the story narra-

tive's management of disorder, its imbrication with sexuality, and its ironical failure. "The Secret Woman" exposes what is missing in narrative theories.

Structuralist accounts, as I show in chapter 2, discern narrative origin in yet another performance of a trajectory from parts to a joined synthetic whole, reproducing narrative's heteroideology. And again, the nature of narrative depends upon an unwitting estimation of narrative's proper (re)productive end, not as a specific outcome but as a shaping presumption. It is clear from this theoretical dependence on this end that the narrative middle, as in Freud's narrative of sexuality, provides the scene for doubt, risk, and uncertainty. The middle, as Freud suggests, is the locus of homosexual suggestion, the place where such a possibility is made visible on the way to a reproductive end.

In chapter 3, "Coming Apart," the middle of this book, I focus on the nature of this middle, the realm where the perverse and the normal intermingle and where the lesbian becomes visible, attempting in analytical fashion to wrench sexuality and narrative apart at the point where they seem to come together. Using cross-gender narratives such as *Victor/Victoria*, *All of Me*, and *Switch*, and the more celestial *Star Trek: The Next Generation* where the middle terms are particularly manifest, I examine how the metaphorically perverse both threatens to short-circuit and leads toward a satisfying, very heterosexual closure. In other words, I look to where the coming together might fail, and I find the lesbian.

As part of this middle, the lesbian constitutes some threat to the story but also provides the pretext for the heteronarrative's spectacular return. This pattern accounts for many mainstream representations of the lesbian as temporary, immature, and titillating. But its suggestion of a possible opening in heteronormative hegemony also provides a rationale that underwrites overtly lesbian tactics for employing, negotiating, and/or exploding the heteronarrative. If the lesbian is visible and viable in the narrative middle, why not exploit that visibility as a way of devising a lesbian story? At the penultimate fourth chapter, where narrative typically reorganizes its perversities into a heterosexual mainstream, I analyze whether and how it is possible to divert that mainstream into a lesbian narrative without having that narrative simply reinscribe the heteronarrative with lesbian players.

Chapter 4, "The Second Coming," examines mainstream narratives; various lesbian narratives, including coming out stories, narratives of lesbian sex, lesbian detective novels, and the experimental narratives of Monique Wittig and Nicole Brossard; and such "perverse" fictions as *Nightwood* to see how playing on the middle's perverse works to avoid heteronormative recontainment. Mainstream narratives such as *Roseanne* that deliberately include lesbian characters try to exploit the virtues of visibility ostensibly for politically laudatory reasons, but at the same time they tend to reproduce sexual ideology all the more insidiously. While they appear to be open and supportive to diversity, they recontain the lesbian resoundingly, publicly, indubitably within the spectacularly heteronormative family.

Some of the forms written for a lesbian audience—the coming out story in particular—also reiterate a version of the heteronarrative by making the recognition of identity the victorious product of a struggle with self, locating the lesbian again within the overweening heteronarrative. Other forms such as the lesbian detective story try to alter the narrative's valence by simply replacing most characters with lesbians; this may produce a better story for lesbians, but it also inscribes heteronarrative for dykes, since the story itself doesn't change. Lesbian experimental writing tries to shift narrative practice and expectations with perhaps better, but more limited success and certainly with a smaller audience. What these deliberately lesbian stories reveal is how difficult it is to surmount narrative's reproductive ideology as long as the writer aims only at form and content.

The final chapter, "Come As You Are," the place where narrative should end in its satisfying product, extends this understanding of the relation of narrative and sexuality into the realm of social action, reading political strategies as already motivated by the same narrative heteroideology they try to combat. Examining the rhetoric of visibility, the strategies of outing and role models, and their reliance on identification and identity reveals their dependence on a particular coming out story narrative of victory. Since the coming out story in fact serves to locate homosexual characters within the larger heteronarrative, it also unwittingly returns bids for homosexual rights to the system that denies them in the first place.

The purpose of this final chapter is not to denigrate political efforts but rather to analyze why those efforts have not worked as well as they might and to suggest a different way of thinking about praxis. If narrative and sexual ideology are interwound, then perhaps finding ways of shifting the very understanding of story would effect small changes in ideology. The end, thus, has no answer, only questions about how to disimbricate sexuality from narrative as a strategy for potentially altering oppressive social conceptions. If narrative is the representational ideology that glues discursive fields into insurmountable fortresses, then perhaps via narrative it will also be possible to take them apart.

COME As You Are

CHAPTER ONE

The End Is Coming

1

She leaned over me and put her mouth on mine. I felt her exploring my mouth, taking it, drawing me into her. I would have been afraid except that I felt her warm hand on my back reassuring me. Then her hand found my breasts and began to find all my reactions. I couldn't stop a funny squeaking sound from escaping. She had my hands clasped over my head with one strong arm and her other hand went further and further pursuing all the boundaries, taking me so far along in the excitement it was nearly pain. And she went on and on, almost methodically except that I felt her own breath rising in response. I fought with the passivity but it was only fun to fight it. I let her go wherever she wanted. I let her find things I didn't know were there. I was so wet, with her hand between my legs. Her finger slipped inside me and my body rose. She held me for two minutes or ten minutes. Then it was my turn (Wings 67).

2

A leather seat clung to Simone's bare cunt, which was inevitably jerked by the legs pumping up and down on the spinning pedals. Furthermore, the rear wheel vanished indefinitely to my eyes, not only in the bicycle fork but virtually in the crevice of the cyclist's naked ass: the rapid whirling of the dusty tire was also directly comparable to both the thirst in my throat and my erection, which ultimately had to plunge into the depths of the cunt sticking to the bicycle seat. The wind had died down somewhat, and part of the starry sky was visible. And it struck me that death was the sole outcome of my erection, and if Simone and I were killed, then the universe of our unbearable personal vision was certain to be replaced by the pure stars, fully unrelated to any external gazes and realizing in a cold state, without human delays or detours, something that strikes me as the goal of my sexual licentiousness: a geometric incandescence (among other things, the coinciding point of life and death, being and nothingness), perfectly fulgurating (Bataille 33).

3

The end is in the beginning and yet you go on.
—Samuel Beckett, *Endgame*, p. 69

How is it that stories are marked by the illusion of an end to come? How is it that the anticipated and delightful orgasmic sexual end comes like the end of a story? This chapter begins with openly sexual narratives as a way to flesh out the relation of narrative and sexuality. The stories' impetus suggests the urgency of an end whose meaning resounds beyond mere structure or real experience. Beginning with the end will be my end, though at this point in the project, there is no end in sight. To get to the end, we must range through discussions of narrative, psychoanalysis, and narrative theories, a wearying proposition, unending in its complications and permutations, apparent indirections, and irrelevancies. But the end is coming, better for its delay.

This chapter begins a two-chapter examination of the structural and ideological relations between narrative and sexuality; I hope to show that narrative theories themselves demonstrate narrative's heterosexual ideology. A discussion of Freud and narrative theorists is necessary to illustrate not only that narrative is figuratively heterosexual but *how* it is so and—perhaps even more important—*why* it is so in a particular social-historical context. The purpose of this presentation is to provide a foundation for my later investigation of heteronarrative's relation to the representation, understanding, and narration of lesbian characters.

Beginning with an analysis of how narrative ends shape our concepts of the whole story, this chapter undertakes discussion of ten issues central to the relation of sexuality and narrative. Recommencing with the relation between end and orgasm, the chapter continues with a brief discussion of cultural understandings of narrative in texts by Walter Benjamin and Vladimir Propp, an inquiry into the interrelation of narrative and psychological processes in Peter Brooks's "Freud's Masterplot" and Sigmund Freud's *Beyond the Pleasure Principle*, and a consideration of the structural and psychical dynamics of narrative, again through Brooks and Freud.

Just when this chapter feels as if it should end, it continues with an analysis of the narrative relation of sex and death; a scrutiny of narratives about sexuality and reproduction as they appear in Djuna Barnes's *Nightwood* and again in Freud; and an examination of narrative, gender, reproduction, and sexuality in Freud's rendering of Aristophanes' myth of the creation of sexuality. The chapter finally ends with a consideration of narrative in commodity culture through the work of Jean Baudrillard and an outline of the historical connections between narrative and sexuality as explored by Michel Foucault.

Outcomes

The passages I cite from Wings and Bataille are coming stories, narratives whose end, we assume, is orgasm, whose point is to get to that point. Neither, however, literally ends in orgasm but rather in something else: the brief, suggestive rising of Mary Wings's lesbian detective or Bataille's cosmic metaphors of universal epiphany. Despite their inevitable drive through the libidinal world of beginning, middle, and anticipated climax, the two narratives do almost anything but come. In fact, everything is important but coming even though the overriding specter of an anticipated climax shapes how we read these passages, what we look for, how we organize them, and how we understand that they are narratives at all.

For example, though we read for orgasm in Mary Wings's narrative, coming—"my body rose"—comes too soon, before but not at the end. The passage actually terminates with the invitation to another narrative of coming, one produced by the first narrative, one that is implicitly coming but that is never told: "Then it was my turn." The sexual sequence dallies in the middle, wandering through body geography and playing out a detached reciprocity through details of method and passive/active struggle. The segment's middling indirection, in part a product of a split between the first-person narrator and the third-person body she watches, frustrates progress toward the anticipated end by enacting a delaying tension between the narrator's ignorance and her knowledge of the elements of the story. It is as if the narrator's body, her lover, and the reader all know where the story is going, while the narrator, as the innocent recipient and gullible reader of whatever suspense is depicted, can appear to give her body, lover, and reader what they want without knowing exactly what is coming. The narrator's ignorance is a necessary part of the story, signifying as it does that which is beyond—the "funny squeaking sound," the "things I didn't know were there"—which apparently cause the ultimate orgasmic effect. Just before the end, innocence, new knowledge, and bodies come together in what turns out to be a productive rising that generates a story to come.

The narrator's simultaneous ignorance and consciousness of the coming end of sex and the story perpetuates suspense in a narrative with a known and pleasurably anticipated end. We know and she pretends not to; we all suspect and yet we aren't quite sure. By casting the narrator's aura of winking innocence against our own knowing assumptions, the narration's distanced quality flirts with our certainty about the end.[1] While the potentially deflating effects of knowing the end too soon are deferred through the narrator's feigned ignorance (a feigning that parallels our own provisional acceptance of the narrator's affected unawareness), our understanding of the style of the narration as well as the narrative's structure is still entirely dependent upon our knowing and anticipating orgasm as the story's ultimate conclusion. Although a relatively vast middle occupies the narrative's space and time, and though the story's end produces an avowed repetition of a similar story, the idea of orgasm is still the end-all of the scene; without it, the women's coming together, the nature, sequence, and timing of events, and the story's building excitement would be without context and meaning.

Rather than dallying in disavowal like Wings's story, Bataille's narrative emphasizes the meaning of the end, but his end becomes equally indirect through the accretion of frames—sky, stars, life, death—that lead to a cosmically aggrandized orgasm, the coming together of the narrator, his lover, death, the universe, being, and meaning to produce the "coinciding point" itself, "perfectly fulgurating" in the oscillating twinkling of the perfect combination of opposites. This infinite orgasm's narrative foreplay is as fulgurating as its conclusion, consisting of the image of genitals on leather flickering within the pumping, spinning, whirling, and jerking actions of the orgasmic velocipede, the machine that produces the suggestive action the narrator views. The passage's final indirect climactic fanning out is the product, as in Wings's account, of the narrator's passivity. He is the recipient of a vision that causes an erection and renders it metaphorical. The literal center of the story, his detached erection becomes the actor that "plunge[s]" into Simone, and whose "sole outcome" is death on a cosmic scale.

The "outcome" that occupies the entire second half of Bataille's passage is, despite (or because) of its indirection, the perfect end, the coming together of "life and death, being and nothingness" all pumped up with no further need for foreplay or narrative. This end, complete in itself, and "fully unrelated to any external gazes and realizing in a cold state, without human delays or detours, something that strikes me as the goal" is the ideal culmination, the aim of the narrator's "sexual licentiousness." Bataille's end is a hyperbolic totality created by joinder and synthesis, figuring not just the end of the story but the end of all narrative drawn into and contained within the "perfectly fulgurating" moment that embraces all. The merger of orgasm and death in Bataille's narrative leads to the exposure of the end's ultimate, most explicit function as the receptacle for everything, the locus of all meaning, and the self-contained moment where desire fulfills itself.

In its very exaggeration Bataille's coming story suggests what is really at stake in the ends of narratives: the impossible, amplified totality of complete joinder and cessation of desire that are perpetually denied in favor of the seeds of another story, another potential coming elsewhere, a coming to come. Coming is the illusion of an end, not an end to end all ends, but one, like Wings's, with coming attractions. Bataille's end is the platonic, prototypical, visionary end to which the ends of narratives refer but that narrative never achieves, not even Bataille's *Story of an Eye*. Instead this coming passage comes near the beginning of the narrative, figuring the end while the protagonist and Simone must proceed through the murder the narrator envisions in the impossible (and failed) quest for the insight he has on the bicycle. Just as Bataille's final image of the paradoxically twinkling figure of still movement is the overly explosive ending to an insufficient, but figuratively appropriate beginning, so the end of narrative is the overemphasized cause and effect of narrative's pumping and whirling with its pretext, its image of self-reproductive agency on a leather seat coming into and disappearing from view.

These ends, these comings, these stories of sex reveal something about our late-twentieth-century Western cultural sense of what an ending should be, for in the 1990s it is the ending that moors the story, or so we, despite postmodern gestures otherwise, think. Without the expectation of an ending, we have difficulty discerning a story, its pleasures, terrors, lessons, its making sense of things, its usefulness as catharsis or panacea. If there is no end we normally identify as an end—orgasm, death, marriage, victory, salvation, the production of something (insight, a child, another story, the story itself, knowledge, identity)—we ask, "Is that all there is?" and regard the apparently truncated story as ironic, as an unsatisfying failure, as a metanarrative commentary on narrative, or as no story at all. But as the coming stories illustrate, the end isn't quite the end; it is more a product, a promise, a potential that occupies the stopping-place before the next story. Orgasm is not the end, though most of the time we think so.

How is it that orgasm and the end are taken for one another, conflated in our narrative expectations? What drives this infatuation with the end, our almost childlike belief in it, not only as a necessary part of stories but also in our criticism, reception, and definition of them? Is this overinvested end a feature of a particular historical configuration of narrative and sexuality, read already through a narrativized history that follows a similar trajectory and has a similar end? Does some intrinsic quality of an end encourage our emphasis on it or does the end's significance come from its structural position in narrative? Does emphasizing the end come from the shape of individual stories or from an idea of narrative itself? Whatever the cause, the nature of this highly significant end might reveal contemporary ideologies of narrative and narrative structure, narrative's role in culture and its place in history, and the relation of our ideas of narrative to sexuality and other cultural ideologies and dynamics.

Dead Ends

As I write this, I want the payoff, the intellectual correlate to the comings I have been describing. I want this narrative to come together, to
produce knowledge and pleasure (and pleasure in knowledge) as the
end becomes the perfect joinder and alibi for the analysis I am constructing. But alas, it can never be. Just as in Wings's and Bataille's narratives, the anticipated orgasmic ending is not the end; so considering
the virtues and necessities of the end only begins a discussion of the
whole story, a story that, like sex, always escapes its end even as the end
always seems to define the story's direction, scope, aim, and the relevance of its terms and actions. The various means by which orgasm and
its analogies become the end of the story in narrative and psychoanalytical theories reveal the nature of the ideological connection of narrative and sexuality.

On the surface, our comfort in the end is produced by a cause/effect
logic where the end promises an ultimate result. Our very idea of an
end is dependent upon a concept of chronological, linear, unidirec-
tional time that positions the end as the cumulative locus of completed
knowledge. In a seeming tautology, our pleasure in knowledge and
meaning is connected to our pleasure in the end, to what Roland
Barthes calls "an Oedipal pleasure," a mastery seemingly located at the
end that governs our reading throughout.[2] The whole story takes pleasure in the fact of an end, in the possibility of an end toward which the
story goes, its specter there as a promise, a reaffirmation of the mastery
we think we have from the beginning (if, as Beckett's Hamm declares,
"the end is in the beginning"), a coming together in the climax.

This narrative pattern imitates our narrative of life: birth, passing
time, reproduction, death. It is analogous, as Robert Scholes has
observed, to our narrative of orgasm.[3] The structural analogy among
the various ends explains why it seems that totality, knowledge, and
meaning coincide in the end, the end simultaneously providing some
insight or meaningful pattern to the rest of the narrative and some sense
of a stopping point constituting an end to a series of events that separates one narrative from another. The connection among these three
narratives—oedipal mastery, life and death, and orgasm—where knowledge, death, and coming all occupy the structural position of the end is
made not only through the metaphorical and paradigmatic equations
of the various ends but also through some ideological link among

them. Reflecting finally a belief that meaning can be had at all, the fact of an end appears to give us a sense of mastery over what we can identify as a complete unit. At the end of the story, the story's time is now separate from ours; we, having known it, have also survived it. What is at stake in the ideological connection of narrative and sexuality, reproduction and death is the subject of the rest of this chapter's analyses of Brooks's (and Freud's) explorations of narrative meaning and dynamics.

Just as Scholes links narrative to a paradigm of sexual intercourse, Walter Benjamin links stories to the perceived pattern of lived existence, locating the rationale and motivation for narrative in the fact of death.[4] But this quintessentially terminal death, like the orgasm with which it is associated, is in turn a mask for something else, for other more complex narrative processes that determine both the primacy and positioning of death as an end and its structural analogy to birth, production, insight, and the promise of more narrative.

Narrative mastery over death results in endings about mastery, knowledge, and victory on the one hand and about birth, production, and more narrative on the other. The facts of life that are overcome or transformed by narrative become themselves points of narrative transformation that often denote a transition from myth to life, from one state of being to another, from one mode of time to another. Marking thus the boundaries, the end becomes performative of not ending, effecting the point of change, and hence functioning as cosmically and socially therapeutic. The payoff of the end, then, would seem to be some kind of narrative transcendence over life's inevitable mysteries.

But rather than imitating or responding to life, narrative might determine our notion of the shape of life and what is important in it—birth, love, reproduction, achievement, death. Vladimir Propp suggests something like this, hypothesizing that folk tales "do not directly 'reflect' a given social order, but rather emerge out of the conflict, the contradictions, of different social orders as they succeed and replace one another."[5] Narrative, then, might also be a creature of a more social response to change, its forms reflecting the discursive tensions that result from ideological and social shifts.

If we understand narrative and life as reciprocal, which is itself both an ideological and a psychological conception, then the end becomes the overdetermined symptom of a complex ideological negotiation. While Barthes observes that "ideological systems are fictions . . . novels—but classical novels, packed with plots, crises, good and evil characters" (27), narrative is ideological and also psychological in the sense that it reflects and shapes both intrapsychic and interpsychic processes and relations. If we understand narrative as a part of a complex dynamic among life, ideology, and psychical processes, there is, as we have seen, no real end; the end is only the appearance of one that lightly masks the fact that the end is both cause and effect, beginning and end in an unending cycle that moves endlessly backward and forward through narrative and time, only appearing to end in what is typically a resounding reaffirmation of dominant ideologies or, in the case of Bataille, cosmic truth. The end that justifies the means is the node where the interactions of narrative, ideology, and psychology are both contained and made visible, the various forms of this relation reflecting the ways both the end and narrative are conceived.

Endgame

If we suspect that ideology, psychology, and narrative are somehow interwound, we might investigate what this connection means by looking at the texts of Sigmund Freud and Peter Brooks. Looking at Freud's attempt to see beyond the story in *Beyond the Pleasure Principle* and at Peter Brooks reading Freud reading in "Freud's Masterplot" provides not so much clues about the "real" nature of narrative but, rather, a fairly transparent rendition of the ideological stake narrative has in sexuality and vice versa. Psychoanalysis has the uncanny virtue of seeming to be only one step from life and at the same time being completely infused with narrative. And narrative, it seems, must reiterate some psychology to make any sense at all. Theories of both psychological and narrative dynamics are interdependent; they share the same features (beginning, middle, and end, plot, characters), are dubious about the middle (the middle in which we are presently ensconced), and emphasize the end, which, according to both theories openly allies sex, knowledge, and death. Although taking a detour through Freud and Brooks may seem a tortuous kind of foreplay (or fore-work), texts that align the psychical with the narrative and the social are the most fertile ground for understanding the ideological stakes represented by the narrative conflation of sex and death.

In a deceptively simple way, Benjamin's generalizations about death and narrative really depend upon a very psychoanalytical understanding of narrative, one initially and perhaps most fully developed by

Sigmund Freud, who came to Benjamin's conclusion (or Benjamin came to his) that death was the story's authority, but in a way that hypothesizes more openly the mechanisms by which death, sex, and mastery are linked to narrative and its ends. Freud's work generally centers upon a narrative pretext: that the telling, reconstruction, and dynamics of stories provide the clues by which the unconscious might be discerned.[6] In his early work on hysterics, dream interpretation, parapraxes and jokes, and even sexuality, Freud relies upon an idea of narrative as sensical and complete, but never as a true, transparent, or faithful representation of a reality.

Premising his psychoanalytical readings upon the idea that narrative is a normative chronological history of a patient's previous experience, Freud deduces the existence and structure of the unconscious from the mistakes, gaps, ellipses, associational illogic, interruptions, and digressions made by patients recounting their experiences and dreams.[7] As Freud remarked in the Dora case, "the patients' inability to give an ordered history of their life in so far as it coincides with the history of their illness is not merely characteristic of the neurosis. It also possesses great theoretical significance" (31). The "theoretical significance" of the "inability to give an ordered history" is entirely a function or dysfunction of narrative conceived as a whole, total account. The patient's refusal to tell a complete story signals either that the patient is holding back or that the patient is subject to symptomatic amnesias.

But the science of psychoanalysis, as Roy Schafer points out, is already reciprocally appended to an underlying narrative operation:

> [T]he claim that these normative life historical projects are simply fact-finding expeditions is . . . highly problematic. At the very outset, each such expedition is prepared for what is to be found: it has its maps and compasses, its conceptual supplies, and its probable destination. This preparedness (which contradicts the empiricists' pretensions of innocence) amounts to a narrative plan, form, or set of rules. *(48)*

Narrative defines the parameters of analysis, setting an imagined whole story against the patient's partial one. The mistakes in the patient's story provide the clues to the underlying existence of another structure—the unconscious. Organized through displacement and condensation, the unconscious insistently interrupts and transforms the surface story. This unconscious seems irrational only in relation to the overlying story; it also has a logic of its own, not only structured by condensation, displacement, and repetition but also comprised of repressed material having mainly to do with sexuality and trauma. It is, finally, another story.

These two structures—narrative and the unconscious—relate to one another through an interpretive dynamic. The surface story provides hints about its unconscious genesis and motivation. At the same time, applying sets of narrative rules (reversal, hyperbole, metaphor, metonymy, repetition) exposes an unconscious that accounts for the surface story's appearance, shape, and problems. The reciprocal relation between narrative and the unconscious constitutes a narrative psychodynamic where even if the unconscious is not narrative, it is perceived, interpreted, and made to function as if it is. When the conscious story and the unconscious join, the result is a complete story that provides the answer to whatever mystery the patient has presented. This answer—this knowledgeable narrative end—has curative power; knowing the whole story of what is repressed and why makes repressed material manifest and the patient is rid of the symptom. The end of the whole story becomes the answer, the goal of analysis, and the possibility of health.

Freud's deployment of narrative as the means to a masterful end requires that he locate and redefine the beginnings—the beginnings of human development, the starting point of analysis, the originating premises of psychoanalytic theories—in order to get to the end at all. The end to Freud's psychoanalysis is only enabled by finding the beginning, the origin of the mistake in the story, the event or repression that, in fact, has often initiated the story (and the analysis) in the first place. The end, hence, *is* literally finding the beginning, which is then relocated as the end, in the position of mastery instead of mistake, of knowledge instead of mystery. The beginning's rescue in the end magnifies the end's importance as it appears to culminate and fulfill the narrative process through which the story is generated. This focus on the end makes the beginning look like a lapse, a false trail, and a bad story that is recuperated through good narrative sense and corrected by the end's insight.

The apparent end to Freud's stories is, thus, not death, but mastery, a mastery that supplants death and motivates the knowledge quest. That knowledge displaces death or that knowledge and death coexist is linked to Freud's emphasis on the story of Oedipus, the same narrative upon which Aristotle formulated his theories of tragic plot. In his appropriation of the Oedipus model, Freud omits Sophocles' play's episode of final suffering—its end—focusing instead on what Aristotle proclaims to be "the most powerful elements of attraction in Tragedy, the Peripeties and Discoveries."[8] Following Aristotle, who prefers the felicitous coincidence of a penultimate Peripeties and Discovery ("The finest form of Discovery is one attended by Peripeties, like that which goes with the discovery in *Oedipus*" [237]), Freud actually prefers this penultimate reversal of fortunes created by knowledge *as* the end instead of the moment of suffering that actually constitutes the end of Sophocles' play. Freud's elimination of the play's terminal anguish dismisses any contemplation of the ultimate effects of tragic action in favor of the masterful moment when all parts seem to join together.

Freud's omission of the literal end to *Oedipus Rex* makes the moment when Oedipus gains knowledge of his identity the end of the oedipal narrative. This shift from the original to a more triumphant, figuratively orgasmic end constitutes both the radical insight of Freud's recovery of the oedipal and Freud's personally triumphant moment of insight into his own life. Comparing Oedipus's narrative with his own development, Freud sees that he and Oedipus are the same. Freud's new self-knowledge makes self-knowledge the oedipal story's new end. In this way, coming to know oneself is coterminous with the high point of Oedipus's drama, effecting the very reversal of fortune and acquisition of knowledge that is itself the conclusion to Freud's quest.

The new end to the story—knowledge, mastery—becomes important not because it is the end; it comes to occupy the end position because it is already important in a post-Enlightenment scientific culture that believes that knowledge is the antidote for death. Instead of Oedipus's suffering and blindness, Freud discovers psychoanalysis, eliminates terminal anguish, and substitutes knowledge for death. This transformation exposes a cultural shift toward a coalition among knowledge, mastery, and ending where death is displaced offstage, and Oedipus rewritten becomes the narrative model—the Plot—for human development.[9] In Freud's transposition of the end, Oedipus's knowledge becomes that which in itself overcomes death while acknowledging it. Oedipus doesn't die but becomes a seer; Freud becomes a knowing analyst; the patient can go on.

While the narrative of Oedipus seems to delay death, the story is still driven by death both in the murder of the father that takes its place throughout the narrative as prophecy, deed, and recognition and in the death of the mother, killed by the knowledge that the story was true. Freud's recognition of the relevance of Oedipus's final knowledge of identity incorporates and subordinates death to the familial, sexual entanglements that become the impetus for murder and revelation, identity, and insight so important to Freudian psychoanalysis. In Freud's work, the omnipresent death of the father becomes a metaphor for self-knowledge and social order, displaced in favor of what Freud envisions as the psychosexual dynamics of human development and socialization. Death's displacement enables a focus on sexuality that returns to an open narrative dynamic with death in *Beyond the Pleasure Principle*.

The oedipal narrative that underlies Freud's work is both the product of and premise for his conclusions about the relation of sexuality to narrative, especially in cases of hysteria and paranoia, where knowledge and mastery are the appropriate, curative ends to fragmented stories whose mysteries are always sexual. As it supplants death, knowledge transforms narrative from any simple mimetic connection with the narrative of life and places it within the dynamic of psychic processes that attempt to manage fear, anxiety, trauma, and reality as they are linked to repressed sexual desires. Narrative's end weds mastery and sexual knowledge as narrative becomes a tool for both psychical survival and psychoanalysis—not an end in itself but the means to a knowledgeable, masterful end.

The End-All and Be-All

What Freud does in shifting the end from Sophoclean suffering to knowledge parallels the way we tend to assume that orgasm, rather than death or another story is a more fitting end. Making the end a higher high seems to provide a more exciting justification for the story, but the end's modern displacement from suffering to mastery is determined by more than just a need for good kicks or a right to a return on our narrative investment. Any rhetorical emphasis on the end—the end where knowledge is located according to some ideology of narrative—may distort its magnitude and make it difficult to see the importance of the story's other parts and their possible relation to sex and death. Where the end represents some sense of a story's totality or wholeness, criticism relating the parts to the whole also tends to focus on the end, not as the subject of, but as a precondition to criticism, even while the parts themselves are equally important.[10] But if an emphasis on the end is a product of the ideologies by which the story is formed in the first place, it is difficult to find meaning in the rest of the story without reference to the end. And so I go on with the end, though it seems as though we should be at the end, beyond the principle of any pleasure.

Sex, death, and endings involve their own dynamic, not one separated from the reciprocal dynamics of narrative but one that tells part of the story of the story. Freud took up the connection between sex and death as the dynamic of instincts in *Beyond the Pleasure Principle*. Employed by Peter Brooks as a model for the dynamics of narrative, Freud's hypotheses about the interrelation of apparently opposing instincts provide a paradigm for the connection between sex and death as narrative motivations, alibis, and subject matter. In "Freud's Masterplot" Brooks links narrative theory to psychoanalysis in an examination of the relation between metaphor and metonymy, repetition and sequence in narrative theory. In the beginning of his essay, Brooks quickly comes to a consideration of the end as that which "continues to fascinate and baffle" (282). Linking the end to death, and desire to the beginning of the story, Brooks conceives end and beginning, death and desire as dynamically interwound, particularly in the middle "whose relation to originating desire and to end remains problematic" (284).

In the middle point in his essay, Brooks introduces Freud's *Beyond the Pleasure Principle* as an "investigation of ends in relation to beginnings" in order to commence consideration of a "properly dynamic model of plot" (285). Already Brooks means more than just plot if plot is simply the story's events and their order. Narrative's dynamism and plot are not analogous, which may account for many of the problems theorists have had understanding the end, which, if Brooks is right, is already more than just an element of plot.[11] Brooks first takes up repetition, the aspect of the dynamic that begins both narrative and *Beyond the Pleasure Principle*. Arguing from Freud's example of the child's *fort/da* game with the reel of thread that repetition is "the movement from passivity to mastery," Brooks interprets mastery as "an assertion of control over what man must in fact submit to—choice, we might say, of an imposed end" (286). In other words, narrative's repetitions are analogous to the child's *fort/da* game. Narrative mastery, thus, is not the end but a response to an end beyond our control. The combination of narrative repetition and mastery enables us to enact in narrative the very choice we would like to have in life.

In Brooks's review of Freud's other suggestions about the function of repetition, Brooks proposes the idea of repetition as "return in the text":

> [W]e cannot say whether this return is a return *to* or a return *of*: for instance, a return to origins or a return of the repressed. Repetition through this ambiguity appears to suspend temporal process, or rather to subject it to an indeterminate shuttling or oscillation which binds different moments together as middle which might turn forward or back. *(288)*

Freud understands repetitions as "daemonic" and "primitive"; Brooks relocates repetition as a structural and temporal feature of narrative's middle where he sees repetition recurring the most. Identified thus with the daemonic through its identification as the primary site of repetition, the middle is a point of uncertainty that refers both forward or back to an end that is in both places. The site of no end yet, the middle nonetheless refers to an end; the dynamics of getting to the end or returning to the beginning are visible in the suspended ambiguity of the middle's *fort/da* oscillations. Suggesting that this middle represents a "tantalizing play with the primitive and the instinctual," Brooks posits the middle as the site where repetition serves as a "binding" agent for "textual energies," the principle through which "similarity" and "substitution," metaphor and metonymy play out.

According to Brooks, narrative repetition exists in a tension with another force that drives either forward or backward in the story. Having linked narrative repetition to Freud's notion of a "daemonic" repetition, Brooks connects the narrative drive to end to Freud's life (sexual) and death Instincts (*Trieb*). Brooks associates the drive to end with Freud's formulation of the pleasure principle: the "tendency operating in the service of a function whose business it is to free the mental apparatus entirely from excitation or to keep the amount of excitation in it constant or to keep it as low as possible" (294–295). He correlates the drive to continue with Freud's "détour called life" that forces the organism to delay death until the right time, to plot its life according to a narrative timing that allows its choice of the correct end. Following *Beyond the Pleasure Principle*, Brooks defines narrative as a departure from and the desire for a sometimes eroticized and always delayed return to the quiescent—"the normal," "the unnarratable" of the beginning and end (291). The terms of this dynamic are, not surprisingly, sex and death where sex as the desire to reproduce sustains the story and joins with death as a state of quiescence, of low excitation.

The idea that narrative is not life enables Brooks to rewrite these forces through a very narrative notion of temporal structure with its distinct beginnings and endings. Brooks, however, also compares narrative to life as that space between a natal excitation and the correct death. Narrative is a series of repetitions with difference that threaten to return to the beginning instead of move toward the end, or that threaten to end prematurely, that pass time, and sustain tension until the right choice of end comes into view. Brooks's "dynamic model," consisting of the tensions between life and death, Eros and quiescence, and stasis and detour, "structures ends (death, reproduction, quiescence, non-narratability) against beginnings (Eros, stimulation into tension, the desire of narrative) in a manner that necessitates the middle as détour, as struggle toward the end under the compulsion of imposed delay, as arabesque in the dilatory space of the text" (295).

The tension of the "dilatory" middle inevitably returns to a consideration of ends, even as Brooks tries to salvage the middle as a potentially subversive site. The middle's "deviance and détour" continue "for a certain time," generating energy, oscillating, but always bound through repetition that functions in reference to the end, working "toward the generation of significance, toward recognition and the retrospective illumination which will allow us to grasp the text as total metaphor" (296). The narrative's play is all finally in relation to the end, not only as that which the text desires but also as the theme that recovers the middle's wandering repetitions. These repetitions are characterized by the choice of an "improper" (and premature or short-circuiting) end or a "mistaken erotic object choice" (296–97). While the middle always threatens a wrong choice, is always in "a state of temptation to oversameness," threatens a "premature discharge," and often, through its provision of false ends, supersedes any "fear of endlessness" a protracted middle might threaten (296), the end's combination of correct erotic choice and death functions as the narrative object of desire. As we saw in Freud's "Three Essays" and as we shall see later, the definitive heterosexuality of the end both forces and enables multiple sexual possibilities in the middle, a locus seemingly occupied by the bad object choice, the homo, and the perverse.

Just as the middle refers to the end, so the end refers back to the middle: "A narrative . . . wants at its end to refer us back to its middle, to the web of the text" in a temporal interreferentiality that ultimately subverts both ends and beginnings (297). The terms and structuring narrative of Brooks's analysis suggest the sexualized nature of the assumptions behind the federation of ends, death, and "correct" erotic object choice as that plays against the middle's tendency to sameness. Associated with the potential cessation of desire, the middle's sameness refers to the quiescence associated with both the end and the time before the beginning. Brooks associates this sameness with a mistaken object choice, examples of which are either frigid or overly perfect brides (both of which stop desire in its tracks by their lack of performative difference) or incest. The danger offered by either of these sexual choices is premature cessation, the "pleasure principle" part of the larger narrative tension between quiescence and a driving forward or back. The dynamic of narrative thus becomes a tension between sameness (defined as a species of incorrect sexual partnering) and difference, between quiescence and desire figured structurally as the middle versus end (and beginning) and as interminability versus the terminable and terminating.

These oppositions and tensions suggest that the connection between erotic energy and death, which Brooks suitably attributes to Freud's need for a symmetry between the two, is ultimately based upon the opposition between sameness and difference with which Brooks begins his essay. Brooks defines sameness/difference in the course of his argument as a species of both repetition and metaphor. The combination of sameness and difference becomes aligned with the duo, narratability and non-narratability, both pairs reiterating the tension between difference and the same-but-different that enables narrative. Sameness (bad object choice, quiescence, premature ending), then, threatens to stop narrative precisely because it is the same as erotic object achieved, as the end of desire, as death. Identifying fulfilled desire with death aligns death and desire through a connection between desire's objects and the story's end. The correct erotic object choice (one that presumably has a potential for reproduction) is located in the same place as death as the delayed object of narrative desire. This connection between death and fulfilled desire also links desire, the force of Freud's Eros, to the end, marshalling what appear to be opposing forces—desire and death—to the same end, arranging them in relation to this end, and subordinating the potential perversity of repetition to the conservation of the proper (i.e., most resounding, total, and pleasurable) end.

Analysis Terminable and Interminable

Here I am at what must be the end, or at least one end, the end where desire, sex, and death seem to come neatly together. Unfortunately this is not yet the final end of the discussion because, like Wings's end, this end hints at another end, the larger end that justifies our looking at ends in the first place. This end—the joinder of death and Eros—leads back to the rest of the story, to just how sexuality becomes a specifically (re)productive activity aligned with ends and death. More dilatory analysis is necessary to determine the ideological investment in the terminal coincidence of sex, correct object choice, mastery, and reproduction and to understand the vicissitudes of metaphor that combines these terms and provides the engine that drives through the story.

Brooks describes metaphor as the productive formulation of "the same-but-different." Stimulating progress or change, one element of narrative successively replaces another similar but different element. Throughout narrative, this successive substitution mediates the deployment of sameness and difference linked to repetition, structure, delay, and desire. Metaphor's intercessions are implemented like the various drives of Freud's pleasure principle: the "difference" that incites excitation goes toward the sameness that characterizes death, the energies of excitation being "bound" by the repetition of a continuous transformation effected by metaphor. As Brooks notes, the larger metaphors of narrative organization, both the death drive and repetition, "serve the pleasure principle" by working toward quiescence and sameness (295). At the same time by limiting excitation, the pleasure principle serves the death drive. Finally, both the pleasure principle and the death drive serve the end.

The dynamic model of excitation, delay, and discharge that Brooks correlates with narrative's beginning, middle, and end produces and/or is premised upon the extended metaphor of orgasm. Freud employs this same orgasmic analogy to prove the truth of the pleasure principle:

> We have all experienced how the greatest pleasure attainable by us, that of the sexual act, is associated with a momentary extinction of a highly intensified excitation. The binding of an instinctual impulse would be a preliminary function designed to prepare the excitation for its final elimination in the pleasure of discharge. *(56)*

Appearing in the last chapter of Freud's discussion of what is beyond the pleasure principle, this orgasmic narrative has shaped his assumption of the seemly order of events throughout the argument. His accounts of the life, reality, and death instincts take place within the narrative of properly productive sexuality he had already fashioned in "Three Essays on the Theory of Sexuality."

What is *beyond* the instinctive urge toward low excitation that constitutes the pleasure principle includes 1) the existence and location of "life instincts" that "operate against the purpose of the other instincts" (34); 2) the possible connection between repetition and reproduction as something that resists ending; and 3) the distribution of Eros and death instincts throughout the psyche that constantly reiterates the little drama of resisting and threatening to end throughout life. While life instincts, like metaphor, work to "combine organic substances into ever larger unities" (37), the self-preservational impetus of the reality principle follows a more strictly preordained, completely nonperverse narrative path:

> They [instincts of self-preservation, self-assertion, and mastery] are component instincts whose function it is to assure that the organism shall follow its own path to death, and to ward off any possible ways of returning to inorganic existence other than those which are immanent in the organism itself. We have no longer to reckon with the organism's puzzling determination (so hard to fit into any context) to maintain its own existence in the face of every obstacle. What we are left with is the fact that the organism wishes to die only in its own fashion.   *(33)*

Like the widely flowing channel of Freud's earlier story of sexuality, self-preservation is in the service of ending properly. The predetermined story "so hard to fit into any context," is still the coming story, the narrative of excitation and release. This, however, is most insistently the story of good release and sufficient foreplay, of not coming before the right time contrasted with the perverse story that comes too soon. While coming to this end is imperiled by the operation of life instincts and Eros in the middle, all comes together in the ending discharge of excitation and return to quiescence attributed to the pleasure principle in the proper nonperverse, reproductive story. No matter how hard Brooks tries to retrieve the middle, the orgasmic subtext still privileges the coming Freud takes as the natural order of life. While Freud examines and questions this order, he also reaffirms it through his assignment of the roles various instincts play.

The orgasmic metanarrative provides one model for the coming together of sameness and difference, not finally in the same-but-different of metaphor but in the synthetic ending accomplished by the various forms of the life instinct and death. The narrative of coming with its underlying sequence of excitation, delay, discharge, and synthesis is a narrative of production (and reproduction) instead of a narrative that leads only to death and cessation. Unlike the real-life end, the end of narrative is not death but a production that replaces death just as in Freud's work knowledge and mastery supplant oedipal death and suffering. In both Freud's and Brooks's accounts narrative leads to the pleasure of cessation but also to knowledge, a child, or another story as the potential products of the synthesis of same but different, of life and death, of the pleasure principle and beyond. Narrative thus oscillates between the same-but-different of metaphor and the different/same of terminal synthesis. Complete sameness or complete difference each threaten narrative but also sustain it.

While Freud associates sex and death through the stubborn insistence of hetero-sex, Brooks's rereading of Freud suggests that the association of sex and death at the story's end has its own little story; the interrelation of sex and death clarifies just what is ideologically at stake in this end that keeps escaping under some other guise. Whether narrative follows orgasm or orgasm follows narrative, the orgasmic narrative beyond the pleasure principle orders the drama of Eros, reproduction, and death, where Eros, which can lead to both intercourse and death, serves finally as their link. While intercourse may result in a reproduction that appears to overcome death by intimating a kind of immortality, it also, and at the same time, leads to the discharge of excitation in death. As the end of the orgasmic story, the coalition of reproduction and death situates the two in an ambivalent relation, reproduction staving off death and death the simultaneous enemy and/or product of reproduction, and both the outcome of coming.

These connections between coming, death, reproduction, and the end are not something Freud and Brooks discover but are rather already a part of the orgasmic ideology of narrative employed by both as a presumption. One way death and reproduction are already associated is through an intergenerational narrative of immortality and perpetuity through which individual death is supplanted by an appeal to family and species survival. Georges Bataille, for example, traces this relation between reproduction and death on a cultural level in *Erotism*. Discerning the complex interplay between the significance of reproduction and death, Bataille sees each as the inevitable and corrective end to the other. Reproduction in its promise of continuity also signals individual discontinuity or death; and the deaths of individuals enable the continuation of a group liable to excessive production. Bataille's vision of mortal/immortal cooperation is similar to Edmund Burke's (and according to Fredric Jameson, Roland Barthes's) connection/opposition between the deathless "beautiful"—"that sinking, that melting, that languor, which is the characteristical effect of the beautiful as it regards every sense"—and the transient "sublime," the fearsome, which arises from the "instinct of self-preservation."[12]

Now I have come to what looks like Freud's end, some knowledge produced by the joinder of elements, a joinder that still oscillates, like Bataille's, between the beautiful and the sublime, the immortal and the mortal as the effect of this ending. But perhaps after all of this, the end is somewhat beside the point or is finally a product of a particular way of thinking about narrative that is aligned with ideologies of production, sexuality, meaning, etc., by means of a particularly literal sexual figuration. The end's position and characterization load it with victory instead of the battle, with the coming of instead of the coming to. Where is the pleasure in the pleasure principle: in the discharge or in the moment just before, or in the many preceding moments of building toward and anticipation, in the beginning so to speak, in desire? As Barthes observes, "so-called 'erotic' books . . . *represent* not so much the erotic scene as the expectation of it, the preparation for it, its ascent; that is what makes them 'exciting'; and when the scene occurs, naturally there is disappointment, deflation" (58). The end is a pretender promising what it can't give by holding out the moment of what has already been happening in the process of coming to the end, hiding the death it cannot occult no matter how many times the spool is retrieved, no matter how grand the victory, prodigious the cum, or auspicious the child.

4

She named him Felix, thrust him from her, and died.
—Djuna Barnes, *Nightwood*, p. 1

If the end functions as the inevitable referent of the story, if it is the orgasm, the synthesis of Eros and death, and the locus of knowledge and mastery, and if the misleading prominence of the end is produced by a narrative of desire and (re)production, how do we understand the stories of desire and (re)production that get us to the end? How do sexuality, orgasm, reproduction, and death become the analogical elements by which narrative is explained: in other words, how much is the story already dependent upon itself in an infinitely recursive circle? Even distinguishing among the terms *sexuality*, *reproduction*, and *death* is difficult without recourse to the narrative paradigm by which they are arranged—and even that paradigm is difficult to separate from its terms, since both terms and narratives are bound up with the ideologies by which the end is already construed as mastery, totality, and conclusion. All this in turn is connected to a pattern of binary opposition, synthesis, and wholeness as it functions within the gendered and sexualized laws of modern Western patriarchy. How do I know this is so without reading through the lens of the narrative I think I shall find? What elements of specific narratives reveal and ratify this reading?

One species of narrative expression that might confirm the ending concatenation of reproduction and death is literary narrative. Unfortunately, the literal combination of sex, reproduction, and death in literary narrative is unusual even though the elements themselves are pervasive. Another major source might be tabloids, television, and media gossip, which are so replete with literal versions of sex and death that we do not even see them; such "real-life" narratives pose as natural fact, so that their very status as story is obviated. The nature of the reproduction/death end is perhaps most clearly manifested in the self-conscious irony and/or melodrama that accompanies overt literary combinations of sex, reproduction, and death. Djuna Barnes's *Nightwood*, for example, begins with the death of Hedvig Volkbein in childbirth. In its diction, descriptions, and in the increasingly ludicrous effects it generates, this introductory moment is heavily ironical. Hedvig Volkbein's age (forty-five), her proud Teutonic stoicism, the desperate pretension of her already dead husband, and all of the false Prussian grandeur for which the patriarchal family stands come to a tiny and uncertain end/beginning in the orphan, Felix, at whose advent the narrative shifts quickly back to a lengthy description of his dead father. As conclusion to and motive for such (albeit false) fanfare, including the sacrifice of his mother, Felix is insufficient, his weakness creating a disparity between cause and effect that produces a constant sense of narrative imbalance embodied by irony and the grotesque. The lopsidedness of Felix's story provides the novel's last patriarchal moment whose parody serves as ironic referent and comparison to the conjunction of sexuality and destruction in Robin Vote.

The obviousness of reproduction and death constitutes the tragedy of the all-too-literal in a narrative world that tends to function metaphorically. The irony of *Nightwood*'s literalized metaphor of death and reproduction is associated with our knowing too much already, not only about the cultural investments of narrative but also about the basic sex/death analogies of narrative employed by Freud, Brooks, and Barthes as a means of understanding it.[13] This knowledge is not some tiresome tautology but rather an example of the rampant prominence of narrative's ideological underpinning. While *Nightwood* plays sardonically with our consciousness of the terms of narrative as well as with a timeworn philosophy of generation, heredity, and patriarchy, the irony produced simply by a surplus of knowledge about narrative—a kind of narrative dramatic irony—is a more typical association of tragedy, irony, and narrative savvy. Thus, we know that the soldier will die as the bells for victory toll, or the inventor will succumb as he perfects his life's work (never living to see its benefits to mankind), or that the prostitute who ruined so many men's lives will be killed (murdered or struck down by disease), or that the adulterers who have believed their success will die or their love will fade. The very literal points excessively to the fact that we all already know the story.

But if sex, reproduction, and death often do not constitute the story's literal end, how, other than through irony or sensational realism do narratives manifest these terms? According to Brooks's more metaphorical reading, narratives embody the tensions a sex/death interrelation epitomizes. As a metaphorical operation, narrative substitutes terms according to a dynamic (the pleasure principle, the death instinct) that itself represents the substitution of terms—sex for death, for example. Narrative is thus constantly displaced and different from itself, chaining same, different, and same-but-different into metaphorical narratives such as orgasm and death that come back, in one way or another, to the metaphors through which narrative is understood—such as orgasm and death. This circularity means that there is no narrative "origin" per se, no beginning point or preexisting pure pattern from which the metaphors of narrative derive; rather, the common principles of their interrelation define the mechanisms and investments of their interchange. In other words, since sex, reproduction, and death are seldom literal, the specific metaphor of sex and reproduction must reveal something about the ideological operation of narrative.

It may seem as if I have always been talking about metaphor if we understand the orgasmic figuration of narrative as a metaphor. But there is an important difference between a sexual metaphor and an ideology of sexuality. Metaphor is artful; ideology is naturalized. Ideology infuses and is inseparable from discourse. Metaphor denaturalizes and draws attention to the terms of the comparison it makes in order to emphasize the insight of its comparison. My argument is that it is impossible to think about narrative without engaging ideologies of sexuality. While my initial analogy of orgasmic narratives and narrative dynamics might have exploited the expectations of metaphor, the metaphor's insight, or the insight that produced the metaphor, led to a more deeply ingrained ideological connection between narrative and sexuality located in the very ways we conceive of narrative.

If we plumb the mechanics of narrative sex/death metaphors, we can find the ideological impetus for this particular combination. Metaphor, as a condition of the discovery and production of meaning and as a basic element of the working of language, requires (and like the fetish, signifies) a loss. Metaphor's shift from term to term always leaves something behind, an ideological detritus precipitated and lost during each substitution. What is lost tells us what has been sacrificed to continue the story, what "same" has been supplanted by what "difference" to continue the chain. Tracing the particular metaphors and substitutions employed in analyses of narrative(s) reveals the differences and losses from one metaphor to the next. That which is replaced by successive metaphors tells the story of the repressed that both drives and impedes the narrative.

So one more time back to Freud as he attempts to untangle the various metaphors of sex and death—sexuality, life, Eros, reproduction, death, the pleasure principle—that become interwound and confused with one another in his formulation of what is beyond the pleasure principle. In this circle of metaphors the distinction between Eros and sexuality, for example, is not so easy to make, despite the fact that sexuality seems to be both a small part of Eros (synecdoche) and to stand for it (metaphor).[14] Untangling Freud's soap-operatic snarl of key terms reveals exactly what ideology sustains their particular relation and function in the scheme of life (and its story), even though Freud's progressive refinement of the definitions of Eros and sexuality tries to differentiate that which can not easily be differentiated. Their differentiation, in fact, might be a symptom of an attempt to keep them separate only because their separation is necessary to a particular notion of structure that requires separate (and separable) dynamics. In the process of separation, Freud must lose those terms that get in the story's way.

In his narrative of instinct dynamics, Freud substitutes Eros, a more generalized, metaphorized version of the sexual impetus, for both the *sexual instincts* and *life instincts*, the terms with which he begins his account. The relation between Eros and the sexual instincts is additionally complicated by another metaphor in which Freud reads the sexual instincts as biological, reducing them to literal reproduction. Appending a clarification of the terms *sexuality* and *Eros* to an explanation of his use of biology as source of convincing analogies, Freud must elucidate the difference between the sexual instincts and Eros because the examples of cellular biology he employs tend to muddle the two, reducing Eros to sex and sex to a reproductive onus and death. To disengage them, Freud explains that the development of the postulate of instinct in psychoanalysis required that the "concept of 'sexuality' " "be extended so as to cover many things which could not be classed under the reproductive function" (45). Sexuality plus the "many things" becomes Eros, while sexuality by itself remains ambivalently allied with reproduction.

To clarify his terminology once and for all, Freud narrates the genesis of the term *Eros* in a footnote:

> We came to know what the "sexual instincts" were from their relation to the sexes and to the reproductive function. We retained this name after we had been obliged by the findings of psychoanalysis to connect them less closely with reproduction. With the hypothesis of narcissistic libido and the extension of the concept of libido to the individual cells, the sexual instinct was transformed for us into Eros, which seeks to force together and hold together the portions of living substance. What are commonly called the sexual instincts are looked upon by us as the part of Eros which is directed towards objects. Our speculations have suggested that Eros operates from the beginning of life and appears as a "life instinct" in opposition to the "death instinct" which was brought into being by the coming to life of inorganic substance.   *(54–55)*

Although sexuality is the origin of Eros, Eros supplants it to become itself the originary force, operating "from the beginning of life." Freud thus constructs a shifting circle where sexuality, the origin of life as it is originally linked to the reproductive function, is the origin of Eros that in turn becomes the origin of life on a slightly less literal level.

Sexuality becomes a subclass of Eros in a relation analogous to that between reproduction and Eros where reproduction unites specific substances into a specific unity and Eros combines "substances into ever larger unities"(37). Eros is the sum of what has been retained from both sexuality and reproduction in their separate metaphorical transformations to the apparently more all-encompassing libido. While Eros and the sexual instincts are related, they are also opposed to one another in the amount of delay they permit; Eros enables a long and well-timed delay, while the sexual instinct, even though conservative, threatens to acquiesce all too precipitously to the pleasure principle. The addition of other "things" slows Eros down, delaying reproduction to the end. Through this issue of timing, which is also a question of proper narrative, Eros becomes the opposite of the sexual instinct, prolonging and preserving what originally wanted instant release.

The product of combined "substances" in another biological analogy, Eros (itself an "ever larger unity") also depends upon what is lost in making sex/reproduction a metaphor. In the substitution of Eros for sexual instinct, Eros carries forward the sexual instinct's combinatory impetus, while its urge toward gratification is lost in favor of delay. Also lost is the pleasure of the pleasure principle. Another loss is gender, the specificity of the germ cells of the biological analogy as well as the "distinction between the sexes" Freud appends to sexuality (34).

The End in the Beginning

While repressing gender would seem to open up the story, permitting a unifying Eros to function in many ways beyond simple oppositional joinder, a binary concept of gender is really the underlying principle driving Freud's presumptions about all of these terms. Gender's centrality is apparent in yet another narrative circle where Freud returns to the "origins" of sexuality in order to reconcile sexuality, which has lost its link to the pleasure principle, with the death instinct. To do this, Freud undertakes a consideration of the origin of sexuality, not by recourse to science where, he notes, "not so much as a ray has penetrated," but rather to Plato's quotation of Aristophanes' mythical narrative of the origin of sexual union in the *Symposium* (51). Selecting

Aristophanes' story of the beginning of sex because it already links the sexual instincts to the pleasure principle ("I should not venture to produce it [the story] here, were it not that it fulfills precisely the one condition whose fulfillment we desire" [51]), Freud provides his own, somewhat truncated rendering. For his purposes, Aristophanes' story recounts "original human nature" where there were three sexes instead of two: "man, woman, and the union of the two"(51). With everything on these beings doubled (four hands, two faces, two sets of genitals, etc.), Zeus decided to cut them into two and "the two parts of man, each desiring the other half, came together, and threw their arms about one another eager to grow into one" (51–52).

This rendering is slightly, but significantly different from Plato's version of Aristophanes' story where the original beings are excessively whole, balloonlike creatures, descended from and looking like their mythical progenitors, the sun (male), the earth (female), and the moon (androgyny), whose doubled features face opposite directions.[15] In their celestomorphic form, according to Plato, these beings were powerful and attacked the gods, so Zeus cut them in half to diminish their strength and increase their numbers. But their " 'parts of generation'" were still in the back, and as they died from grief, a merciful Zeus decided to shift the genitals to the front so that " 'by the mutual embraces of man and woman they might breed and the race might continue'" (101).

Freud omits two important features in his narrative tailoring of Aristophanes' story; one is, as happened with Sophocles' play, the story's end. The other is the beings of the same doubled gender. Curiously, Aristophanes' conclusions lead to a formulation of something like Freud's notion of Eros (Aristophanes' "Love") as a productive coming together, but Freud omits this terminal breeding so that he can end with the beings' nostalgic reunion, the point that proves the viability of the pleasure principle: in its original form the sexual instincts are linked to the pleasure principle as a desire to return to an originary state of things. Repeating his truncation of *Oedipus Rex*, Freud changes Aristophanes' end in order to gain his own end, reshaping the story by omitting anything extraneous to his argument, most crucially the end, thus changing and emphasizing his new end as a moment of joinder and mastery.

Freud can premise the pleasure principle on a return to an originary state only if the majority of the original alternatives are omitted.

Including those homosexual alternatives treated explicitly by Aristophanes would divorce a sexuality linked to reproduction from the urge to return to the origin. Sexuality would, thus, again be split from the death instinct that is where Freud began. To make sexuality fit death, therefore, Freud must tie sexuality to reproduction already seen as a combination of opposites, omitting all instances of sameness, including the sameness represented by homosexuality. Freud thus includes only the odd androgynous term of Aristophanes' story, losing what is really the story's point (and conclusion). He disregards the sexualities created by the originary beings' redoubling, forgets the coming back together that produces joy, loses again the pleasure already lost in the shift from sexuality to Eros. The omission of joy, sameness, and homosexualities suggests that they are all somehow connected to one another in their exclusion from the causal circle, a circle that, in order to function as a circle, must include heterosexual reproduction, the odd but necessary term that provides the mechanism for the perennial production of difference from difference that drives metaphor and the story.

Having left out Zeus's affirmative, specifically reproductive anatomical reconstruction that succeeds his conclusion (Zeus moves the parts of generation from the back to the front), Freud also neglects Aristophanes' own conclusion, which is an explanation of the origin of multiple sexualities as a logical derivation from the originary doubled wholeness of three different genders. In fact, Freud completely neglects the problem of gender altogether, partly because the apparently ungendered impetus to originary wholeness in his account of Eros is already heterosexual, but also perhaps because Freud's schema of instincts already belongs to an oppositional paradigm that Aristophanes' story undermines.

Because reproduction, in Freud's view (and despite all of his examples from cellular biology) depends upon an oppositional union, reproduction becomes the paradigm for the binary combination of differences that delays life until the proper end. Reproduction, which embodies difference in its presumed binary opposition, is thus in the service of Eros, of that which extends life. This link between reproduction and Eros splits sexuality into two parts: a primitive one that follows the pleasure principle and stops the narrative—the joyful, overly same, homosexual with bad timing—and a conservative one, linked to heterosexual reproduction, which extends it. The interrelation of hetero and the primitive perverse and homo parallels Freud's earlier narrative of sexuality in *Three Essays*. The first genus of sexuality—the homo, the perverse—is the repressed upon which the second, heterosexual reproductive story ultimately depends.

Reproduction thus exceeds and represses sexuality, while sexuality is always already more than reproduction, coming closer in Aristophanes' account to Freud's notion of Eros. The circle between sexuality and reproduction must omit sexuality that is not reproductive as excessive and dangerous to the healthy continuation of life and the story, but include it as that which is necessary to the progression of same-but-different that continues the story. The relation between the sexual instincts and Eros is parallel to the relation between reproduction and sexuality; but while the sexual instincts stand in as only a part of Eros, reproduction substitutes for sexuality, eliminating all nonreproductive sexuality (seen as sameness) to keep the story going. But the sameness attributed to the unexpressed remainder of sexuality and the doubled originary beings is necessary to produce the narrative/life dynamic in the first place as the sameness hetero difference must repress. The result of the elision of sameness is a turn toward what appears to be an originary heterosexuality that serves as the combinatory principle of both metaphor and life.

The confusion about the relation between sexuality and Eros, played out around the origins of sexuality and the source of the instinct to return to a former state, is ultimately linked to the hidden but pervasive binary oppositional premise cached in this footnote about which story is the original story. But while it seems obscure, Freud's binary premise openly emerges on the metaphorical level of life dynamics. Freud's scheme for the tensions of life depends upon oppositions, actually ignoring the sexual aspects of Eros that exceed the reproductive binding of germ cells. At the same time, the oppositional germ cells that combine become the model for an indiscriminate binding force that is covertly, and oppositionally, gendered. The binarism of these life dynamics exists not only at the expense of other possibilities (such as the quite logical homosexual component to Eros that Freud omits from Aristophanes' story) but also as a result of the influence of a narrative of completion and wholeness that can result only from having all of the parts and none too many. Binary oppositions fulfill the role of completion without excess that precedes and shapes the dynamics Freud identifies. While he thinks he is proceeding from scientific evidence and empirical observation, he is already conforming to a necessarily binary ideology that locates wholeness as both beginning and end and appends it very specifically to a process of combination analogous to his renderings of sexual reproduction.

Gender binaries are ensconced in Freud's account even though (or because) joinder and wholeness, as Aristophanes' story illustrates, are not necessarily linked to opposition, nor is the originary wholeness of the sun, earth, and moon beings a wholeness in the sense that it is a product of binaries. Rather, theirs is an excessive wholeness, a dangerous doubling or repetition whose excess cannot be recreated. Only the Androgynous Beings' rejoinder is productive; and it is their productive model that holds sway throughout Freud's choice of what he tells of these stories. Thus the entire range of Aristophanes' origins and wholeness is really too much to constitute the originary state to which Freud wishes instinct to return. He displaces the excessive wholeness of Aristophanes' original into the heterosexually productive model, leaving the other alternatives as by-products. The by-product of this hetero-logic is the sameness that governs the ambition of the originary beings and the homosexuality of their attempts to reunite. Like Zeus, Freud cuts them apart since their halves suffice better than their wholes.

Despite his locating heterosexuality at the origin, Freud's own logical maneuvers demonstrate that the return to an original wholeness is not as simple as it seems, in part because that origin, like death, threatens the return of sameness. Employing, for example, the origin as the source of Eros means defining the origin in the first place and flirting dangerously with the premature return of the repressed. The form of the return, in the case of Eros as a binding instinct, is related to the supposed originary state described by Aristophanes and at best linked to some version of the pre-oedipal, but Freud has trouble finding the correct state without inadvertently conjuring the excessive sameness of the same-sex doubled beings. He must therefore seek an origin that anticipates his end instead of employing Aristophanes' origin, which verges on the pathologically same. Freud thus rejects Aristophanes' story because it is already second-hand (told by Plato) and is not really about the origin of sexuality after all but about the "power of Love" for which originary wholeness accounts and not necessarily through sexuality at all. Aristophanes' heavy emphasis on the causes of homosexuality cannot finally be the origin of the origin for Freud (even though he has already omitted this). Instead, in a footnote, Freud traces "Plato's story" to what he claims to be the even more originary Upanishads, which in his description includes only the androgynous being, resulting in a completely (and totally) heterosexual version of a return to originary wholeness (52).[16]

Freud's covert reliance upon a narrative of opposition and joinder (or rejoinder) and reproduction completes the circle of narrative and psychical process. Narrative is the product of tensions that are like psychic tensions, and psychic tensions are like the tensions of a very specific notion of narrative that is in turn dependent upon a certain comprehension of opposition, joinder, and reproduction. The opposition working within this circle is linked to gender and heterosexuality as a naturalized assumption made through the narrowing of sexuality into reproduction at the expense of other options. Through reproduction, a specific heterosexuality supplants the broader possibilities of binary opposition as the operative mechanism of joinder. Occupying the place in the story where same that has become different becomes same-but-different, the model of heterosexual reproduction becomes the way to a correct and timely end.

But which comes first: the beginning and end in wholeness or the binaries that come between that define the character of this beginning and end? Aristophanes' story shifts from a wholeness that is doubled, to doubles, to a desire for unity. Perhaps his story is a specimen story in a much more telling way than Freud suspects, as he supplants it in favor of the simple oppositions of the Upanishads. The division into twos produces a drive for unity, "a longing to grow into one" (101), which is different from the original doubled wholeness, the two together becoming a closed system. Jean-François Lyotard observes that the division Freud makes between Eros and death instincts is a way of separating and opposing what may be inseparable pulsions into a binary scheme dependent upon the "unicity" of the function of each, a separation and opposition that are the necessary structural precursors to any idea of wholeness.[17] As Freud appropriates Aristophanes' story, it becomes the story of how intrinsic the narrative relation is between binary oppositions and unity and how the production of difference diverges from deathly sameness and in turn produces a new unity and an appropriate end. His analysis also demonstrates how completely sexualized this process is in its conception.

5

Termination of the analysis signals the dissolution of certain fantasies as well as of the analyst, whose omnipotence is put to death.
—Julia Kristeva, *In the Beginning Was Love*, p. 9

The underlying sexual ideology of narrative survives despite claims that we are in a poststructuralist (and perhaps postnarrative) age. Although various metanarratives of knowledge, according to Lyotard, might be disrupted, the structuralist character of narrative with its adherent binarisms and presumed productivity still holds sway not only as a comforting relic of more certain times but also as a thriving defense against poststructuralist skepticism, systemic failures, and grandiose multiplicity. The structuralist sense of narrative, in fact, fits nicely into a commodity cultural sense of product where narrative becomes another part of the economy. But it also survives exactly where we might not expect it: as the narratives accounting for knowledge, progress, and consumption in poststructuralism and commodity culture.

If we are in a poststructuralist age, this means, among other things, that the weaknesses, processes, investments, and blindnesses of structuralism are visible.[18] In this narrative of the history of thought, poststructuralism takes the knowing position of the end (even if it knows it doesn't know), signaling the termination of a structural analysis whose fantasies of wholeness are finally dissolved. But as Lyotard's comment about Freud implies, all is not quite as certain as that hindsight that can at last identify such enemies as binary opposition and self-repeating structure and expose their error. While a late-capitalist avant-garde might fashion narratives without closure or end or with polymorphous sexualities beyond the reference of the family (and that is usually somewhat doubtful), the idea of narrative as a cause-and-effect sequence with conflict and a conclusion still dominates not only literary narratives—and the very idea and process of narrative—but also the positioning of poststructuralism itself. The end has not yet come.

Justifying the Means

It takes little stretching to engage a needs/pleasure narrative in service of commodity culture, since this narrative has always been the narrative of capitalism, sexualizing and reordering profit and production (coming and reproduction).The concepts of narrative and sexuality evolved together within the frame of developing capitalism and the rise of the bourgeoisie. In broad historical terms, the word *narrative* meaning "history," or "story" linked to the telling of a history and the formulaic recitation of legal facts, appears in the late sixteenth century.[19] With the industrial revolution, the term shifts slightly, connoting less a recital of facts and becoming more a species of tale, an independently existing, separable genre. This latter idea of narrative becomes institutionalized with the novel; only in the twentieth century does *narrative* become a term that connotes a specific shape and dynamic existing separately from any particular narrative instance.The evolution in the concept of narrative from the Renaissance to the twentieth century is also coincidental with the enlargement of the concept of sexuality as something separable from reproductive sex, the discrete identification of male homosexuality, and the rise of the bourgeoisie.[20]

Sexuality appears in English, according to the *OED* in the early nineteenth century, a noun deriving from the adjective *sexual*, the use of which began in English in scientific treatises in the mid-seventeenth century. Originally referring to gender, particularly as it plays in the sex lives of plants, sexuality's meaning is enlarged to include sexual intercourse as well. *Sexual* from the start means hetero-sexual; remaining for a long time within the scientific/medical vocabulary, only in the mid-nineteenth century is the term *sexuality* separated from reproduction, referring to the "possession of sexual powers or capability of sexual feelings" (*OED*). One of the examples offered by the *OED*, however, is neither scientific nor medical; rather, it refers to pleasure:"1893. C.A. Clarke *Knobstick* xiii, 137. Under the unsteady inspiration of . . alcohol, there was rude and uproarious bawling of music hall ditties . . and chuckling sexualities were tossed to and fro."

If the appearance of these terms in English is indicative of the emergence of their concepts, the roughly contemporaneous emergence of the terms *narrative* and *sexuality* suggests a connection that is not so much causal as coincidental. Aligning power and production, three terms—1) sexuality defined as strictly reproductive; 2) "excess" sexuality that is not reproductive; and 3) narrative as a form of organizing information within a dynamic that is curiously mimetic of both human reproduction and industrial production—come together in the burgeoning of a print culture that was already anxious about reproduction.[21] When production is linked to reproduction, sexuality becomes the "cause" of both in a narrative where the failure of increase is tragedy. Before twentieth-century commodity culture, this narrative was naturalized, part of an enlargement of scientific discourse into literature. Zola's *Nana*, for example, is exactly about how a nonreproductive sexuality—that of the courtesan Nana—is financially ruinous to her suitors. Nana's wealth, pried from these lovers, is wasted on ephemeral luxury. In the end, an impoverished Nana dies of smallpox, her dangerous beauty and sexuality destroyed. The "lesson," which is apparently about the dangers of immoral women, is also about the relation between nonreproductive sexuality and economic waste and the very alluring dangers of both.

The link between commodity and sexuality, which reaches its first apotheosis in the pornographic/scientific narrative of the prostitute, also informs the more hidden analogy between production and reproduction and the already operative dynamic of production and power.[22] Tracing the history of sexuality and its relation to discourse and power, Michel Foucault argues that the very concept of a sexuality as a "set of effects produced in bodies, behaviors, and social relations by a certain deployment deriving from a complex political technology," is linked to the "self-affirmation" of the bourgeoisie as it developed in the nineteenth century with the overtly reproductive end of improving and sustaining bourgeois family lines.[23] Foucault's history of sexuality makes visible the narrative disposition of sexualities and the sexual disposition of narrative in terms of power and discourse. His analysis of the intricacies and perversities of power enlarges the sway of sexuality to all narrative, not as itself the specific cause but as the specific pattern of the discovery of knowledge and mastery in narrative.

Sexuality, according to Foucault's history, exists in a complex and contradictory relation with power, conceived not as monolithic but as playing in several places at once. Sexuality, whose narrative is quickly appended to the family, is perceived as the site of the effects of power: "It [sexuality] appears rather as an especially dense transfer point for relations of power: between men and women, young people and old people, parents and offspring, teachers and students, priests and the laity, an administration and a population" (103). Sexuality functions as the principle of transfer, the logic of a plot of history and power. And that logic is binary, even if sexuality is not: "Power is essentially what dictates its law to sex. Which means first of all that sex is placed by power in a binary system: licit and illicit, permitted and forbidden. Secondly, power prescribes an 'order' for sex that operates at the same time as a form of intelligibility: sex is to be deciphered on the basis of its relation to the law" (83).

The self-perpetuating motives of bourgeois capitalism rope sexuality into the service of the family, which must restrict sexuality to a non-incestuous heterosexuality. Sexuality's position as licit or illicit depends upon its reproductive use; its intelligibility exists in relation to the reproductive narrative. In the narrative of familial productivity, homosexuality and other "perversions" quickly become the enemies of healthy reproduction; "sexual perverts" descend from afflicted ancestors and in turn produce degeneration. Thus, while healthy heterosexuality produces the proper reproductive narrative—like reproducing like and increasing (similar to well-invested capital)—perversions produce the wrong story: decrease, degenerescence, death. This perception is supported by the narrative logic of production, a logic of combination and increase, and both are susceptible to a deplorable short circuiting through pleasure (bad investment) and the seductive but unprofitable delay of perverse "détours." The bourgeois need for the correct narrative, one effected by proper heterosexual, reproductive sexuality and good timing, positions sexuality as itself causal: perverted sexuality is the cause of the bad narrative, familial disfunction, low production; and good, reproductive sexuality is the cause of profit, continuity, and increase.

Sexuality becomes narrative, particularly, Foucault argues, confessional narrative, where the confession of sex becomes the truth of subjectivity. Sexuality's position as cause is a product of the expansion of the confessional mode into broader cultural discourse. Sexuality produces the techniques of narrative and surveillance by which its own truth is extracted. But while confession of sex leads to the truth of the individual, the truth of sexuality remains the victim of a discursive duplicity:

> Underlying the difference between the physiology of reproduction and the medical theories of sexuality, we would have to see something other and something more than an uneven scientific development or a disparity in the forms of rationality; the one would partake of that immense will to knowledge that has sustained the establishment of scientific discourse in the West, whereas the other would derive from a stubborn will to nonknowledge. *(55)*

Perverse sexuality causes the narrative of degenerescence, ensuing from and producing this "will to nonknowledge." At the same time, the perverse rejoins the narrative of familial production as its hindrances, as that which can make the family pathological and non-(re)productive. In the second half of the nineteenth century, psychoanalysis rewrites the narrative of the perverse and the properly reproductive into another cause/effect narrative. Resituating the perverse as normal, psychoanalysis relates the family to perverse as well as healthy sexual causes, engaging a much broader range of sexual causality in a circular family narrative where the family causes perversity and is the result of its cure. Psychoanalysis's de-pathologization of perversions occurs via a recognition of their role in production: the production of the sexually normal individual who passes through various stages of perversion on the way to a reproductive future. Perversion is normalized as it is narratively subordinated, but it is permitted to play in the field of pleasure that constitutes part of the narrative's "détour." In this way the family comes to contain and neutralize nonreproductive sexualities within its own reproductive aegis, subordinating and burying the "unhealthy" sexual narrative within the narrative of production.

Foucault's analysis of the emergence and functions of sexual discourses requires a series of reciprocal relations among sexuality, power, the family, and production that include narrative (and its inherent heterosexual premise) as the already functioning though highly complex cause/effect logic of combination. His suggestion that sexuality becomes the cause of a confessional disclosure and at the same time becomes the truth—the knowledge gained at the end of the story—enacts a circular relation between sexuality and narrative where as both cause and effect, sexuality's truth becomes the "truth" of a history of discourse, even though Foucault has rendered provisional the idea of truth. "Having to tell everything, being able to pose questions about everything, found their justification in the principle that endowed sex with an inexhaustible and polymorphous causal power" (65), he says, while sexuality as the object of investigation becomes its own answer. In a sense, this is his point: the complex and polymorphous relations between discourse and power mask themselves with a sexuality that, itself polymorphous, is structured and naturalized into the binaries that serve as the organizing matrix and combinatory model for its own operation, creating a seamless circle where sexuality and its hidden narrative of production become cause and effect of themselves and each other.

The causal power of sexuality in turn reverts to the story of sexuality itself, informing the conflict between perverse pleasure and reproduction and the division of sexualities into the two historical trends—

"the deployment of alliance" and the "deployment of sexuality"—
Foucault discerns. For Foucault,

> the deployment of alliance is attuned to a homeostasis of the social
> body, which it has the function of maintaining: whence its privi-
> leged link with the law; whence too the fact that the important
> phase for it is "reproduction." The deployment of sexuality has its
> reason for being, not in reproducing itself, but in proliferating,
> innovating, annexing, creating, and penetrating bodies in an
> increasingly detailed way, and in controlling populations in an
> increasingly comprehensive way. *(107)*

His identification of these two sexual systems divides sexuality into
two concepts whose terms reenact the conflict/synthesis narrative of
production. The "deployment of alliance," roughly aligned with familial and reproductive forms, and the "deployment of sexuality," aligned
with a more polymorphous perversity, reproduce a binary not unlike
Barthes's division between the oedipal pleasure of cultural acquiescence
and the perverse pleasure of that which disturbs it. Neither Foucault
nor Barthes link their binaries within a logic of combinatory reproduction; rather, they see them as interdependent and interpenetrating,
cause and effect of one another. This enables them to locate pleasure in
the middle, in the place where the law of closure and reproduction is
both challenged and given in to—in the place of interpenetration and
multiple unresolved possibilities constituting desire.

Terminal Knowledge

While terminal knowledge tends to foreclose all pleasure but its own
pleasure in ending, this pleasure of the middle, of Brooks's "détour," is
of another species. For Foucault, there is pleasure in power and power
in pleasure in the exercise of what seem to be the controlling regimes
of social institutions and the family:

> The pleasure that comes of exercising a power that questions,
> monitors, watches, spies, searches out, palpates, brings to light; and
> on the other hand, the pleasure that kindles at having to evade
> this power, flee from it, fool it, or travesty it. The power that lets
> itself be invaded by the pleasure it is pursuing; and opposite it,

> power asserting itself in the pleasure of showing off, scandalizing,
> or resisting. *(45)*

This pleasure/power play is a flirting rather than a fucking, like Barthes's "pleasure of the text," a pleasure produced in abeyance of an end, on the way to closure and in the place of its impossibility.

The interdependency of pleasure and power, like the relation of narrative's middle and end, is constituted by interpenetrating binaries—heterosexuality, homosexuality—situated in relation to particular cultural positions defined according to shifting "techniques of power." The specific terms of the middle, while we know or suspect they are sexual, may change, but their larger relation to the oedipal or the "deployment of alliance" shifts only over longer periods of time. If this is the case, then narrative's deployment of sexuality would reflect the techniques of power that hold sway at a given time in history. By reading the deployment of sexualities, we might also understand what idea of narrative governs and how its dynamics and ideology both produce and conform to the techniques of power that dominate. While the end seems to be the locus of power's play, the truth of sex and the sex of truth, the middle holds the cues.

Commodity culture, in fact, seems to suspend us in a perpetual middle, where each simulation only leads us to another while making us believe that our urge is for the "Real," a twenty-first century truth mercifully and delusively distant from the death and void the Real might import. Closure of consumption, at best temporary in its orgasmic purchase, serves the dynamic of perpetual desire that sustains consumption but is itself sustained by the overriding, sexualized narrative of desirability. Consuming seems to fulfill our desire and make us desirable; desire interwound with itself creates a narrative whose only reference is desire. The end of the story, thus, serves the middle's scenario of desire by perpetually holding out another end: the ultimate and paradoxical end that in the end we will ourselves be the commodified objects of desire. What this means is that the desire of commodity narrative is to sustain itself by producing the impossible narrative of the desire to be desired, a desire sustained and fed by consumption as a version of joinder modeled on sex. Being the object of another's desire means finally being the commodity, being in the locus of power as the narrative leads to an illusory ending in self.

This pattern of desire and commodity is the hypertext of Foucault's analysis of sexuality, power, and discourse, taking the terms to their most logical extreme, translating the romance of familial reproductive sexuality into the subtle realm of late-capitalist productive desire. This desire is finally not as polymorphous as it might seem; rather, it still makes sense only within a strained reproductive logic that nostalgically situates the entire process as patriotic, moral, right-minded, and natural. Hence the commercial emphasis on authenticity: "natural" food, public confession, the biologization of homosexuality (i.e., the hypothalamus, the gene), the emergence of artificial reproductive techniques whose end is a "natural" child, the panic of family values. But this conservative gloss and the survival of the reproductive narrative are dependent upon precisely that perversity of desire typical of the commodity system, the desire perpetually misled, that where the homosexual man (known or unknown) becomes the object of heterosexual female desire, where males can (and sometimes wish to) claim they are lesbians, where mainstream lesbianism is whisperingly tolerated at least in public figures, and where gay studies have a commercial "place" in academe. Only in contrast to the "authentic" narrative of production represented by the old story of heterosexual reproduction do these new perversities make sense. They are produced by it and in turn perpetuate it within the shifting realms of need and object.

Family turned commodity, the family narrative still contains and employs perversion as causally useful even (especially) in the commodity narrative. Perversion has its place as always in the still-dominant and omnipresent heterosexual story, the story we can see in our "post-" position, which is itself the product of the convergence of sexuality and truth.[24] Homosexuality, of all the perversions, is permitted as narratively useful, necessary to stir up the middle, to sustain consumptive desire, to make us believe that the hetero no longer holds sway while it holds more and more frequent sway in the commodity narrative, where, as rumor would have it, the best consumers are homosexual males. The story is now "perfectly fulgurating," like Madonna, the perennial orgasm that masquerades as desire, the perpetual short circuit of gratification that becomes an end in itself. But this narrative of "geometric incandescence" is not, as Bataille envisions, a narrative of life and death; it is the narrative of a narrative of a narrative of . . . that perpetually defers the end in the name of the end: the perfect orgasm, the perfect product, the ultimate bliss of being desired.

Despite (or because) of commodity culture, the structuralist notion of narrative that governs Freud's and Brooks's analysis still operates—although, as commodity culture demonstrates, it may appear to play more in a narrative middle comprised of illusory endings. If the orgas-mic end is now the middle of a commodity culture narrative whose end is perpetually deferred in favor of profit, then sexuality becomes the middle in reference to an unreachable but always referenced end that is either more sex or real death. Only in the narrative of romance does this unending end continue to function, its anachronistic shape comforting and its imaginary dynamic governing even the explanation of that which might diverge from it as it occupies the middle of a more overweening narrative of commodity consumption. Our fantasies are still not dissolved, poststructuralism is not the end of the story, the ana-lyst is still alive.

If Propp is correct in his understanding of folk tales as reflecting both cultural shifts and the tensions between coexisting but perhaps incom-patible orders, then the link between sexuality and narrative may reflect the tense coexistence of two orders represented by the change from a feudal to a capitalist economy and from blood to affiliation as the basis for family organization. In this context the sexual ideology of narrative is like the "winged horse" Propp uses as an example of a "hybrid" char-acter; appended to one another, ideologies of narrative and sexuality produce a compromise form: narrative whose heteroideology moors failing familial forms and a sexual ideology whose narrative persistently underwrites production. Foucault locates the rise of sexuality in the nineteenth century, and the heteroideological narrative may date from then. We may now be facing a new shift in social orders from produc-tion capitalism to a commodity culture detached from labor; their over-lap may effect a new narrative hybrid and shift narrative ideology. If that is the case, then it is important to understand the narrative/sexuality configuration as a way of anticipating and employing any new shifts to the advantage of those the current narrative regime has left flounder-ing in the middle.

CHAPTER TWO

Come Together

1

The passage from scission to "synthesis" consists not in some productive act of reconciliation but in a simple shift of perspective by means of which we become aware of
how what we mistook for scission is already in itself reconciliation: the scission is not
"overcome" but rather retroactively "undone."
—Slavoj Žižek, For They Know Not What They Do, p. 165

If "the end is in the beginning," then the middle is the continuation, the site of interplay, the locus where contingent conflicts and alliances are formed, dissolved, reformed. In Brooks's and Freud's account, the middle is the site of tension and threat, a dynamic vista full of exchange, substitution, and desire. It is also the region where Eros's urge to combine into larger units essays but does not yet dominate. Unlike the synthetic mastery associated with ends, the middle's mediate scrambling may operate in the same way that, according to Foucault, the term *sexuality* functions in discourse. Like sexuality, the middle demonstrates, unbound and visible "mobile, polymorphous, and contingent techniques of power" (106). The perceptible orchestration of narrative elements—their definition, disposition, investment, and employment—in the middle might evade the gathering rigidity of binary opposition aligned with narrative's (re)productive terminal impetus. Unless of course, our notion of conflict or even looking for a middle, is, as Žižek suggests, already a retrospective product of the end. It might also be the case that the middle only makes sense as a middle if it is structured in anticipation of an end whose reconciliations depend upon the middle's discernible sorting, opposing, dividing, and conjoining under the guise of mobility and contingency. Or both.

This chapter will investigate how structuralist theories of narrative understand narrative. It is too easy to declare that narrative is heterosexual simply on the basis of the plotting habits of industrial culture; to understand why heterosexual, marital, reproductive plots are so pervasive and insistent requires looking at our very understandings of narrative as those exist in theories and narratives about narrative.[1] As deliberate examinations of the nature of narrative, narrative theories might reveal whether and how narrative is metaphorically heterosexual, the forms such heterosexuality might take, and how the inflection of sexual ideology influences our understanding and reading of narrative.

What we find is that structuralist theories of narrative assume a heterosexual ideology. Coy, disappearing in attempts to avoid overt conflict or head-butting oppositions, and ghostly without the support of openly gendered positions, evidence of narrative's heterosexual ideology can be found in those places where theorists finally attempt to account for just what brings narrative together—for what transforms narrative from a series of dissociated events into a cogent form. This combinatory principle (and the idea that there should even be some such form of combination) occupies narrative's center. Confusion reigns in this narrative heart until an often unspecified, but very fecund attraction comes to save it, providing a magical mechanism (remember Freud?) by which disparate parts come willingly together.

This analysis is necessarily protracted, since locating the subtleties of ideology demands multiple examples. I focus in this chapter on how and where the narrative theories of Claude Lévi-Strauss, Tsvetan Todorov, A. J. Greimas, Roland Barthes, Teresa de Lauretis, and Freud (as well as a host of narratologists) expose their heterosexual presumption; I also show how narrative's heteroideology depends upon gender and the oedipal construct as naturalized paradigms. I begin with an analysis of Colette's short story, "The Secret Woman," whose metanarrative commentary exemplifies narrative's intimate relation with gender and sexuality.

Sexual Healing

Narrative's middle exposes its sexuality most alluringly not in narratives about sexuality, but in those narratives that are literally about *narrating* sexuality. In Henry Miller's *Tropic of Cancer*, Vladimir Nabokov's *Lolita*, or Kathy Acker's *Portrait of an Eye* narrative appears to be the story's focus and sexuality its secret. No longer the sexual substitute that effectively performs a libidinous dynamic, narrative is the middle's preoccupation, blocking and exposing sexual dynamics, standing in their stead. One of the most economic illustrations of this interchange of narrative and sexuality is Colette's very short, short story, "The Secret Woman." In its metanarrative consciousness of narrative's necessary relation to gender, sexual fantasy, and desire, "The Secret Woman" exemplifies how narrative substitutes for sexuality, raising questions about the nature of narrative itself.

In "The Secret Woman" an omniscient narrator recounts the ironic tale of a doctor husband who produces the alibi that he must be out of town so he can attend the purple and green masquerade ball without his wife. The wife, pretending to find the idea of attending the ball alone distasteful, histrionically feigns resignation to an evening alone. The story's irony is linked to the characters' overcompensatory manufacture of deliberately fictive narratives of sacrifice. These cover stories of professionalism and social frigidity generate opportunities for sexual freedom at the same time as they mask desires that both characters wish to hide.

The story's middle is occupied with the third-person narrator's retrospective rendering of the husband's shifting perceptions and ensuing narratives of his wife's apparent promiscuity at the ball. Thinking he sees through his wife's lie when he encounters a masked Pierrot that resembles her, the husband tries to construe what is under the mask. He manufactures a series of alternative narratives to account for his "wife's" behavior as she wanders from person to person in a series of flirtations, caresses, and embraces. Fabricating a progressive set of sexualized subjects in the place of his enigmatic wife, the husband invents stories that are either quickly contradicted by her actions, thus requiring another narrative, or that conceal some question his stories can never answer, also requiring more narrative. What the husband does not recognize is that his uxorial narratives are about his own desire.

The husband's blindness about the real subject of the story disenables any masterful ending—any "real knowledge," dénouement, or even literal unmasking. Resolving finally that his wife's disturbing instances of random sexuality have no significance whatsoever except to indicate their lack of significance (or that she is characterized by lack), the husband's final conclusion is that there is no conclusion. He becomes the postmodern apologist who substitutes the narrative of a lack of masterability for his failure to master; in knowing the secret of his wife's lack of "secret," he believes he is somehow wiser than when the story began. And while the husband doesn't know what he doesn't know, we, from the privileged frame of third-person distance, think we do know how silly his knowing is.

Making the husband's narratives the subject of another narrative—that of an omniscient narrator—"The Secret Woman" rather cleverly imbricates narrative and sexuality on several levels at once, each of which implicates the narrator as reader and the reader as narrator. On the level of the story's manifest content or cause/effect arrangement of events, the husband becomes the suspicious reader/narrator of his wife's actions. The story of the husband's stories and their certain end in uncertainty invites a skeptical rereading of the husband. A consciousness of our own reading (and now subsequent narrative) of his stories reiterates the circle among sexuality, knowledge, and narrative as we think we know that what the husband thinks he knows he does not really know.

We are thus bound into this story, not only by a kind of readerly mimesis that imitates and extends the husband's attempts to account for his wife but also by the tightly drawn relation between narrating and desire. Rather than describing desire, the story constructs it through the interplay of multiple projects of narrating (including the level of the reader) that cannot quite answer the questions the wife's behavior raises. The apparent impetus for all of this is a fleeing sexuality affixed to a masked, perverse character who appears to frolic in the perfect, joyfully polymorphous, uncertain, present, and deferred, middle. "The Secret Woman" is a narrative in which the middle and its "secret" finally seem to escape the end.

Our knowledge of this escape is premised upon what we think we know about the relation of narrative, gender, and sexuality. We know, for example, that the husband has been fooled; his blindness is apparent as he futilely seeks the "real" sexuality of his wife. His narratives are sexual, both in the suspected (but already presumed) object of his search and in the process of his voyeuristic narrating. And so we are fooled. Voyeurs like the husband, we also seek the secret of the woman, safely distanced from her by the narrator's rendering of the husband's narratives. In an apparently privileged position, we "know" the husband is both right and not right: right in the sense that the wife's secret is still unknown, not right in the sense that its unknowability constitutes its essential quality, not right in the sense that the husband is even posing the right question. We think we see the husband's blindness because the story appeals to our own sense of a sexual answer, simply the more correct one of polymorphous pleasure and freedom, purchased at the cost of a necessary lie. For us as for him, the narrative's sexuality exists in the search rather than in the answer.

Suggesting that narrative blindness is an intrinsic part of narrative, the story is about the compensatory process of story-making. "The Secret Woman" 's final refusal of mastery (though itself masterful) privileges a middle that repeats itself in the end, exposing how sexuality is produced both in and by narratives that are themselves the products of a libidinous dynamic—an urge to know (to bring parts together)—akin to Eros. The ultimate insufficiency of any "objective" narrative exposes the causal link between our investment in the narrative's illusion of knowledge and a sexuality produced not as knowable answer but in the desiring dynamic generated by the narrative's knowledge quest. "The Secret Woman" 's failure to produce certain knowledge raises questions about the assumed process of narrative upon which the story and its readers depend. What is it about narrative that inveigles us to arrange information into "knowledge"? Why don't we question whether "The Secret Woman" is a narrative at all, as it illustrates narrative's potential failure? Why are we so certain of its parts when they circle around one another? What shape informs our shaping?

2

It Takes Two, Baby

I assume "The Secret Woman" is a narrative, since I found it in a collection of short stories, since it is "prose," "fiction," and can be analyzed according to the various schematic terms invented to define, explain, and analyze literary narrative. Using generic categories such as "short story" as a basis for definition, my initial presumption that "narrative" literature is narrative by-passes threshold issues of ontology—what is a narrative and is this one?—that might bring the nature of narrative more sharply into question. And since I rely on some idea of what a story is to identify and discuss narratives, the terms of that idea shape any conception of narrative I might assume, utilize, and perpetuate.

Yet the question of what narrative is occupies fewer narratologists than one might expect, and those it does interest, as Tom Leitch observes, have "not yet defined narrative with the authority of Aristotle on tragedy."[2] Gérard Genette admits that "we currently use the word *narrative* without paying attention to, even at times without noticing, its ambiguity."[3] The definition of narrative as a discrete, definable thing (whether entity or process or both) is curiously absent from most of its analyses (literary, theoretical, and more broadly cultural), which focus largely on accounts of narrative structure, evolution, and aesthetics and/or politics.

Structuralist/formalist, broadly literary, or psychological critical traditions tend to rely upon the assumption of some evanescent proto- or "primitive" narrative we all know, the unarticulated "model" or "logic" upon which discussions of narrative rely. As Tsvetan Todorov remarks, this ur-narrative functions as the point of comparison and digression, that from which later narrative practice is thought to develop and that it perverts. But, just as there is no origin accessible for argument, "there is," Todorov asserts, "no 'primitive narrative' " (55). Like the illogic of all originary arguments, the appeal to an originary, but undefined protonarrative enables the displacement of most of narrative's operative assumptions, avoiding any explanation or direct definition of what constitutes narrative in the first place.

In the terms of those who do try to define narrative, "The Secret Woman" clearly qualifies, and their mainly formal definitions tell us something about the assumptions that underlie twentieth-century Western concepts of narrative. Gerald Prince describes narrative as "the representation of *at least two* real or fictive events or situations in a time sequence, neither of which presupposes or entails the other" (4). David Bordwell and Kristin Thompson define narrative as "a chain of events in cause-effect relationship occurring in time and space."[4] Robert Scholes and Robert Kellogg define narrative works as "distinguished by two characteristics: the presence of a story and a storyteller."[5] Gérard Genette outlines three meanings for the term *narrative*: 1) as "the narrative statement, the oral or written discourse that undertakes to tell of an event or series of events"; 2) "the succession of events, real or fictitious, that are the subjects of this discourse, and to their several relations of linking, opposition, repetition, etc."; and 3) to the "event that consists of someone recounting something: the act of narration taken in itself" (25–26).

"The Secret Woman" is clearly more than one event in a time sequence; it has a story and a storyteller (more than one of each): in fact it fits into each definition quite easily and obviously. Yet none of these definitions or their application to "The Secret Woman" tells us very much about the propelling dynamism by which narratives engender narratives and by which reading and narrating become entwined, about the nature rather than the form of the process understood as narrative, or about the story's metanarrative sexual cast. What can these definitions tell us about how these elements become a narrative? What do they provide other than rules for pattern recognition? What do they tell us about the very ideologies of narrative?

Each seeking some irreducible minimum, some combination of essential elements, and some essential mode of combination, these structuralist definitions of narrative all depend on some manifestation of a binary structure. Prince and Bordwell and Thompson require at least two events, Scholes and Kellogg and Genette insist on a teller and a tale, a mode of representation and its content. The relation between the subject of narration and narrating, between cause and effect, or Genette's "relation of linking, opposition, repetition, etc." suggests that some binary combination of active and passive, of opposition, or of vertical and horizontal series of pairs underwrites these ideas of narrative. Narrative is never only one and always, so far, really only two. This binary is perhaps the effect of Žižek's "retroactive scission," but what principle demands that split?

The insistent presence of binaries in these minimal definitions of narrative may be due to the structuralist cast of the discussion, a structuralism that tends to understand structure itself as the product of irreducible binaries. If narrative is understood as a structure and if structure is inevitably binary, then binary logic is bound to repeat itself in definitions of narrative. And if all attempts to define narrative are themselves finally also narrative, narrative cannot be defined except through its own binary terms. This means that defining narrative is always a tautological project where the question of a narrative "logic" is preempted at the very moment one tries to answer it. The *idea* of narrative, the assumed but rarely articulated "model," is thus perhaps always in abeyance, always just beyond its own narrative like Colette's woman's "secret."

The elusive nature of the idea of narrative is analogous to what Tsvetan Todorov points to as the "supplement" within narratives:

> Each narrative seems to have something excessive, a supplement which remains outside the closed form produced by the development of the plot. At the same time, and for this very reason, this something-more, proper to the narrative, is also something-less. The supplement is also a lack; in order to supply this lack created by the supplement, another narrative is necessary. *(76)*

Narrative's definitional difficulty recalls a familiar trait of the signifier: it refers to other signifiers rather than to a simple signified; its metonymical slide through other signifiers points to a lack it stands in for and never fills.

Narrative always requires another narrative; all narrative definitions are narrative; narrative's tautological definition is never an explanation. All of these observations reflect the perpetual disjunction between the premises of narrative and its performance. Narrative can never say what it is and narrative is always more than what it says it is. These incongruities mean that narrative definitions of narrative a) always refer elsewhere; b) never succeed in defining narrative logic; and c) always return to that upon which they depend but never define. Colette's story replays this problem of narrative definition; the "secret" of the woman is the logic that can never be found but can always be narrated.

And even here, I, too, look for an origin as the place that might reveal narrative's shaping ideologies. While I look to definitions of narrative for hints about what narrative is, I might more readily locate its founding ideologies both in the significant absence of any definitive understanding of narrative and in the way narrative definitions perversely transform any essential explanation of narrative into descriptions of its structure and operation. However, despite narrative's seemingly inherent tautology—or perhaps because of it—definitions of narrative do reveal some underlying organizing principle that distinguishes, aligns, and relates binary terms to one another. Narrative's narrative premises would suggest that this principle not only determines how elements are combined but also determines what counts as an element in the first place. The ubiquitous presence of two elements in the definitions implies, at a minimum, some kind of combinatory logic that is more than merely additive or sequential, since a simple sequence neither requires binaries nor can account for any representational relation. And such a relation is more than Freud's Erotic "urge to combine into ever larger units."

Just an Imitation of Love

Where does one begin, however, if the same logic governs the choice of elements and the principle of their combination (or even the principle that they do combine in the first place)? Putting aside for the moment those accounts of narrative that are mainly literary (those of Wayne Booth, Northrup Frye, and Scholes and Kellogg) because they tend to define narrative within a more limited and formal literary context, many of the remaining accounts of narrative derive from modern linguistics and begin with the premise that language and narrative are somehow both linked and analogous to one another.[6] Using structuralist descriptions of language as a model, Claude Lévi-Strauss, for example, likens the structure of myth, a species of ur-narrative, to the structure of language, though "*above* the ordinary linguistic level."[7] For Lévi-Strauss, the analogy of language enables a linguistic definition of the elements of mythic narrative. If myths are like language, then like language, they are "made up of constituent units" (210); and in myth, those units, which "belong to a higher and more complex order" (211), consist of a relation between what Lévi-Strauss calls a "function" and a "subject." The "higher" level of myth is distinguished by its use of "bundles of such relations" (211). Lévi-Strauss organizes these "relations" within a bipolar scheme; he contrasts myth's diachronic or historical ordering of such bundles to their synchronic reiteration of a common element. This scheme enables him to bring together all versions of a myth; he can, thus, analyze myth without worrying about which version is the original.

The principle by which elements combine in myth, though Lévi-Strauss does not define it, is presumably also analogous to the linguistic relation between a function and a subject. Although this linguistic analogy may provide a way of understanding a species of mythical narrative structure, it does not address the question of what myth (narrative) is in the first place (nor does it pretend to), nor does it provide, outside of its hierarchical analogy between myth and language, any basis for determining what the combinatory qualities of a "function," "bundle," or "relation" are. As in definitions of narrative, Lévi-Strauss's analysis of myth circles around itself: myth is like language because it can be analyzed like language. Like language, myth is propelled by some deeper need.

Lévi-Strauss's equation of language and myth does provide the useful link between language and narrative employed by such other structuralist theorists as Todorov, Greimas, and Barthes, all of whom use Lévi-Strauss's adaptation of a bipolar model to account for the structure of narrative. Todorov, who takes up a "Grammar of Narrative," begins with the premise of a "universal grammar" that, if it is to be universal, must no longer apply only to languages. Adopting George Boas's view that there are "certain fundamental psychological processes" that are reflected by the universal appearance of certain grammatical structures in language (109), Todorov sets out to discover if any such grammar works in symbolic systems other than language. Avoiding from the start any strictly analogical argument, Todorov favors "a two-way relation" where grammar influences the understanding of narrative and vice versa. Despite his caution, his reasons for bringing together language and narrative are premised on the conclusion that narrative is a kind of symbolic activity that employs a "grammar."

Todorov does locate psychology as a possible "cause" for the cultural repetition that enables this sweeping structural view of narrative, seeing psychology as the connection among the structure of language, narrative, and subjectivity. The notion of a psychological analogue (developed by Brooks), however, drops out rather quickly as Todorov elaborates the ramifications of the grammar/narrative comparison. He begins by parsing narrative into two parts: an agent or subject, which is by definition devoid of characteristics, and two kinds of predicates, which bear the weight of all of the plot's movement. These predicates divest the subject of meaning; "the agent cannot be endowed with any property," he says, "but is rather a blank form which is complete by different predicates" (110).

The "completion" of the subject by the predicate comprises quite a classical binary, where the passive, acted-upon subject (which looks almost feminine) gains all meaning from the active predicate. But this twosome only begins Todorov's binary scheme. He also divides plot into two parts. Todorov characterizes "the minimal complete plot" as "the passage from one equilibrium to another" (111). The two parts of the plot, equilibrium and disequilibrium, correlate with the two "classes" of predicate: those that "describe a state (of equilibrium or disequilibrium) and those which describe the passage from one state to the other" (111). Those pertaining to state are "static," "iterative," and essentially adjectival; those having to do with the transitions between states are "dynamic," "non-iterative," and verbal.

Having deferred strict notions of active and passive from the first binary separating the subject and the predicate, Todorov recovers it among the predicates, basically dividing narrative predication into the categories of description (passive) and "passage" (active). His "ideal" narrative "begins with a stable situation [adjective] which is disturbed by some power or force [verb]. There results a state of disequilibrium [another adjective]; by the action of a force [verb] directed in the opposite direction, the equilibrium is re-established [adjective]; the second equilibrium is similar to the first, but the two are never identical" (111). The equilibrium/disequilibrium formula seems to avoid any strict notion of opposition in its alternation between state and passage; however, while an equilibrium becomes disequilibrium through the action of some force, moving back to equilibrium requires an "opposite" force. This binary suggests that Todorov's notion of narrative, as Brooks has noted, minimally requires agents perceived as sameness (adjectives) and difference (verbs). The relation between the iterative adjective and the dynamic verb implies a binary between the adjective's species of repeating sameness and the "verbal" difference represented by successive forces that come from outside to effect change.

This outside force is like Todorov's notion of the "obligative," or the "coded, nonindividual will which constitutes the law of a society." What catalyzes the "verbs"—the passages—is "always implied, never named (it is unnecessary)" (114). Although Todorov never directly links the obligative "law of society" to the force that motivates the passages from equilibrium to disequilibrium (or vice versa), the implication of a "force" whose source is never specified is much like both the absent cause of narrative he later identifies as driving some of Henry James's stories and the "Secret Woman's" secret.[8] This "secret cause" is the very essence of narrative as well as its driving force and its link to psychology. It is also the missing center of Todorov's own account.

The progressive alternation of equilibrium and disequilibrium, the interplay of sameness and difference, and their shift through the application of opposing verbs effects a model of production, where the raw material of an adjectival ground is progressively changed through the strategic application of opposite forces. This narrative, as Todorov points out later in his argument, is inherently reproductive, spawning other narratives. And doing so in more ways than he is aware.

A. J. Greimas, who writes about narrative from the position of a linguist and semiotician, further elaborates a bipolar dynamic in his own narrative grammar.[9] Greimas locates a narrative ideology as both antecedent to and embodied in language, distinguishing what he calls the "immanent level" of narrative—"the common structural trunk where narrative is located and organized at the stage preceding its manifestation"—from narrative's "apparent level" manifested in narration where "the diverse manifestations of narrative are subject to the specific requirements of the linguistic substances through which it is expressed" (64). The idea of narrative exists before but can only be expressed through some linguistic dimension. This supposes an interdependent relation among narrative, language, and discourse; "the *linguistic structures of narrative* correspond, at the level of manifestation, to *narrative structures*, and the analysis of narrative has discourse analysis as its corollary" (64).

Complicating Lévi-Strauss's analogy to structural linguistics, Greimas's reciprocal relation between language and narrative permits him to question the ways both language and narrative are understood. Rejecting the idea that narrative or language could be analyzed by a formula, by "putting into a place a combinatory or generative mechanism that, starting with simple elements and original kernels, would account for the production of an unlimited number of utterances, with the latter in turn being transformed and combined in order to create successions of utterances in discourse," Greimas suggests that the reverse might be the case. We can, he asserts, begin with "agglomerations of meaning that are as little articulated as possible" and, by descending through increasingly specific levels of signification, "obtain more and more refined significative articulations (64). The result is neither mechanical induction or deduction; rather, it is narrative itself: "the generation of meaning does not first take the form of the production of utterances and their combination in discourse; it is relayed, in the course of its trajectory, by narrative structures and it is these that produce meaningful discourse articulated in utterances" (65). Narrative structures the meaning of meaning that structures narrative.

In the chicken-and-egg game of meaning and narrative, Greimas does however determine an "autonomous instance" of narrative. Although narrative may be like language and operate in a dynamic relation with language's structures, structures of narrative rather than structures of language determine meaning. Seeing narrative structure as one instance of a general semiotics, Greimas devises a narrative of signification that proceeds from what he terms an "*ab quo* instance," the moment of representing, "where the semantic substance receives its first articulations and constitutes itself as a signifying form," to an "*ad quem*" instance, which is the meaningful organization of representations, "where signification manifests itself through multiple languages" (65). Between the beginning and the end, the word and its reproduction as meaning, lies the middle, the "vast area" of the "*mediating instance*" where all of this takes shape, a kind of grand passage "where there would be developed complementary articulations of content and a sort of grammar that would be both general and fundamental and that would regulate the setting up of articulated discourses" (65).

Greimas's story of signification is much like Todorov's narrative of narrative; like Todorov, Greimas focuses on the predicate, on the mediating instance, which he divides into "semantics" (meaning) and "grammar" (the rules of combination), reminiscent of Todorov's adjective (state)/verb (passage) dichotomy. Greimas links semantics both "to the process that makes explicit the conditions under which meaning can be grasped" (the "language universals" or "deep grammar" of signification) and to an "elementary structure of signification" where meaning and signification intersect.

Growing from the binaries implicit in the semantic understanding of a simple term, this elementary structure is derived from the "logical development of a binary semic category . . . whose terms are in a relation of contrariety and that can also, each one, project a new term that would be its contradictory" (65–66). This results in a four-term rectangle divided by relations of contrariety (opposition, i.e., male v. female) and contradiction (negatives, i.e. male and nonmale) that are sustained, as meaning, by the tensions of multiple conflict:

S_1 (white) S_2 (black)

S_2 (nonwhite) S_1 (nonblack)

This represents the possible relations to one term, or what J.- A. Berthoud calls a "correspondence of differentials;" it distinguishes between two kinds of opposition while bringing them into one structure and one signifying instance.[10] In this way Greimas freezes the sequential, serial oppositions of metonymy and the paradigmatic, concurrent oppositions of metaphor into an instantaneous dialectic.

As both the structure of meaning and the formal model of more "manifest structures, such as those governing sexual or narrative relations" (Berthoud 102–103), Greimas's structure is both "the basis for the organization of contents" and a "formal model that, thanks to its constitutive categories manipulates the organized contents without becoming identified with them" (67). If this is the "enabling model" of signification, the very *ab quo* of language and meaning and, by extension, of narrative, then Greimas succeeds in showing the metaphorical link between signification and narrative suspected by Lévi-Strauss and Todorov. Narrative oppositions work like the contradictions and contrarieties that produce meaning.

What exists, however, at this schematized junction of differences in their first bloom of differentiation depends upon some meaning that has already attached to the signifiers that come to meaning through their opposition, contradiction, and contrariety to other signifiers. If Greimas's theory is correct, we only know that white contradicts black because we know what white means, even if we only know what white means because of its complex, quadrated relation to its contradiction and contrary. These relations do not arise automatically from the meaning of a term (if the term's meaning is defined by sets of contradictions and contraries) but, rather, by a preexistent understanding of the narrative logic by which meaning is generated as opposition or differentiation, by the values of the social milieu and cultural comprehensions of power relations (which Greimas takes up in a later discussion of "values" in narrative), and by the operations of derivation and combination that result in contradiction and contrariety. In other words, meaning and value are not semantically innocent but ideological and narrative from the *ab quo* start. Thus, even in Greimas's model of the *ab quo* instance, signification and narrative already relate in the kind of epistemological circle typical of narrative, for it is only through a narrative process that any term's oppositions and negatives can be derived in the first place. As in all stories that depend upon an originary moment, this narrative of meaning is retrospective; it can account for an imaginary moment before meaning only by recourse to mean-ing—and to narrative.

While Greimas's starting point is clearly the impenetrable essence of the binary as (to use his term) *ab quo* constitutive of meaning, this binary is also the essence of the narrative by which the binary opposi-tion can both make meaning and can emerge as the site of meaning. Like Todorov, Greimas ends up with a bipolar model of narrative struc-ture; he links this to his "taxonomic model" (82) and derives narrative's basic action from the "hypotactic relations" between the negatives (i.e., white/nonwhite). Thus,

> the triggering of narration would be represented here as being the establishment of a *conjunctive* contractual relation between sender and receiver-subject, followed by the spatial *disjunction* between these two actants. The completion of the story would be marked, on the contrary by a spatial conjunction and one last transfer of values, this time setting up a new contract through a new distrib-ution of values." *(82)*.

Greimas's appeal to what Todorov calls the "obligatory," to a sense of law and contract, results from the injection of legal discourse into his taxonomic model. His contractual metaphor evokes the idea of equal, willing parties to a voluntary agreement; contract is a specific way of joining two parties in a bond of mutual interest premised on the trans-fer of value within the ideological system of property-based, patriarchal law. While the addition of a legalistic vocabulary appears to clarify the reciprocal relation of narrative elements, it actually defers again any specification of what this narrative relation might be. Greimas modifies the contractual with the term *conjunctive*, which becomes retrospec-tively spatial but, in its connection to the contractual, implies marriage (as a conjunctive contractual relation) or something like a marriage. He further defines and separates this "conjunctive contractual relation" with the terms *sender* and *receiver-subject*; this metaphor simultaneously implies a spatial figuration of narrative's movement through time and introduces a gloss of activity/passivity that redefines the elements rejoining in the contractual conjunction that completes the story.

The introduction of a notion of contract and its delineation through sender/receiver roles provides an ideological capitalist gloss to Greimas's binary framework, which is represented suspiciously like a marriage, the

meeting of opposites, and the fulfilling of roles in production/repro-
duction. Greimas's description of narrative also ends up looking like
Todorov's equilibrium/disequilibrium model, where the motivating
force is a promise and a debt and where disequilibrium is resolved when
opposite parties meet and fulfill the contract. Greimas concludes his
essay on the problem of value in narrative with a description of narrative that clearly parallels Todorov's: "Narrativity, considered as the irrup-
tion of the discontinuous into the discursive permanence of a life, a
story, an individual, a culture, disarticulates that discursive permanence
into discrete states between which it sets transformations" (104).
Narrative is thus some introduction of difference onto the ground of
sameness or stasis that cannot change or move without the catalyst of
difference from without.

Through the ideas of Lévi-Strauss, Todorov, and Greimas, we have
come from origins to binaries to a suspicion of marriage or at least the
sight of some contractual maneuvers appearing at the very spot where
the principle of narrative combination must finally be defined. These
accounts of narrative structure always defer any definition of what
might characterize the structure or artifact they are describing. Their
main feature is a putting-off—putting off difference and opposition,
putting off the principles by which narrative's parts interact, putting off
any definitive idea of what narrative is while depending upon the very
principle they avoid. Since this evasion is probably not deliberate, there
must be something in narrative that is frightening, elusive, or so obvious that we need not mention it. The little leap between formal binaries and narrative is suggestive in its absence, evading theories, seeming
just out of sight and around the next logical bend.

The next bend is Roland Barthes who, in his "Structural Analysis of
Narratives," adapts the parallel between Greimas's "deep structure" and
narrative form. Borrowing from all of his structuralist forebears, Barthes
attempts to bring together the problems of homology, level, classification, and combination Lévi-Strauss, Todorov, and Greimas introduce,
developing their notions of the role of metaphor/metonymy and inves-
tigating further the problem of narrative logic. Like the others, Barthes
consistently divides the elements of narrative into binaries whose functions refer to one another and to similar binaries on levels organiza-
tionally above and below. Barthes, however, is more attentive to the
hierarchy of operations introduced by Lévi-Strauss's notion of "bundles." He says, for example, that

> narrative is a hierarchy of instances. To understand a narrative is
> not merely to follow the unfolding of the story, it is also to rec-
> ognize its construction in "storeys," to project the horizontal
> concatenations of the narrative "thread" on to an implicitly ver-
> tical axis; to read (to listen to) a narrative is not merely to move
> from one word to the next, it is also to move from one level to
> the next.   *(87)*

Barthes bases his idea of level and hierarchy on two complementary
operations: 1) the division and classification of narrative into its smallest units (the linguistically informed process used also by Lévi-Strauss,
Todorov, and Greimas); and 2) a principle of re-organization by which
these basic units are combined into ever-larger, interdependent functional groups. He sees the "function" as the basic unit of narrative.
"Meaning," he says, "must be the criterion of the unit," and "narrative
is never made up of anything other than functions" (89). Borrowing
from "the Russian Formalists," including Tomachevski and Todorov,
Barthes describes "the essence of a function" as "the seed that it sows in
the narrative, planting an element that will come to fruition later" (89).
Referring to the same kind of productive logic as Todorov, Barthes
characterizes the smallest separable narratively significant acts as reproductive. Narrative consists of the proliferation of functions in a hierarchy ordered by a binary logic that divides functions into two classes:
true "functions," or "metonymic relata" corresponding to "a functionality of doing"; and "indices," or "metaphoric relata" corresponding to
"a functionality of being" (93). While this duo nicely parallels Todorov's
discrimination between verbal and adjectival predicates, Barthes discerns yet another division among the functions; some are "cardinal,"
"hinge-point," or "nuclei" functions and others "fill in" or catalyzer
functions. These catalyzer functions are the connectors, the transitions,
the cement between narrator and addressee. While their designating
rubric makes them seem something like Todorov's notion of a "force,"
they are more like a state or ground that fills in in a "complementary"
way around the real action of the cardinal, "doing" functions. In a sense
both "fill-in" catalyzer functions and "being" indice functions are produced by the "hinge-point" nuclei, which act as the real "seed" of the
narrative. As Barthes explains, "Nuclei . . . form finite sets grouping a
small number of terms, are governed by a logic, are at once necessary
and sufficient. Once the framework they provide is given, the other

units fill it out according to a mode of proliferation in principle infinite" (97). Nuclei are narrative in small.

The complementary "doings" and "beings" come together according to a logic of production/reproduction without any motivation other than meaning (the same already-narrative motivation employed by Greimas). Citing the work of Claude Bremond, Lévi-Strauss and Jakobson, and Todorov, Barthes mentions three possible "directions" through which we might resolve the problem of a missing motivation for this coming together.[11] Bremond understands that cardinal functions combine according to a logic of character choices in a kind of personality match, what Barthes calls an "energetic logic" based on "alternatives" (99–100). Lévi-Strauss, Jakobson, and Greimas see this logic in terms of oppositions—the naturalized assumption that opposites attract—and Todorov tries to determine ever more minutely the rules by which predicates are combined. All of these comprehend narrative's coming together as a species of combination that follows a more or less heterological model of conjoinder.

Barthes, however, locates narrative logic not in what he calls the "implied" complementary relation between nuclei and catalyzers (between hinge-point and fill-in) but, rather, in the logic of "solidarity" that links nucleic functions to one another. Barthes says, for example, that "a sequence is a logical succession of nuclei bound together by a relation of solidarity: the sequence opens when one of its terms has no solidary antecedent and closes when another of its terms has no consequent" (101). *Solidarity* here means "the Hjelmslevian sense of double implication: two terms presuppose one another" (101 n.). But this is very much like the narrative-dependent circle of Greimas's meaning structure. Terms relate because they relate; meaning presupposes combination and a logic of opposition, and the presupposition of meaning determines the logic of combination, which in turn supposes meaning. The logic of solidarity superficially seems rather homologous: "a function of this type [cardinal] calls for another function of the same type and reciprocally" (98). Evoking the Aristophanic bonding of previously unified beings whose coming together is a meaningful return to a previous state, this narrative epicenter also resembles Freud's magic moment of heterosexual attraction. With the force drawing them together still undefined, the cardinal functions bond and reproduce, their nucleic seedy natures finding their way to one another through the crowded vista of functions that litter the narrative scene.

Why they must come together is unclear, however, if each nuclei is a story in itself.

But Barthes does add another element to solidarity, an element of risk or threat that suggests that something operates outside or beyond the solid unit of cardinal functions. "A sequence is thus, one can say, a *threatened logical unit*" (102). This element of threat or risk justifies the narrative, pushing like Todorov's "force." Like Todorov's "force," risk does not account for the internal oppositional dynamics of solidarity or equilibrium but represents the chance that things won't come together again, that a narrative won't be made, that meaning will fail. In a sense meaning always fails; risk lies in not sufficiently covering that failure with structures of meaning that succeed in eliding the emptiness at their core.

Circling around mysterious narrative logics, these structuralist accounts of narrative illustrate the binary premise of structuralism even as binaries are suspended in sequence or space or dislocated into indirect oppositions. But their reliance on binaries may not be the most significant clue to structuralist ideologies; rather, structuralist analyses of narrative bring to light how covert metaphors of (re)production dependent upon binaries inflect our understanding of narrative. While these theorists offer a dynamic rather than a static model for the interaction of the binaries they discern, their hypothetical systems are undercut by an unspecified but omnipresent appeal to an underlying narrative where opposing forces combine. While they are all probably correct in asserting that there is no primal narrative, all employ some primal notion of narrative in their narrative mappings. Although their analyses focus on the narrative middle—on the organization and dynamic that characterizes narrative—the middle is still produced by a knowing reproductive end, by functions that are inextricably intertwined with binaries, which are produced by and that produce deferred oppositions, and that know when to join.

Todorov, Greimas, and Barthes all refer in one way or another to either reproduction or marriage as a metaphor for narrative at the point where the issue of an essential narrative logic is most acute. Todorov's "supplement," Greimas's "social contract," Barthes's nucleic "seed" all import a similar conjunctive and/or reproductive metaphor around the disciplined edges of their discussions. Sneaking in while the writers try to avoid positing direct opposition, simple binaries, or conflict as narrative's essence, this contractual, heterological, reproductive model informs the otherwise unspecified mechanisms by which narrative elements are combined. The assumed process of combination upon which all of the discussions depend tends to remain the mystery site in these accounts, supplanted by such mechanisms as the force from outside, hierarchical grouping, "bundling," the spontaneous generation of meaning, or solidarity; the binding factor of narrative (if there is one— none of these really discuss such a thing but all depend upon it) is either a narrative deus ex machina or a narrative self-production that, in tau-tological glee, generates itself by virtue of some internal dynamic that perpetually reproduces the relation it pretends to contain.

Although Lévi-Strauss, Todorov, Greimas, and Barthes all pointedly ignore the end of narrative in favor of its middle, like Brooks and Freud their understandings of narrative are dependent upon both this end and on a very sexualized metaphor of the whole narrative process. Preferring the categories provided by linguistics, they never discuss gender as a metaphor in any of their classifications; even so, oppositions between passive and active, field and force, subject and function, and adjective and verb connote the same binary division of qualities employed in the male/female pair. But even without specific evocations of gender, we are halfway to heterosexuality; defining oppositions in terms of complementary differences creates a heterology, a play of dif-ferences that seems to be minimally necessary for any narrative activity to occur. While notions of hierarchy or the cooperative intersections of metaphor and metonymy seem to avoid the direct clash of binaries by spreading their association through time, they, too, share in the dynamic of sameness and difference that underlies all discussions of narrative. While the possible delays, deferences, and alternatives of the middle may make it appear to have and even momentarily participate in a polymorphous mobility, that mobility itself is a lure, a kind of fetish that, already representing a duplicity, both contributes to and enables a heterological (re)productive organizational aegis. And when these oppositions are gilded with a gloss of gender, their covert heterosexual ideology is finally exposed.

3

A Man and a Woman

You have written me all your loving tenderness, dear giant, without saying a word to me about Rézi, without telling me: "You did with her just what I did, with so little

difference . . ."Yet that would have been very reasonable, almost flawless as a piece of
logic. But you knew that *it was not the same thing* . . . and I'm grateful to you for not
having said it.

—Colette, *Claudine Married*, p. 510

Hidden, the model merger produces, but its productions and reproductions come after the flirting and indirection of structuralist analyses'
various classifications, disjointed oppositions, and hierarchical match-
ings that operate on an apparently genderless ground. Why is gender
missing from these accounts, even as a metaphor? Is gender simply not
a consideration, or are structuralist theorists conscientious nonsexists?
Or is gender always present, haunting otherwise "neutral" characteriza-
tions (such as passive/active), pervading the drama of narrative dynamics with an insistent if denied gloss?

The function of theories' elided gender becomes visible in specific
narratives. "The Secret Woman," for example, provides an allegory of
the structuralist dilemma, enacting theory's inability to discern the
essence of narrative, while setting out the terms of a narrative logic
organized according to some binary, combinatory principle. "The
Secret Woman" exposes the gendered premises of narrative's binary
principle by arranging the husband and wife as narrating subject and
narrated object. Playing with an openly gendered logic, the story dramatizes how gender generates (or significantly fails to generate) both
narrative and meaning.

The openly gendered binaries of "The Secret Woman" locate sexuality as narrative's mystery. The bad fit between the wife's behavior and
her gender makes her actions confusing. Although the husband initially
believes that his wife is "here for someone, with someone" (40), her
alluring walk, her enjoyment of embraces from a "big brute" of a
Byzantine figure, a group of men, and "an almost naked wrestler"; her
clinging dance with "a warrior"; the bemused placement of "her little
satanic hands, which were entirely black, on the white bosom of a
Dutch woman wearing a gold head-dress, who cried out nervously";
and her kissing "the panting, half-open mouth" of a "savage, handsome
young face" convince him that "she was neither waiting nor looking for
anyone" (41). Her behavior, in fact, is reminiscent of the perverse middle of Freud's account of sexuality, except that her perversity leads to
no resounding "right" conclusion.

As the narrative "force" that appears to motivate the husband's story-
telling, the wife's behavior and the narratives it inspires fail to mask

emptiness, the gaps in meaning, and the lack founding signification. The husband's narrating also depends upon a gender logic, enacting an apparently masculine imperative to cover over the wife's feminine meaninglessness by continually producing narratives that explain her. When the feminine wife also becomes a subject, she duplicates the "active," "cardinal," verblike function of the "do-er" husband, producing the narrative crisis reflected in the husband's obsessive, frustrated, and unproductive narrating.

The husband's inability to account for her actions forces him to conclude that his wife enjoys "the monstrous pleasure of being alone, free, honest in her crude, native state, of being the unknown woman, eternally solitary and shameless" (41). Rather cleverly playing the narrative game by the rules, the husband sees that if there is no narrative, there is no meaning; he transforms the impossibility of narrative (within the rules) into his own triumph of understanding. At the same time, the wife's mask performs the alluring polymorphous mobility of a narrative middle that is all the while being redrafted into a sensical, gendered, oppositional attempt at terminal meaning.

The narrative politics of "The Secret Woman" expose what Teresa de Lauretis so brilliantly argues in *Alice Doesn't*: that it is not a difficult leap from the active/passive dichotomies of structuralist accounts of narrative to the active/passive stereotypes by which sexual difference is understood and narrated. De Lauretis observes that

> opposite pairs such as inside/outside, the raw/the cooked, or life/death appear to be merely derivatives of the fundamental opposition between boundary and passage; and if passage may be in either direction, from inside to outside and vice versa, from life to death, or vice versa, nonetheless all these terms are predicated on the *single* figure of the hero who crosses the boundary and penetrates the other space. In so doing the hero, the mythical subject, is constructed as human being and as male; he is the active principle of culture, the establisher of distinction, the creator of differences. Female is what is not susceptible to transformation, to life or death; she (it) is an element of plot-space, a topos, a resistance, matrix and matter. *(81)*

Although the rigid binaries of sexual difference and gender are produced and reinforced by countless narratives that link, reiterate, and oppose active/male and passive/female, their intrication is also part of narrative's mechanisms and intrinsic ideology. Reflected in what is narrated, gender role ideologies do not exist separately from the shape and logic of their narration and of narrative itself. Narrative depends upon these gender categories as part of the "meaning" upon which accounts of gender depend. Although never specifically evoked, gender is an underlying narrative assumption, part of the ideology of binaries and combination that underwrites structuralist narrative theory.

Naturalized in the distribution of narrative roles, the relation between sexual difference and narrative's binaries completes narrative's ideological scenario of heterosexuality and reproduction. Gender ideology and narrative coalesce into an insistent form that reiterates a tension between male and female as occupiers of particular narrative (and [re]productive) functions—the male as "creator of differences" and the female as "matter" or undifferentiated space. The similarity between the logics of narrative and Western ideologies of gender partly explains the real difficulty of establishing a female protagonist who is not somehow recuperated by the narrative; narrative logic, combined with entrenched gender ideologies, works more or less invisibly against her. Simply changing the gender of the players or shifting their positions, therefore, does not alter cultural conceptions of gender and sexual difference, because their oppositional structures are entangled with and produced by a narrative heterologic whose shape both reflects ideologies of gender and limits the ways genders may interact and combine.

Here Comes the Son

Tracking the gender intrinsic to structuralist accounts of narrative suggests three possible readings of the relation of narrative ideology to gender and sexuality: 1) gender is produced by narrative's heterologic in its appeal to a distinctly heterosexual ideology; 2) gender precedes and produces this heterologic; or 3) both happen at the same time and are so complexly intertwined that they cannot be separated. What is important for the purposes of this discussion is that both gender and a narrative heteroideology shape our assumptions, perceptions, and understandings of narrative, casting their metaphors as narrative's lens. But this alliance among narrative, gender, and sexuality is nothing new; the metaphors of gender and heterosexuality are already figured in the oedipal, Freud's ur-story, the narrative that distributes genders within a heteroideology that connects the production of narrative to mastery. Or it could be that the oedipal was revived at a particular point in the late nineteenth century because it embodied particularly effectively the ideological intrication of narrative production, gender, and sexuality.

As the narrative of the subject's coming to culture as a gendered subject, the Oedipus story is the myth of gendered oppositional transformation from indeterminacy (from that indifferent matrix) to nascent subjective independence. Its gendered structure dominates Western imaginings about narrative and subjectivity; it links mastery and ending to the discovery of difference, situated as a specifically sexual difference and to a gendered identity in relation to mother and father. Registering difference through gender reflects the oedipal dynamic that de Lauretis observes in her consideration of the connections between studies of myth and narrative; "It is neither facile nor merely paradoxical . . . to state that if the crime of Oedipus is the destruction of differences, the combined work of myth and narrative is the production of Oedipus" (120). The destruction of differences disallows narrative; only their reinstallation—their perpetual rediscovery—allows the story to go on. While de Lauretis's link between Oedipus and gender is primarily cultural and ideological, Oedipus also, as she later points out, becomes the structuring narrative of identity and subjectivity in the work of Freud.[12]

As a quintessential narrative pattern in Western culture, the pattern of Oedipus is not only a narrative adopted by Freud to account for human development, it is coterminous with Western understandings of narrative. It is the "ur" narrative of narrative as well as the "ur" narrative of subjectivity, standing in for the lost origin of both, functioning as the point of origin for stories of origins and accounting for the production of individual meaning. It is difficult to tell whether some preexisting oedipal substratum prompts oedipal readings of narrative or vice versa or both. In any case, the critical reiteration of variously named integrative patterns by which difference is separated from sameness suggests that the link between subjectivity and differentiation is read, devised, and narrated as oedipal.

It is, thus, no accident that like Freud before him, Lévi-Strauss selects the Oedipus myth as the sample story for his "Structural Study of Myth": its pervasive oppositions conveniently illustrate the linguistic principles that he believes underlie myth and its very centrality as a story has to do with the way it reproduces the already ensconced ideological configurations of gender, subjectivity, and social identity. In his essay, Lévi-Strauss analyzes the extended series of stories that comprise the Oedipus myth; his purpose is to explain myth's structure, define the methods by which such structure can be discovered, and discern the pervasive anxiety the myth represents through concepts offered by structural linguistics.

By means of a paradigmatic analysis of analogous elements in various versions of the myth, Lévi-Strauss concludes that the Oedipus myth is bound up with two dialectics, one concerning over- or under-rating blood relations, the other affirming or denying the "autochthonous" (aboriginal, earth-bound) origins of humanity. Together these two dialectics lead, Lévi-Strauss concludes, to a basic underlying problem about reproduction: whether man is "born from one or from two," from the earth or from two gendered beings, or "born from different or born from same?" (216). Lévi-Strauss understands the Oedipus myth as an ambivalent structure that resolves a cultural contradiction between experience (birth from same, the "two" represented by human parents, or non-autochthony) and cosmology (birth from different, from the "one" of the earth, or autochthony)—between biology and the social. Lévi-Strauss's analysis recalls Freud's use of Aristophanes' account of the origins of sexuality, which also juggles the dialectic between one and two; Freud, however, resolves the story's ambiguity into a balanced heterosexuality ("born from two") there from the start.

Lévi-Strauss's interpretation of Oedipus as an ambivalent myth of origins reflects the operations of the linguistically oriented narrative logic he employs, which privileges the derivation and combination of binaries. His almost-obsessive return to origins as the resolution to problems of mythical structure also suggests a connection between a heteroideological imperative and something basic to conceptions of narrative. His analysis illustrates the stake of narrative in reproduction (where do I come from?) at the very moment of its denial of it (I am father to myself). This ideological nexus of patriarchy and narrative is expressed through a tension between filiation and authority, the written (named) and the author (namer), the character in versus the originator of the story of identity. Although according to Lévi-Strauss, the Oedipus myth is about the origins of humanity, it is also about the origins of narrative in so far as narratives of narrative's origins almost always deny narrative's production from same—from another narrative—leaving the empty place of autochthony as the default source of their generation.

While Lévi-Strauss's analysis deemphasizes sexual difference as a significant element (swallowed by the patriarchal exigency of the myth of patriarchy), gender lurks within the problem of reproduction as the essential element of the non-autochthonous (born from two humans) origins whose repression the social sphere demands. Even though Lévi-Strauss defines biological reproduction as a birth from same, this very definition (and perhaps the myth itself) denies sexual difference. The oedipal myth displaces the male/female opposition necessary for the human male's birth from the realm of biology into an opposition between biology and cosmology. Oedipus represents the clash of human reproduction (non-autochthony) with the exigencies of culture (autochthony) in relation to patriarchal law that requires both non-autochthony for filiation and autochthony for power and precedence. The narrative of Oedipus, then, is produced by the oppositions inherent to the relation of a male subject to his origins; the terms by which origins are understood displace and deny the binary of sexual difference whose specter threatens the cosmological (autochthonous) status of man. The gender of the myth's protagonists is never in question: Oedipus is the originary narrative of men and patriarchy.

Freud's earlier appeal to Oedipus denies the male's non-autochthonous origins (his mere biological birth and existence as helpless, passive, and dependent [though happy] being) in favor of a myth of self-authorship and cultural inscription that takes place through opposition and desire. The very lack created by his separation from his non-autochthonous, too-same mother is denied and healed by a secondary, retrospectively originary self-inscription in the social paternal sphere as an autochthonous challenger of the father. Literal biological birth is superseded by the metaphorical birth of the subject into culture, a subject made in part by the assumption of a gender but also by the operation of a paternal Law already dependent upon gender and the reproductive uncertainty of the father. In this second oedipal birth, the subject is finally stripped of his natal origin in favor of a legal one (he enters the Lacanian Symbolic). The law of social order, of paternal reproduction identified with cosmology, supplants the non-autochthony of maternal sameness. The Oedipus narrative thus reveals and performs narrative's function of covering over one origin in favor of another as well as the process by which that second origin becomes originary and the way both repress the feminine in favor of the masculine.

My return to Oedipus at this point in my argument about the heterosexual ideology of narrative is also related to this oedipal covering
over, insofar as the Oedipus narrative both obscures and exposes an
intrinsic heteroideology identified with a narrative of birth and the
birth of narrative. This oedipal moment stands in as an account of the
birth of gender, the family, and culture. As a screen narrative of birth, it
simultaneously covers up and represents that moment, but it also
engenders the idea of a telling origin in the first place. Oedipus is a suspicious story, not only because it seems to anchor a gendered binary
heteroideology in the reproductive, familial triangle but also because it
seems to situate origins as both the story's cause and the locus of the
answer to its questions. As a site of mastery, origins are a product of narrative rather than narrative's source; explaining narrative via its oedipal
"origin" is to try to account for narrative via narrative. But, as I have
already noted, the sites of narrative redoubling are the places where narrative reveals its ideological investments.

Freud employs the Oedipus narrative to confirm his discovery of
the dynamic of the childhood desires he unearths in his self-analysis.
Again, the oedipal myth refers to an origin, this one the temporal
childhood origin of the desires that shape the subject's psychic life.
Writing to his friend Wilhelm Fliess, Freud comments, "Only one idea
of general value has occurred to me. I have found love of the mother
and jealousy of the father in my own case, too, and now believe it to
be a general phenomenon of early childhood."[13] This "discovery," he
says earlier in *The Interpretation of Dreams*, "is confirmed by a legend
which has come down to us from classical antiquity: a legend whose
profound and universal power to move can only be understood if the
hypothesis I have put forward in regard to the psychology of children
has an equally universal validity. What I have in mind is the legend of
King Oedipus and Sophocles' drama which bears his name" (294).
Discovering the tension between non-autochthony (love for mother)
and a desire for autochthony (jealousy of the father), Freud both
affirms and generalizes this tension by recourse to Oedipus.

Connecting his desires to the cultural myth of Oedipus enables
Freud to link structures of subjectivity to narrative, and narrative, in the
form of Oedipus, enables a universalization. Thus the play *Oedipus Rex*
works because we are all oedipal. Although in Freud's story of his "discovery," the discovery comes before he likens it to the story of Oedipus,
it is only after he can link his desires to Oedipus that they make sense.

The Oedipus narrative resituated becomes both a personal and a "universal" cultural hypothesis, not only about the nature of unconscious structures but also about the reasons for the story's power and appeal. Narrative allows us to name desire; through narrative, desire becomes theory; or, as Shoshana Felman observes, Freud's "transformation of narration into theory" transmutes "not just the questions of the story but the very *status* of the narrative, in investing the idiosyncrasies of narrative with the generalizing power of a theoretical validity" (1022). Narrative becomes the conscious form of unconscious desires, identifiable and comprehensible because of the narrative to which they can be appended.

This story about origins, about childhood as the bearer of the adult subject, and about the matrix of passions that shapes the child is also the story of the essence of psychoanalysis as the symptomatic reading of stories. Freud remarks in *The Interpretation of Dreams*: "The action of the play consists in nothing other than the process of revealing, with cunning delays and ever-mounting excitement—a process that can be likened to the work of a psycho-analysis" (295). "The process of revealing" the story behind the story, the story that constitutes the truth of the subject, is the story—the very ideology of narrative and its link to subjectivity—that underlies Freudian psychoanalysis's reliance on narrative. This reliance is coupled to an understanding of subjectivity as a distinctly *narrative* field; subjectivity is imparted and constructed through narrative, understood through narrative, in fact, even structured like narrative. The subject makes itself through narrative; as Anthony Kerby argues, "one's identity is that of a character in a narrative and that self-understanding is accordingly a matter of the emplotment of one's experiences."[14] Or as Roy Schafer observes, analysands narrate themselves in character roles which belong ultimately to "the regulative narrative structures that one person, the analysand, has adopted and used simultaneously with the others, whether in combination, opposition, or apparent incoherence" (40).

The problem, as Schafer implies, is that this narrative process is both retrospective and already narrative, occurring after the subject can speak through some sense of identity. In other words, narrating oneself can only occur after the subject already functions—even if problematically—as a subject. The point at which the subject ceases being a creation of narrative and begins to narrate its creation is the point identified as oedipal. As we have seen, the oedipal narrative of origins substitutes one origin for another, screening the moment of division and castration and separating the postoedipal fiction of the complete subject from the pre-oedipal production of a subject with particularly narrative propensities. This moment (narrated as a moment, though it is not a moment at all) marks the difference between an ego with a "complete" identity and place in culture and the always incomplete subject who persists in the place where meaning and subjectivity are continually produced in reference to castration, separation, and lack. The former is the gendered myth of the subject in culture whose function is to forget the latter.

The former, too, is gendered in a particular way. The subject's position in relation to sexual difference partially defines the narrative roles the subject may assume; narrativized gender positions define the roles that may be taken and the story that can be told. As both Barthes and de Lauretis assert, Western narrative is oedipal in the sense that it replays the triumphant discovery of identity and moves toward an end that resounds with a sense of completion and fulfilled desire. If that oedipal narrative links masculinity with completion and identity (as Lévi-Strauss's version of the myth certainly does), then the grand narrative within which subjects locate themselves positions genders in relation to particular places in the story and, by extension, to particular loci in relation to subjectivity and identity. The female, then, is lost by the wayside, unaccounted for by this oedipal story unless she assumes the position of the oedipal son, in which case she no longer adheres to the sidebar narrative of the female subject.

Another tautology, gender is shaped by the narrative it shapes; the dynamic of the gender story reinforces the myth of wholeness in the place of the son through the authority of the father, while the mother is lost in the denial of the son's non-autochthonous origins. The story of gender also engenders a psychology, an ideology of narrative, and subjectivity not unlike those deduced by structuralist accounts. The story of the story is the combination of opposites that concludes with a completing merger and a new equilibrium. The opposition represented by gender, already generated by the oppositional impetus of narrative, does not, however, exist in a closed narrative/gender circle; rather, its terms shift through history and cultures in relation to the discourses of sexuality and power. While sexual difference is assumed in the naturalized reproductive activity associated with sexuality, the categories *male* and *female* only comply with the sameness/difference dynamic of narrative as opposed to their being some natural state of affairs depicted by narrative. While as a complementary and contrary pair, male and female seem to fit neatly into the kind of active/passive bipolar dynamic characteristic of most accounts of narrative structure, the pair does not align with the sameness/difference tension that underlies and informs the dynamic of equilibrium and disequilibrium. Female is not same to male's difference. Instead, male and female together constitute a primal difference pervasively manifested in the surface level of narrative; heterological gender's very performance of difference defeats the stasis and death represented by sameness as a lack of difference. As a basic category of difference, gender is thus also a basic functional category of narrative.

Coming to Term

Screening the very process it pretends to arrange, the oedipal myth is a cover story, like all accounts of narrative, obscuring the very nature of the logic by which it is generated. Narratives of origins (and narratives of the origins of narratives) displace the founding logic and ideology of narrative into an empty originary moment where narrative itself appears to fade. In so doing, originary narratives substitute temporal structure and series of oppositions—an entire dialectical organization—for narrative's logic and impetus that remain undefined. The "originary" moment appears in the guise of a lack of difference, chaos, non-autochthony, pre-oedipality, sameness, stasis, or equilibrium that precedes meaning, law, the mirror-stage initiation of a coming to subjectivity, movement, and disequilibrium. Difference somehow deranges or violates sameness, like Todorov's "force" that enters and changes an equilibrium, disenabling this aboriginal sameness to which one can never return but can only imagine through the gloss of difference that both destroys and enables it. At the same time difference creates a lasting breach, a lack that difference and narrative move perpetually to fill. Difference is proliferated in oppositions that appear to sustain meaning, change, plot, and narrative in a perpetual displacement of an origin that was already only produced by narrative. This narrative of displacement is the originary narrative repeated in Oedipus, in accounts of meaning, in analyses of narrative, in stories of the emergent subject; it repeats and enacts the mistaken conflation of origins, lack, and sameness. Origins become a lack of origin, which in essence is simply a lack masked by the story of an origin.

The narrative structures created to supplant and obscure the breach (this lack of origin, meaning, law) are highly elaborated narratives of meaning and fullness. Fullness means destiny, the complex passions of Oedipus, the endlessly embroidered categories of narrative functions, identity, or a table of laws. The heroic passage from empty to full, described by de Lauretis, might be understood as driven by the origin. This origin is the end that exists before the beginning, the fate that seals the child before it is born, the postoriginary shape of things that situates the origin in its place and function as sameness—the difference to difference over which difference triumphs. And all of this depends upon an ideology of heterosexual reproductivity where the "female" sameness of the originary ground is invested with meaning by the "male" difference that results in the production of law, culture, narrative, meaning.

The narrative circle is evidently endless; its apparent endlessness obscures that which its seamlessness already hides. Origins and the forms of their representation reflect the politics by which their stories of commencement and closure cover over what it is that narrative and meaning screen: the lack in being that drives representation, narrative, signification, and subjectivity. The certainty of an origin sustains the more-or-less incomplete accounts of narrative logic; these obscure the even less certain dynamic by which lack, desire, culture, and difference instigate narrative, both as a cultural form and as an organizing medium for subjectivity. What Oedipus hides is not the truth of identity but the fact that this identity, this unoriginal origin, this non-autochthony is always with us. And what Oedipus expresses in a most convenient form is not only the shape of our ideas of narrative, the gendering of roles, and the ideological primacy of the male protagonist but also the link between an oppositional structure, the dynamic of sameness/death/stasis and difference/change/production that sustains it, and the lack it all hides.

The interplay of sameness and difference, as those terms are loaded with ideological baggage, characterizes our ideology of narrative but requires for its deployment a coexistent heterosexual ideology by which its terms are organized into sense. What this means is that while specific narratives might play out the sameness/difference dynamic in a variety of terms (including terms apposite to their ideological positioning, such as a female hero), narrative as an idea already conforms to a metaphorically gendered, heterosexual arrangement. The insistence of this idea of narrative and its ideological vestments preserve the idea of narrative even as its surface terms change.

I come to a stop here, at least with the analysis of structuralist theories of narrative. If the origin is no place to look, then the story is. But which story? Any narrative or narratives of narrative? If our understandings of narrative are both gendered and heterosexually inflected, then how can we look at narrative at all outside of those terms? And if we can't, how can the story ever change?

CHAPTER THREE

Coming Apart

Things fall apart; the centre can not hold;
—W. B. Yeats, "The Second Coming"

1

Let us examine a simple, but appropriately embroidered narrative of desires. Boy (Robert Preston) meets girl (Julie Andrews). Girl is very poor, but a talented singer, so boy, who is a homosexual, dresses girl up as a boy so that the girl/boy can dress up as a girl, sing in nightclubs, and make a lot of money. Another very rich boy (James Garner) comes along, sees girl dressed up as boy dressed up as girl, is instantly attracted to the girl the girl/boy is dressed up to be. Upon discovering that the showgirl is supposedly really a boy, rich boy wonders about the nature of his own sexual desire. Rich boy's desire to know the exact nature of his desire (he can't believe that he is a homosexual or that girl/boy is really a boy, though the strength of his attraction makes him almost willing to accept the former) drives him to try to discover the girl/boy's real gender by sneaking around trying to see girl/boy undress. Hiding in a closet, rich boy gets a glimpse of the underlying story; he is comforted because girl/boy is really a girl (as she was in the surface that didn't deceive after all). The truth about gender discovered, the story can continue toward joinder. Everybody gets together: rich boy and girl/boy, now just girl; rich boy's very masculine aide (Alex Karras) and girl's original homosexual boy.

Victor/Victoria illustrates beautifully the maxim that narrative can proceed to closure only after the correctly oppositional, appropriately gendered heterosexual components are sorted out. In relation to its almost Shakespearean end, *Victor/Victoria*'s middle, like that of "The Secret Woman," appears to be appropriately confused and chaotic, as genders, sexualities, identities mingle in an apparently mobile desire glossed by dramatic irony. *Victor/Victoria*'s deployment of gendered oppositions, gender switches, and romantic desire enacts and parodies the metaphorical tensions of sameness and difference by which narrative produces and sustains tension and desire. It also demonstrates narrative's ideologized sexual interplay as the film's circumstantial and mistaken homosexuality gives way to a more correct and satisfying heterosexuality for the main protagonists.

Since sameness, as we have seen, is a threat to narrative, it is important to understand how the sexualized dynamics of narrative *produce* homosexuality as a threatening sameness. *Victor/Victoria*'s gender disorientation elucidates how a homosexuality produced by the play of gender and narrative structure is culturally located as transient, sterile, and perverse. This chapter investigates how narrative's seemingly inadvertent structural production of homosexuality is actually a process necessary for narrative's heteroideological closure. Gender makes a difference in the production of homosexuality; homosexuality makes a difference in narrative's (re)productive ideology. Overcome by the reinscription of the hetero, homosexualities are seen as threatening to narrative closure and/or its attendant (re)productivity. Homosexuality's intersection with the middle's knowledge disparities makes sexual knowledge (or a knowledge about sexuality) one of narrative's primary nuclei. Taking as examples narratives that mess with gender as surface appearance, such as *Victor/Victoria* and *Star Trek: The Next Generation*, and narratives that involve bodies of mixed or layered gender, such as *Switch* and *All of Me*, this chapter explores gender's narrative differences and the "accidental" production of homosexualities. If cultural ideologies of homosexualities are indeed partially an effect of narrative, then understanding narrative dynamics might, at this time in history, enable the inscription of different ideologies of narrative and sexuality or force their disimbrication.

Breaking Up Is Hard To Do

Narrative's mediate confusion, as *Victor/Victoria* illustrates, is highly organized from the beginning. As in the middles of the orgasmic narratives that began both chapter 1 and "The Secret Woman," *Victor/Victoria's* middle is full of the indirection and distancing techniques that play openly with gender and irony; the film feigns a chaos that is produced by the intersection of at least five different mechanisms that seem to divide narrative from itself. First, the film's central boy/girl binary is a complementary opposition that stimulates sequences of equilibrium and disequilibrium as James Garner pursues Julie Andrews. At the same time, an outer/inner dichotomy, reflected in the question of Julie Andrews's gender, is vertical (Julie Andrews is simultaneously boy and girl) in relation to the horizonal, sequential convergence of male/female. Third, an uneven distribution of knowledge about gender creates dramatic irony. Fourth, narrative embodies a tension between extending desire and obtaining gratification (between continuing and ending) appended to homosexual and heterosexual romance and to the desire to know.[1] Finally, all of these divisions are complicated by dynamics of readerly identification that may or not follow the several divisions constituting the narrative; if not, then reading might organize sexualities and binaries differently but in a tension with the narrative's structural oppositions.

In *Victor/Victoria* the coexistence of multiple gender/sex "truths" in one gendered position generates narrative confusion. Who knows about whose gender and when they know it create an extended misdirection—but only in relation to the "right" direction that we already know. Reproducing the story's tension between outer and inner, dramatic irony pits viewers' awareness of the disparity between the characters' appearance and their "real" gender against what they already know to be the narrative's direction. Thus viewers perceive confusion in anticipation of a joinder that depends upon the elucidation of the gender secret they already know. When confusion and joinder coexist, the always-savvy reader discerns what is really a highly organized narrative duplicity between knowing and not knowing analogous to the narrative attached to the fetish: "I know very well, but all the same."[2] In this way, we can permit confusion, knowing that it is always a part of a larger whole in relation to which it has already been sorted.

While dramatic irony appears to order *Victor/Victoria*'s gleefully out-of-control combinations of gender and desire, its control derives from narrative's already-retrospective organization of such binaries as male/female and inner/outer. But the narrative's deployment of the knowledge of sexual secrets—its outer and inner—is never really so divided or neatly reflexive. Like the knowledge disparities of dramatic irony that know and don't know at once, the distribution of knowledge within this narrative exists in a self-contradictory posture. The surface or outer narrative of Julie Andrews's disguise, while misleading, also tells all; that is, it inevitably both hides and leads to a truer "inner" story (her gender) that enlightens outer appearances. But while embodying some truth about the outer (Julie Andrews is a girl), this inner also refers to an even more "inner" savvy: a prior knowledge about the way stories really go (boy meets girl). The reader's knowledge is not really a knowledge of "real" gender that the story then reveals as true; knowledge of gender is produced by a knowledge of the way the story must go. In cross-dressing comedy, knowing gender stands in for knowing the story, but gender is defined by the story and not the other way around, a cause/effect switch that cross-dressing broadly parodies and dramatic irony tends to hide.

The outer, manifest story, thus, is not ultimately the effect of its own idiosyncratic, ironically discerned "inner" but of the "inner" of a narrative ideology whose pattern we know, seek, and find. Maintaining this outer/inner division through time shapes the narrative of discovery and knowledge as the opposition between outer and inner is dissolved by the emergence of an inner knowledge that can be either a specific narrative's truth or the truth of all narrative. This inner knowledge, as Foucault observes, has become, since the nineteenth century, an inner knowledge defined as sexual. Foucault's version of the history of sexuality describes the relative enlargement of this outer/inner binary and its role in connecting subjectivity, sexuality, and modes of production; this occurs at the same time that the "inner" cause of sexuality gradually becomes the answer to "outer" questions about behavior, material success, family longevity, thriving or failing production, and reproduction.

Operating within the narrative, between reader and narrative, and in conceptions of narrative, an outer/inner split organizes other binaries around a pole of knowledge at the same time that it appears to produce and perpetuate confusion in the narrative middle. The outer/inner split works like a narrative masquerade to disavow what it confirms, to mislead from what it leads directly to. Safely organizing the appearance of discrete but conflicting levels, outer/inner is a low-risk way of breaking up, disbursing, and precipitating a few oppositional elements into too many conflicting possibilities. Always already arranged by narrative foreknowledge, these elements—sameness/difference, noncomplementary oppositions (girl and non-girl), odd and multiple terms—constitute a safety-netted dynamic of pseudopotential failure that narrative's heteroideology can spectacularly appropriate, organize, and master at the end.

Enterprise Zone

While narrative itself requires a middling confusion, cultural anxieties about reproduction and difference also produce confusions in the locus we understand as narrative's middle. For example, the extended family narrative of *Star Trek: The Next Generation* faithfully constructs divisions between inner and outer and truth and inauthenticity along the lines of both species and gender. Juggling these jealously maintained distinctions through such clearly marked boundaries as the Enterprise "home" and "space, the final frontier," or the difference between physical attribute and function (the engineer Geordi's blindness, the counselor Deanna's empathic ability to "access" the inner), *Star Trek* appears to reiterate the tolerant lesson that one cannot judge ability by appearance or space by its fearsomeness. To manage this inner/outer disparity, *Star Trek* moors its potentially dangerous, polymorphous, unknown "inner" alien to the familiar secrets and power deployments of sexual difference. By superimposing stereotypical sexual differences upon all examples of aliens and by insisting upon metaphorically gendered and familial terms, *Star Trek* establishes gender as the definitive dynamic of cosmic existence. In the face of its apparently liberal acceptance of all, the show's constant reproduction of superficial "outer" categories suggests an anxiety about rampant otherness and the potential failure of future white bourgeois proliferation in space.

Star Trek's divisions between outer and inner depend upon the establishment of consistent sets of oppositions that are mostly contained within the gendered aegis of the hierarchical starship "family."

The family's metaphorical "children" are characterized by internal splitting or by an external multiplication of disparate traits. Engineer Geordi is black and blind; Worf is a Kling-on raised by humans; Troi is a part-human, part Betazoid empath; Data is an android who wants to be human. The family's "parents" are doubled. Guinan, the ship's bartender and ultimate maternal figure is the knowing and ageless survivor of millennia; Dr. Crusher is doubled by her hyperactive teenage son; the stalwart Commander Riker has a literally coexisting other self (Lieutenant Riker) created in a transporter accident. Captain Picard, father of all, is the recipient of other lives; he is transformed into an alien Borg, mind-melds with Spock's father, lives the entire life of an alien from an extinct planet, and, like Riker, is literally doubled in a space/time incident. The difference between splitting and doubling reiterates the difference between inner and outer; most of the crew members have the internal and warring duplicity of the still-oedipal child, while the command characters exhibit the external self-production and mastery of the parent/reader.

This splitting/doubling of character and character traits sets the pattern for the kind of outer/inner split typical of *Star Trek*'s plots; narrative synthesis always means the victorious, oedipal return of the inner, the genuine, and the always gendered truth that has been displaced by the middling chaos imported by alterity. The resolution of the outer/inner split usually corresponds to the solution of the starship's larger crisis (if there is one), to a moral lesson, and to the wisdom of its various father figures. Multiplicity is always on the side of the nonhuman; for this reason, the narrative's resolution always involves a return to a singular human truth sanctified against too much difference. Only superior beings may retain their multiplicity so long as that doesn't disturb the starship familial hierarchy; aliens who are too powerful often resolve themselves into one visible form, usually characterized by a single bright light, before they leave the ship that has served as their metaphorical womb (they've come aboard to examine humanity, they are in the middle of some giant species mutation). Members of the cosmic continuum such as Q, who are intrinsically polymorphous, may retain their multiplicity as long as they stay off the ship.[3]

The successful negotiation of this medial splitting and doubling— successful in the sense that the duplicity is penetrated, the secret exposed, and the character reduced to manageable singularity—is related to sexuality and to preserving a heterosexual narrative logic.

This productive logic is openly appended to the starship Enterprise's own production narrative proudly stated at the beginning of each show: "Space the final frontier. These are the voyages of the starship Enterprise." Galactic heterosexuality is a product of a capitalist production economy; as the founding paradigm for most *Star Trek* episodes, it preorganizes not only the permissible relation between sexuality and production but also the ways such a relation might appear to be challenged, muddled, or interrupted.

In "The Outcast" (March 15, 1992), for example, Riker is attracted to the inner "feminine" essence of an outwardly undifferent and therefore somewhat fearsome and totalitarian J'naii.[4] The difference between the J'nnai's appearance and essence as well as the difference between this J'nnai and the rest of J'nnai culture fascinate Riker and spur in him a complex of interrelated desires—to certify the J'nnai's "true" gender, to give it (?) knowledge of a passion impossible to the homogeneous, to convert and mark it. The confusing duplicity of the J'nnai is undone as one of their number reveals the inner truth denied by the rest (that they are really feminine), a truth that conforms to the opposition/synthesis model of narrative. Bringing the renegade J'nnai's gender and sexual identities into homogeneous alignment, Riker, the ship's agent of civil liberties, reveals the secret femininity of all androgynes through sexual activity that removes the disturbing distinction between appearance (female) and identity (androgyny) otherwise sustained by the J'nnai. Literal heterosexuality becomes the saving agent of an encounter/synthesis with some "other" whose lack of gender and consequent sameness produces an allegorical rendering of reverse cultural homophobia; the "Same" J'nnai oppress their hetero members in a way analogous to the way heterosexual cultures oppress their homosexual members. The J'nnai thus provide a threatening sameness against which the ship's heterosexuality must defend itself and reign in whatever literal register it can find.

While outer and inner create narrative interest and complication, their motivating anxiety throughout the *Star Trek* narrative is an anxiety about diversity. Diversity is not a question of species but rather the possibility that too much duplicity might result either in too many terms for successful synthesis or in too much sameness that prevents narrative progression, synthesis, social order, and spaceship productivity. In either case the outer/inner duplicity of the alien other (and sometimes of the starship denizen), just like the gender of *Victor/Victoria*'s boy/girl Julie

Andrews, must be reduced to a single term for the conflict to become binary and closable instead of multiple and unmanageable. For example, in "The Host" (May 12, 1991), the story of Dr. Crusher's love affair with the symbiotic alien, the alien is doubly different, since he is already double: two aliens in one, the outer alien, male. This alien is not what he appears to be; when the outer male host body dies and the inner, symbiotic alien transfers to a female body, the sudden disappearance of sexual difference between Crusher and the alien provokes two fears at once: a recognition of the real difference of the symbiotic alien and a fear of no difference like that provoked by the J'nnai's outer androgyny. By transferring from male to female, the inner alien reveals that inside there has never been gender or sexual difference, that what has been passion for Dr. Beverly has been superficial at best, that there hasn't really been the attraction of opposites at all. The alien's transfer to the female body not only dramatizes the inner alien's lack of gender (and a retrospective lack of romance) but also performs a reiterated sameness (linked to its fearsome diversity) that in the *Star Trek* narrative stops passion and the story. Now there are too many girls. Since joinder is no longer possible, Dr. Crusher's only possible choice is to reject the now-female-doubled alien, even though the alien offers continuing passion. Her response reveals the other half of narrative same-phobia: humans cannot cope with too much change and diversity.

It Takes Three, Baby

The moment when the alien offers to continue her affair with Dr. Crusher is the moment when the overt homosexual possibility becomes visible and threatening. It is also the place where the divisions between gendered opposites, outer and inner, and audience and character knowledge seem to coalesce. Produced in the intersection of these three narrative divisions, homosexuality as narrative possibility emerges. A part of what we already know, its appearance imports what seems to be a potentially different logic, the titillating suggestion of a different story. This difference locates it in the manufactured seam of systemic collision where knowledge and desire do not yet correlate in strict compliance to a reproductive aegis. Because it is, however, the effect of narrative's medial dynamic where too many elements converge, homosexuality always appears as a vertical or simultaneous possibility—the inner to an outer, something layered, inherently multiple, and insincere—rather than a linear and "genuine" position such as heterosexuality. And because it is constructed as vertical or simultaneous, homosexuality, both female and male, can never go anywhere in a process that is quintessentially linear.

The sense of a different direction associated with homosexuality is, of course, already a product of the logic of linear narrative. Narrative collapses the homosexual's vertical play of multiple divisions into a flat layer of sequential opposition rendered as sameness standing in the way of reproduction. In *Victor/Victoria* Julie Andrews's sequential gender positions and the conscious knowledge of their effect on the "story" (heterosexual joinder) flattens her multiple, simultaneous differences. She is first a girl, but with a male homosexual, then with a boy with no romance, then a woman with a man, so romance precedes. *Victor/Victoria* actually plays out one of its homosexual stories, the comic romance of Robert Preston and Alex Karras, but locates it as a parasitic parody of the traditional oppositional joinder of the main plot. In *Star Trek* the collapse of multiplicity is rendered as a reduction to homology rather than to a single term. In the case of the J'nnai, the entire culture is relocated into the feminine position of an undifferentiated matrix. Dr. Crusher's alien is still double, but a doubling of a female with an ungendered being that results in the appearance of a female who loves a female, or the doubling of same.

The sexual anxiety of the heteronarrative is thus located in the outer/inner split, the discursive position of sexuality in culture where sexuality has become an inner truth. As the way of organizing knowledge in narrative, the outer/inner split tends to occur in connection to narratives with a pronounced ideological stake in reproduction and survival such as psychoanalysis, and detective, family, romance, and political intrigue stories. The presence of this apparently superficial structural characteristic in such narratives suggests that the narrative ideology by which narrative is already metaphorically heterosexual must doubly reinforce itself when the more literal reproductive terms of bourgeois ideology are at stake—when the normative sexual "cause" seems threatened. At the same time the proposition of the perverse narrative, produced by a controlled "breakdown" in the narrative middle, is already aligned as an element of narrative heteroideology that appears to stimulate the narrative mechanism back to normalcy. This recircling represents some intranarrative drama, a redoubling of narrative's metaphorical base by a more literal threat. Narrative is, therefore, not about literal homosexuality; rather, homosexuality as a fleeting narrative suggestion embodies the nature of narrative's (authorized) instability. Homosexuality already constitutes a part of the narrative system as the metaphorical model for the risky "sameness" that operates as the "difference" to a metaphorically heterosexual difference; this allows narrative to replay its recovery constantly.

The narrative risk of sameness is still linked to knowledge in narrative's sex/gender interplay. For example, the main difference between the discovery of true gender in *Victor/Victoria* and the reduction to homology (or same difference) in *Star Trek* is the function of dramatic irony in the mix. In Dr. Crusher's story, we have not necessarily anticipated the gender switch; it comes as a surprise just at the moment when the other narrative divisions seem to resolve themselves. Unlike *Victor/Victoria*, where the wisdom of dramatic irony matches the narrative's simplification and synthesis, *Star Trek*'s "surprise" creates an irony: the apparent immortality of the alien, which might perpetuate and enable a joinder with Dr. Crusher, turns out to be the very mechanism by which such joinder is made impossible. The effect of the alien's unexpected regendering is to break open and confuse what had appeared to come into alignment; in this moment of surprise and breakage a homosexual possibility suddenly becomes visible. In a moment lasting only as long as it takes the reactionary Dr. Crusher to reject the possibility—a moment coinciding with narrative closure— this new knowledge introduces two different narrative possibilities: 1) that Dr. Crusher accept the alien's proposal and continue her passion; and 2) that she reject the alien's proposal and live with her memories.

The sudden bifurcation of narrative possibility plays on another narrative binary, the tension between the drive to end (death drive) and the urge to come together (Eros). The first of Dr. Crusher's narrative possibilities divides on the side of Eros since its choice would continue the desire and the narrative. The second belongs to the drive to end, in this case both the romance and the episode. Because, however, the ideological narrative of Eros is linked to heterosexual reproduction, the first option is never really possible within *Star Trek*'s narrative heteroideology. The sudden appearance of multiple possibilities caused by a breakdown in the ordering stability of dramatic irony is here really only an illusion of possibilities, since the first narrative promises a series of repetitive and sterile passions with a perpetually unreduced and self-reproducing alien. Only the second narrative has ever really been possible within narrative's heteroideology; Crusher's rejection of the alien indeed permits the story's closure, which comes rapidly in the doctor's sad return to starship normalcy and the celibacy of an honorary maternal figure.

The problem represented by the moment of the alien's homosexual proposal is that in retroactively doubling one side of a gender binary, it appears to provide too many terms in addition to too much sameness. Finding the inner secret in the case of Dr. Crusher's alien means the tragic perpetuation of a homology governed by gender—of things too same to be different. But the threat posed by the alien reveals the narrative risk caused by the contradictory copresence of too many elements on the one hand and too much sameness on the other. Too much sameness and too much difference constitute the same threat. Their literal sexual exponents—homosexuality and heterosexuality—comprise the narrative's diegesis; this literal story appears to present sameness and difference "naturally" as the life-based result of the truth of gender and sexuality.

Narrative sameness manifests itself in the fear of another kind of sameness: the absolute disappearance of difference. The disappearance of difference is actually the displaced fear of a loss of the ability to discern difference. When James Garner panics in *Victor/Victoria*, it is because he can not tell that Julie Andrews is a boy: sameness is a problem of knowledge rather than a problem of biology. And if Andrews is a male, then there is too much sameness, which provides James Garner with another instance of panic. The inability to discern difference and too much sameness are linked in the more suggestively lesbian moments when *Star Trek*'s aliens' inner/outer dichotomies dissolve. Although the conflicting inner essence and outer appearances of the J'nnai and the symbiotic alien work in opposite ways, the disappearance of the difference between outer and inner results in no difference, a no difference whose sameness freezes action, production, and narrative. Fearfully close in both cases to the specter of the lesbian, the disappearance of doubled differences—the aberrantly feminine J'nnai's distinction between appearance and identity and her difference from her culture, the alien lover's male/female copresence—is more threatening than the fear registered through any problematic doubling of terms.

The fear of no difference in *Star Trek* plays out in the field of sexuality, where sexuality certifies gender when gender cannot certify sexuality. The loss of binaries that generates the dreaded inability to discern difference tends to be feminized and hence metaphorically lesbian.

Male homosexuality tends to occupy the position of doubled or excessive sameness, though both lesbian and gay male sexuality may be literally present in both places. While this distinction makes little difference in the relative narrative position of lesbian and gay male characters (they still play in the middle), the difference between too much sameness and no difference does define their very different narrative deployment. The distinction is due primarily to the different roles of gender in narrative whose stereotypes of male presence and female absence generate the difference between doubled sameness (male presence) and a feminized lack (absence) of differentiation.

That both *Victor/Victoria* and *Star Trek* rely on the pretext of a dissonance between inner and outer as a way of addressing a fear of no difference suggests that the anxiety catalyzing the narrative of sexualities, posed as a conflict within self, is actually a conflict about the inability to discern, about a fear of homogeny and homology. But this anxiety is structural, embedded in the idea of narrative itself, for the very real problem of the characters with no difference or doubled sameness is that they threaten to end the tensive conflict of binaries through which the narrative produces and reproduces. On the surface of the *Star Trek* narrative, this fear seems to take the two forms: literal lesbian sexuality as no difference and a bisexuality representing too much difference. This bisexuality implies everyone's potential duplicity; more crucially after AIDS, however, it also represents a fear of contagion. Male homosexuality as a literal possibility is never produced in *Star Trek's* narrative intersections; this absence has to do with the particular no-difference form anxiety takes in the face of multiple diversity and galactic otherness. Although bisexuality implies a flexibility and even a productive difference within, in *Star Trek's* narratives such difference is rendered as the inability to discern difference in an hysterical emphasis on an always-potential lesbian sexuality that threatens to destroy appearances, stop passion, and kill the story.

Outer/inner dichotomy's clash with sequential complementary oppositions is ideologically, historically, and structurally linked to sexuality as the model of an inner, truer narrative—even though sexuality may not always be the literal inner secret the outer narrative hides and exposes. Narrative's ideological link to sexuality also enables another doubling gloss; sameness or homology is already identified with homosexuality through a simple heterologic of gender difference. If heterosexuality is defined as a coalescence of different genders, then homosexuality is the coming together of same genders. Tied to this gendered heterologic, the outer/inner dichotomy perpetuates the sameness already associated with excess, death, stasis, and homosexuality as a threat within narrative. This happens at the same time such homological sameness is already reappropriated by its necessary correlation to the difference (knowledge, heterosexuality, sexual difference) that constitutes the other half of the opposition into which narrative is organized. Sameness, homology, homosexuality thus constitute narrative's difference to difference.

The operation of narrative heterologic produces a retrospective narrative by which the true essence of no difference and doubled sameness have all along been a logic of differences. Both sameness and no difference are functioning parts of a difference that both precedes and succeeds sameness; sameness is the difference to difference, its appearance conditional upon its simultaneous pairing with the discovery of its lie. There is no such thing as no gender; gender always exists to be discovered. Gender's preexistence is defined by the prospective/retroactive gloss of narrative heterologic whose dynamic depends upon the production and defeat of no difference and doubled sameness as the real enemies to difference. And there homosexuality is.

Lost in the Masquerade

> What is it like, secrecy? The secret life. I know it's sexual. I want to know this.
> Is it homosexual?
> —Don DeLillo, *Running Dog*, p. 110

Homosexuality appears as a preliminary reorganization of the middle's confused elements. The point where homosexuality is recognizable is the point that catalyzes the return of the heterosexual and closure. In this sense homosexuality does function as narrative's secret whose revelation enables narrative's productive realignment. Homosexuality's emergence—its summons—at this most intermediate stage situates literal/metaphorical homosexuality as a step in the salvation processes of the (re)productive narrative. Yet this homosexual moment is more than structural, utilitarian, or transitory; it represents an omnipresent anxiety that is beyond simple homophobia, an anxiety about mastery, control, and production that surfaces at the last point where narrative feigns failure. This last point is characterized by mechanisms of disguise, fraud, and delusion that stage both the revelation of an outer/inner disparity and the lie of narrative itself. The structural evocation of a homosexual possibility in narrative's middle marks an anxiety about narrative's ability to continue in the face of death.

Narrative masquerade (as a manifestation of pretend confusion) displaces this anxiety from narrative itself into homosexuality as the moment of vertical fraud; this sustains a veneer of difference in the place of narrative's potential stasis.[5] Masquerade is not simply one of a number of possible ploys by which narrative equilibrium becomes disequilibrium and vice versa; it is an inherent aspect of our idea of narrative itself. Narrative is its own outer/inner; what Brooks identifies as a desire to continue and a desire to end refer to and conceal one another. Absorbing the fraudulent aspect of the masquerade that conceals, a metaphorical (or literal) homosexuality aligns with the narratively inauthentic while heterosexuality aligns with "true" knowledge of the inner, of identity, or of narrative itself. This truth, as we have seen, enables the "correct" reorganization of differences into a productive end.

The narrative crisis homosexuality represents in *Star Trek* becomes even more explicit in narratives that feature masquerades or cross-gender embodiments. In these narratives, the (really not so) misleading appurtenances of a circumstantial surface miscoding produce excesses, confusions, and risks overtly linked to issues of gender and sexuality. As in the "The Secret Woman," the overlayering of narratives permits the licensed but pleasurable chaos of supposed gender misidentification by which a perfectly respectable reproductive end can divert itself, always to be saved in the end by the revelation of an underlying truth and always assuaging the anxiety of the reader/audience through an overdose of dramatic irony.

The fact that our heteroideological understanding of narrative appears in transparently sexualized components does not mean that stories of sexual masquerade are instances of narrative in its own terms. Narratives containing literal gender or sexual masquerade make sense because they refer openly to our knowledge of narrative; reading the narrative of gender masquerade through the narrative of gender and sexuality redoubles narrative through its own metaphors, but two steps removed. Like overt narratives of sex, stories about cross-dressing or transsexuality tend to be a strange mixture of broad parody and the uncanny. As has been the case with other narratives that are too literal in their connection of sex and death or sexuality and narrative, narratives about cross-dressing and transsexuality are ironic and predictable, depending on an overly complex costume baroque to constitute a narrative middle of apparently polymorphous and mobile desire.

In addition to *Victor/Victoria*, two film comedies of the past fifteen years, *All of Me* (Carl Reiner 1984) and *Switch* (Blake Edwards 1991), dramatize in literal terms the interrelation of an Eros/death tension, the metaphorical sex/gender positions of (re)productive narrative, and homosexuality. In all of the narratives except *Victor/Victoria*, homosexuality is not an identity but is, rather, the effect of a circumstantial multiplicity of sameness. Homosexuality is the nexus where the clash of disorganized multiples (too many terms) and sequential oppositions (organized binaries) makes visible narrative's conflicting and multiple dynamics. Structurally produced homosexuality is, thus, a suspiciously desire-ridden, uncertain, and very interesting turning point of unassuaged desire.

Both *All of Me* and *Switch* are narratives about death, essentially about correcting or rewriting a previous sterile, or incorrect life narrative by reinscribing a proper heterosexuality in a second life. This second chance features a gender switch as the ostensible mechanism for narrative correction. This "I've looked at life from both sides now" (the theme music for *Switch*) approach to narrative rectification recalls the nostalgic wish for wholeness Freud identifies as the basis for sexuality in *Beyond the Pleasure Principle*. And literal sex is certainly the mechanism by which the correct reproductive path is reinstalled as a way to overcome or vanquish a very literal death.

All of Me is the story of an invalid rich woman's desire to reproduce herself in another body so that she can enjoy her wealth. Employing a generic eastern mystic, Edwina Cutwater (Lily Tomlin) has cajoled the stableman's daughter into agreeing to act as the "host" body for a postmortem soul transmigration. Keeping the girl and the guru close by her, the dying Edwina plans to transmigrate her soul into a bowl at the moment of her death. Dying unexpectedly in the offices of her attorney, her bowled soul is accidentally tossed out the window and lands on Steve Martin's head, transferring her soul to him instead of to the girl. Cohabiting with him instead of taking over his body, the Martin/Tomlin hybrid manifests an all-too-literal bisexuality as Cutwater and her stereotypical femininity control one half of Martin's body and the masculine Martin the other. With too many terms, Martin's behavior is visibly eccentric: he must give his Edwina-controlled right hand audible directions while urinating; he walks in an awkward, half-highly-effeminate fashion; and he cannot drive, since the warring souls and their exaggerated parodies of gender cannot agree about how his body should operate.

The problem with this bisexual duplicity, or partial gender layering becomes apparent when Martin has an opportunity for sex with the girl who was to have received Edwina's soul. On two different occasions Martin attempts to go to bed with the girl, only to be stopped—the first time by Tomlin's lack of cooperation, and the second time by her too enthusiastic fantasies of Cary Grant. Martin's desire is thwarted by Tomlin's puritanism, innocence (she was a virgin), and dislike for the girl, as well as by the fact that the female Tomlin still fancies men. Because they have different sexual directions, Martin and Tomlin cannot sustain a sexual act together.

The combination of two differently directed heterosexuals, however, produces some homosexuality no matter what he/she does. In overtly sexual moments there are both too many terms—three instead of two—and too much sameness as Edwina's presence doubles the female and creates the possibility of a inadvertent, but de facto lesbian involvement. At the same time, Edwina's continuing desire for men creates the suggestion of male homosexuality. Only when he is rid of Edwina's soul can Martin function again, predictably with Edwina (with whom he has already been joined) after she has been made separate and single via a successful transplant into the stableman's daughter's body. The lesbian side effect in all this is suggested rather than permitted; the fact that Edwina can not actually make love to the girl is never an overt rejection of lesbianism; rather, it is accounted for by the warring heterosexuality of Martin's two parts, the same duplicity that makes the lesbian suggestion in the first place.

While *All of Me* focuses on Martin's problems sharing his body (he loses his job, his girlfriend, etc.), the framing narrative rewrites Edwina Cutwater's life, shifting its sterile, invalid, useless wealth from a premature death to a new life of heterosexual romance and affluence. Openly aligning the perpetuation of wealth with the metaphorically reproductive transmigration, the narrative accomplishes renewal by means of the apparently serendipitous heterosexual agency of Edwina's spiritual cohabitation with a man. She can reproduce herself (and her wealth) in another woman's body only via Martin, whose accidental male intercession produces a vertical heterosexuality that balances Tomlin's spirit and enables Eros and synthesis rather than narrative's premature arrest through quasilesbian sexual gratification or death. The threatened short circuit of the lesbian moment manqué emerges at the moment when bodies and spirits are most multiple, most disguised, most ready to reveal their duplicity. The failure of the second sexual act initiates the process of painful separation, the redistribution of genders and bodies from three in two to two in two, and the realignment of body and soul that leads to a more satisfactory end.

In contrast to *All of Me*'s comically soulful gothic, *Switch* is the story of a grotesque male chauvinist Steve (Perry King), who, drowned in a hot tub by a group of vengeful ex-girlfriends, is offered the opportunity to redeem himself by finding one woman who likes him. The narrative genius devil, claiming that God's deal is too lenient, counterproposes that Steve return to life as a female. Set within this cosmic binary, Steve's life as a female is much like Martin's life as Edwina's corporeal landlord. Instead of a male/female mix, Steve is a man in a woman's body; masquerade becomes literal. Steve's new female body (now Ellen Barkin) constantly betrays its manly innards to others who only read the surface; Steve the woman's masculine mannerisms are thus understood as lesbian, when he/she is attracted to women who pass, or when he/she punches out the men who hit on him/her.

Steve's conscious homophobic anxiety, however, is that a male will be attracted to him. He/she is therefore unprepared when he/she cannot follow through on the inner man's attraction to women. Steve's problem isn't the superficial lack of "relevant" body parts; an intrinsic heterosexuality apparently appended to surface gender makes his inner desire for women disappear. The body follows the "natural" logic of heterosex that governs the outside instead of the inside of an outer/inner dichotomy, making the gendered body the site of ideological regulation. This suggests that in representations of transsexuality the visible regime of gender controls; whereas in depictions of transvestism the inner unseen gender seems to command. In terms of narrative structure, this means that transsexual masquerade is the opposite of transvestism; while transvestism is healed by revelation of an inner "true" gender, transsexuality's binary is resolved only if the inner gender is brought into line with the outer body's naturalized heterosexual desire. While gender governs over mere appearance, sexed bodies rule over gender.

Attempting to win the advertising account of a wealthy lesbian's cosmetic company, Steve the woman attempts to seduce the client. But when the client tries to take him/her up on it (several times), Steve evades, gives excuses, and finally admits that he/she was only using the sex as a way to gain the account. As Steve comments, he/she thought she could go through with it, what's the difference, just like old times. But for Steve the woman there is a difference, and that difference is a lack of difference. Not only does this lesbian no difference paralyze him/her, the very fact that the woman who is seducing him/her is a lesbian finally redefines the relation from covert heterosexuality to the very much too much sameness of open lesbian sexuality. As in *All of Me*, *Switch*'s lesbian moment is produced by the confluence of too many terms—Steve, his woman's body, and another woman. This point of excess is the moment when the masquerade can go no further.

Instead of verifying the man inside with the cosmetic queen, a drunken Steve ends up in bed with her/his best friend, Walter, and somehow, out of sight and filmic consciousness (so there can be neither intention nor desire), Walter impregnates Steve. Genders finally properly aligned with bodies, the reproductive aegis is fulfilled. Still a duplicitous vessel of excess, Steve must die, but his heterosexual reproductivity saves his soul as he gives birth to a daughter whose love for her/him fulfills his return mission.

The two places where homosexuality is suggested in *Switch* are both places of failure—a failure of desire, a failure of the consciousness of desire. This failure illustrates both the difference between narrative configurations of lesbian sexuality and male homosexuality and the function of the homosexual moment in narrative. The lesbian moments, when the girl Steve threatens to become sexually involved with other women, are moments of phallusless heterosexuality, a paralyzing economy of no difference. When Steve finally comprehends that she/he is female, Steve also comprehends that she/he is heterosexual. Steve's discernment of his female heterosexuality at the moment of lesbian capitulation enables him to avoid the wrong, potentially short-circuiting narrative path of lesbian prostitution and seek, albeit unconsciously, a different, heterosexual mode of deliverance. The lesbian moment is, thus, the initiating moment of no difference that throws Steve into heterosexual difference with a vengeance.

Although the discovery of her/his heterosexuality is Steve's social downfall for it precipitates her/his loss of status at the advertising agency and her/his drunken orgy with Walter, it puts Steve on the right narrative track. While at the beginning of Steve's transformation moments with Walter were male homosexual moments to be loudly denied, his relation with Walter loses its threat when Steve begins to recognize his heterosexual femininity. But even as Steve conforms to the heterosexual desire of the surface body, her/his encounter with Walter must be shielded by a lack of intention and desire. Steve simply isn't there when Walter makes love to the female body. Unconsciousness masking its male homosexual suggestion, sexuality between Walter and Steve is only made visible by the evidence of Walter's nudity the morning after. Retrospective and minus the mental factor that is the only way Steve is still male, the hint of a male homosexual moment is lost to the productive heterosexuality that supplants it even before it can happen. While the lesbian moment consists of a the too-visible sameness of multiple women's bodies, the male homosexual moment is masked by heterosexual difference, obliterated by unconsciousness, and represented by a filmic ellipsis. The compromised male homosexual moment is nonetheless productive and reproductive rather than paralyzing, furthering the narrative to its heavenly end rather than stopping it in its tracks.

Both *All of Me* and *Switch* present a sequence of homosexual possibilities in their middles, but the order and timing of the appearance of lesbian and gay male sexuality is important. In both films the specter of lesbian sexuality occupies the site where sequence (the plotted coming-together of characters of opposite genders) and paradigm (the vertical layering of opposing genders) intersect. This produces two correlative narrative moments: the moment when difference is difficult to discern and the moment when differences are sorted out again. While Steve Martin's character has desired the stableman's daughter all along, Edwina's skittish homophobia stops them the first time and his distraction by her fantasied attraction to Cary Grant stops them the second. The suggestion of male homosexuality within the Martin character's body during this second attempt initiates the drive to separate Edwina from Martin. Although *Switch*'s Steve has the calculated opportunity for sex with the lesbian cosmetic queen, his going through with it would be a narrative short circuit. Going to bed with Walter inaugurates the realignment of gendered soul and body that will enable Steve to die and go to heaven. The association of these two moments illustrates narrative's pressure to resolve into heterosexual difference, while enjoying the disparities created by its temporary failure to differentiate.

Spawned indirectly by the moment of lesbian no difference, suggestions of male homosexuality—Martin's inability to function when

Tomlin desires Cary Grant, Steve's unconscious [but nonetheless desired] capitulation to best buddy Walter—are ultimately productive as they mark the beginning of the process of differentiation, separation, and single alignments. While both lesbian sexuality and male homosexuality represent potential short circuits, the lesbian moment structurally precedes and enables the male homosexual moment in both of these narratives. At the same time, the lesbian moment is more overt, more an immediate product of the fully confused array of multiples at their point of reorganization. The lesbian moment stimulates the desire for differentiation, and the male homosexual possibility only appears after such differentiation. The corporeal difference between lesbian sexuality and male homosexuality is the presence of the penis as the finally distinguishing mark of sexual difference. The presence of the penis in male homosexuality, even if redoubled, enables a patriarchal reproductive continuity that the lesbian moment threatens.

What happens, then, in the interplay between outer and inner, appearance and essence, costume and gender, disorganized middle and tidy scission/synthesis, is the production of desire as an effect of the disparity between those things that should (in the good heteronarrative) go together—gender and body, body and heterosexual desire. This narrative desire is the product of at least three different tensions intersecting at the point of gender/body/desire disparity: 1) the perverse pleasure of the disparity itself and its playful, shifting perpetuation of desire and of narrative; 2) the oedipal pleasure produced by the narrative's incipient mastery over gender in anticipation of the known end; and 3) the pleasure suggested by the moments of potential short circuit themselves, a pleasure whose suggestion one might enjoy even if the story cannot go that way. If, as Brooks and Barthes suggest, these moments are moments of risk and wrong choice, their very presence imports another story, which one follows as an alternative in the same way that the husband in "The Secret Woman" follows his wife's varied sexual activities. We get them all; ultimate narrative heterosexual redemption does not eliminate the possible gratification suggested by homosexual moments in the text.

The problems of transsexuality and indeterminate or multiplied gender are also symptoms of the potential failure of oedipal closure, reproduction, production, continuity, immortality, patriarchy, knowledge, and so on. The plurality of narrative that both defies and serves this closure is emblematically treated in literal transsexuality, cross-dressing, or indeterminate gender. These moments of gender confusion and its attendant homosexual possibilities are quickly shut down, their very position as wrong choice subordinating them to the oedipal pleasure associated with dramatic irony. Knowing the outer and knowing or suspecting the inner generates a desire for a synthesis between the two, one that will prove one's expectations correct and hence, prove one's mastery over sexual confusion and over narrative itself even while allowing one the pleasure of the sexual "détour." This finally represents what appears to be, in Western oedipal narrative, a containment.

Everything's Coming Up Phallus

As a vehicle for narrative crisis and also its cure, vertical gender configurations not only refer to the gendered assumptions of narrative heteroideology but also depend upon a relation to the phallus/penis. It does not matter who is cross-dressed or embodied as what; rather, what seems to matter is whether there is a phallus around somewhere. Edwina Cutwater is empowered by her association (quite intimate) with the phallus, while Steve, the woman, has been castrated by death. Until she/he interprets this castration as femininity, he is simply a frustrated, castrated man. The only sexual possibility in *Switch* involves Walter's penis, as Steve's phallic mind simply isn't enough. This one real penis finally gives meaning, love, production, and salvation to Steve and to the narrative. In relation to this penile centrality, the dynamic directing narrative's gender switches is a phallic circulation, where both desire and meaning, dressed in the overtly gendered terms of the narrative disguise, take the form of the phallus whose discovery leads to meaning and wholeness.[6]

The difficulty is discerning what accounts for what. Does the phallus as a signifier of desire structure the interplay of genders? Does the reproductive exigency of narrative ideology situate the phallus in a particular relation to gender? Do gender confusion and the particular narrative forms it takes as cross-dressing or transsexuality arise from an anxiety about reproduction and mastery or from some pleasurable play of the phallic signifier (which such crossing literalizes)? Does the ideological and even psychical centrality of the phallus somehow direct all of this from the beginning? Cross dressing and transgendered narratives suggest that the phallus functions culturally and psychically as that which appears to differentiate the sexes on an imaginary level. The phallus's presence or absence (castration) defines both gender and narrative position; but it can only play its role when veiled. "The fact that the phallus is a signifier," Lacan remarks, "means that it is in the place of the Other that the subject has access to it. But since this signifier is only veiled, as ratio of the Other's desire, it is the desire of the Other as such that the subject must recognize, that is to say, the Other insofar as he is himself a subject divided by the signifying *Spaltung*" ("Phallus" 288).

These cross-gender narratives literalize subjective splitting in gendered terms. Since the phallus is initially invisible, otherness in gendered terms is impossible to determine and desire is actually thwarted. False or layered gender serves as a masking device in cross-dressing and transsexual narratives that literalize and parody phallic veiling in a game of who has the penis. Relocating the phallus to the place of the other and veiling it via gender masquerade sets up a phallic construct of desire where the phallus as distinguishing mark is what is sought. The inability to determine where the phallus is and hence where the Other's desire is, however, confuses this economy. The lesbian moment reveals where the phallus isn't, pointing perversely to where the phallus and a more heterosexual desire might be. The lesbian moments' loss of the phallus also suggests a momentary shift of desire from its focused "petit a" search for specific phallic fulfillment to a phallusless desire that is radiated in all directions.

The confusion the lesbian creates in this phallic economy also suggests another way to explain the narrative structure of the suggested lesbian moments. If the lesbian is "the love that prides itself more than any other on being the love which gives what it does not have," then the narrative masquerade's temporary loss of the phallus results in an attempt to exchange what is lost.[7] This attempt at exchange actually "finds" the phallus again by reference to its discovered absence.[8] The lesbian moments thus constitute a slightly different narrative of exchange (giving "not it" to someone who also doesn't have "it") in relation to the productive narrative that of necessity requires the phallic copula (giving it to someone who doesn't have it and getting it back). Yet the reproductive narrative is dependent upon this lesbian moment, not of inversion or reversion but of an evasion of/reference to copular logic, an indirection "by which to find directions out."

The phallic shell game played through cross-gendering creates an anxiety not about gender per se, since gender is already unreliable, but about the principles of copulation and meaning that give any shell game significance. The "penis," Lacan states, "is the most tangible element in the real of sexual copulation, and also the most symbolic in the literal (typographical) sense of the term, since it is equivalent there to the (logical) copula. It might also be said that by virtue of its turgidity, it is the image of the vital flow as it is transmitted in generation" ("Phallus" 287). And what the phallus imports is a logic of copulation located within the individual and cultural narratives of law and castration. While the penis's migration across bodies in cross-gender narratives may trace an imaginary path of desire, the phallus as a signifier of desire may actually be more representative of the principle of combination by which the narrative comes together. It is also the signifier for an entire narrative, the oedipal narrative we have already seen.

The phallic shifting in these stories, depicted as cross-gendering, does represent some crisis in narrative, one played out in terms of having or being the phallus, or both or neither that in a heterosexual, phallic narrative constitute positions of homo- and heterosexuality. Having the phallus, being the phallus, and castration are functions of the oedipal narrative represented by the assumed presence of the literal penis. As the signifier whose castration represents postoedipal differentiation, the phallus is linked to oedipal appurtenances: separation, individuation, gender, identity, family, social place, fate. In combination with its function as a symbolic copula, the phallus becomes the link between reproduction and patriarchal law. "The phallic signifier is . . . inscribed at the origin of the unconscious meaning system where Law, desire, language, separation, and gender merge in a drama subsequently repressed."[9] This repressed drama is a version of the reproductive narrative that intersects with the narrative of becoming a subject.

In cross-gender narratives, there is a phallus, displaced in a veiled presence chased by the protagonist but present in the narrative copula whose combinatory principle is actually what is sought. In this scheme, real female characters are the phallus, while male characters play out the drama of their castration and desire to return to wholeness. The lesbian moment of two females who each may be the phallus becomes a paradoxical moment of phallic overload that catalyzes a search in the right direction, while the suggested moments of male homosexuality have to do with a reduplicated being *and* having the phallus that threatens to stop the search altogether. This is the opposite of the dynamic produced by narrative's surface gender politics I have just sketched, where lesbian nondifferentiation represents paralysis and homosexuality productivity. Taken together, the contradictory narratives of homosexualities—1) lesbian as nondifferentiation and the cessation of desire, 2) lesbian as redoubled presence and phallic overload fulfilling desire, 3) male homosexual as a redoubled productive sameness, 4) male homosexuality as a castrated, redoubled paralysis—represent a constant oscillation between desire and a lack thereof, castration and plenitude, lack of difference and difference that reiterates the narrative of sameness and difference by circling through the positions that constitute it. In revealing the terms of this narrative economy, the homosexual moments bare the stakes in narrative meaning and closure as not only gender and sexuality but also as problem of resecuring a relation to law, castration, and desire.

In the metaphorically gendered terms offered by a Lacanian analysis of this relation, the role of the phallus as signifier of individuation and castration makes it the signifier of socialization, limit, and law. If castration can be regarded as a "primordial anxiety" caused by the "psychic pain of division and alienation"; if, through the matrix of culture and family, castration is associated with and literalized in gender; and if language and narrative compensate for the lack of wholeness, then the gendered terms of narrative and their relation to castration have to do with the relation between individual lack and cultural law.[10] Narrative legislates the relation between sexuality and the Law-of-the-Name-of-the-Father as the principle organizing both reproduction and social inscription. By either an evasion of castration or the reacquisition of the phallus, homosexualities threaten a premature return to wholeness. The lesbian moments constructed in narrative prove lesbian futility as an effect of *both* no castration and too much castration. The male homosexual moments and their acquiescence to some version of phallic law (it is worthwhile to have one, for example) are productive despite themselves because they intrinsically recognize castration even if they mess around with it (being and having).

Although narrative dynamics would seem to require that gender be represented in terms of the presence or absence of the phallus, sexuality comprises a narrative dynamic wherein the phallus plays a more limited part or a part with greater limitation. The metaphorical heterosexual reproductive narrative is linked to an oedipal narrative about accepting castration as the price of knowledge. Accepting castration produces meaning, a narrative phallus associated with knowledge, closure, endings, and paternity. Castration, thus, is ambivalent in the metaphorically heterosexual narrative, both there and not, occurring in behalf of a greater narrative good. The lesbian moment of paralysis, nondifferentiation, potential death, and literal phalluslessness is a narrative point of imagined noncastration, plentiful possibility, and no limitation that also knows its limits. It is precisely because there is no penis at the lesbian moment that such power is possible—such power to gratify, to end. The lack of literal phallus also explains why the moment must self-destruct, for in the lesbian's rivalry with the real end—the phallic signifier of reproduction, the Law-of-the-Name-of-the-Father (in an oedipal narrative of narrative)—the lesbian's lack of castration (and hence individuation) render her a narrative outlaw. This out-of-law moment is recontained by the law of narrative, by a castration that recognizes the limits of noncastration. The phallus, the law, cannot exist until castration is recognized; that is one reason why male homosexuality tends not to occur until after the lesbian moment.

As a signifier of desire, the presence or absence of the phallus in overtly gendered narratives may mark the trajectories of narrative desire, but like narrative, the phallus is characterized by a disparity between idea and execution. The phallus imports and is imported by the narrative of castration; castration comports a narrative of the origins of law that refers back to Oedipus and the question of origins. While finding the phallus is one way to organize narratives of cross-dressing and transsexuality, the phallus is itself ultimately a lure, a narrative dildo that reiterates the same copulative, reproductive ideology already basic to narrative. For this reason, narratives about gender transgression or confusion tend to appear as if they are playing out a phallic politic that locates meaning and law in gender already defined in relation to the phallus, when they are instead or at the same time, playing out the metaphorically heterosexual (re)production narrative in relation to death. By referring back to issues of identity and origins, the phallic gloss (like a fetish) lures us away from the narrative's deathly stake and reinforces narrative's compensatory function, covering over the lack-in-being created by the splitting of the subject in castration. Lesbian sexuality functions in this drama to constitute the imaginary moments of no difference and all power, replaying the state of no lack that is instantly riven by castration and limit.

3

Right Place, Wrong Time

You have all seen the great abomination of your brother. Now he is no longer my
son or your brother. I will only have a son who is a man, who will hold his head up
among my people. If any one of you prefers to be a woman, let him follow Nwoye
now while I am alive so I can curse him.
—Chinua Achebe, *Things Fall Apart*, p. 128

The dynamics of the narrative middle and their coy suggestions of
homosexualities parallel the various narratives that have been employed
to understand homosexuality since the nineteenth century. Looking for
its origin and etiology, sexual theorists inevitably oedipalize homosexuality, locating it within family histories as the same kind of misdirection that fires the confusion of the narrative middle. Tracing the pattern
inscribed for it by narrative heteroideology, lesbian sexuality functions
as a case of mistaken identity located on the fulcrum between the
before and after of castration, individuation, and socialization, between
plenitude and limitation, between lawlessness and law. The narrative
production of lesbian possibility coalesces with the intersection of four
or five other narrative tensions, making the lesbian a complex and very
middling sort of moment, the kind of moment that necessitates sorting.
And yet the lesbian is also a catalytic site of narrative disequilibrium that
instantiates the "force" necessary to reimport equilibrium, reinvoke the
"contract," and finish the "function." This position is most appropriate;
as Foucault points out, the location of sexuality as the secret cause in a
narrative ideology that becomes increasingly insistent on (re)produc-
tion produces homosexuality as a narrative category, the causal agent of
the bad, nonreproductive story. And finding the "cause" of homosexuality might protect the reproductive interests of the capitalist family
from the danger from within.

Accounts of the etiology of homosexualities arise with the increasing dominance of this sexual "cause" and the installation of a heterosexual ideology of narrative. Although located in scientific discourse,
these etiological accounts of homosexuality reconstructed several different versions of the place of male and female homosexuals in the culturally ascendant reproductive narrative. Beginning in about 1870 with
Carl Westphal's "Contrary Sexual Feeling," the narrative of homosexu-

ality commenced as a simple gender reversal, a symmetrical inversion of bodies and roles that sustained rather than challenged the reproductive matrix.[11] But since gender reversals or inversions could not account for the degenerescence feared to be the effect of such perversions, another cause was necessary. Richard von Krafft-Ebing believed that homosexuality was constitutional, a sort of inborn trait, though other experts increasingly believed that homosexuality was caused by the influence of some childhood event, including masturbation and corporal punishment.[12] Before Freud, this theory of acquisition had been elaborated to the point that unconscious events in childhood were seen to be causal, and homosexuality became an alternative narrative in the story of human development.[13]

The difference between some natural "cause" and a familial one makes all the difference in the way the tragedy of the family is understood. If homosexuality is inborn—lurking somewhere in the character of a family's generations—the family is already suspect and, in a twisted Calvinist logic, deserves what destiny (or predestiny) offers. If homosexuality is a product of intrafamilial relations, then through rigorous discipline, the family can control its sexual fortunes by not producing any degenerate offspring. The family's health is measured by an absence of nonreproductive homosexual members.

The narrative logic of the family reproduces the same mechanisms by which narrative produces its metaphorically homosexual positions; it is the reproductive matrix for either healthy heterosexuality or a short-circuiting, degenerate homosexuality. The connection between narrative homology and homosexuality may be most elementally evident in psychoanalytic narratives of the place of the homosexual in the family narrative. Beginning as a confusion of gender, homosexuality becomes a perverse side-effect of an abnormal parental influence. This in turn becomes an unconscious force in the heterosexualized narrative of development, turning the child/story away from its normal (heterosexual) path and resulting in the bad, nonreproductive narrative that leads to and causes degenerescence of family and wealth. The family, like narrative, is both aware and unaware of what it is doing; the homosexual child is a feigned indirection.

Heir to this narrative, Freud makes it into an overtly familial story, even though throughout his career he was barely able to account for it. To Freud male and female homosexuals are subjects who assume the wrong parts in the family romance at the wrong time. Messing up the tidy binaries of the patriarchal unit, homosexuals occupy the incorrect place in the gendered familial metaphors that represent ideological conceptions of gender and power. The male homosexual, according to Freud's early work, is he who identifies with and assumes the position of the mother in relation to the father, becoming he who is in love with his father, a more powerful version of himself.[14] The lesbian is the girl who loves her father so much that she identifies with him, eschewing all other men to be like her father the oedipal son, loving other women in despair of him.[15] This is not to endorse these versions of Freud's understanding of the etiology of homosexualities but rather to indicate how even in the very stories of their inception, homosexual characters impede heterological narratives by identifying with what is different when they should identify with what is same (defined here as gender) and, in addition, insisting on this gendered "same" when they should move on to difference.

The difficulty with the homosexual's assumption of the wrong place at the wrong time is not that it disrupts the narrative of the family romance; rather, both male and female homosexual, according to Freud, reinforce and sustain the centrality of the father, which is the covert function of familial narratives anyway. Instead, the problem with homosexuals is that they are not perverse enough, not *père-vers* or toward the father enough. Homosexuals are too literal: they desire the father instead of understanding that he must not be desired. In this narrative homosexuals prefer the metonymy of desire over the more important metaphorical power of difference, the limitation on desire that resides in the father's name. Instead of respecting the cultural boundaries inserted in the place of the father, according to this narrative, homosexuals substitute a very different boundary, which, by traversing the father, reverses the polarities of sexual difference and gender. Thus in Freud's several narratives of homosexuality, the gay man is narcissistic and feminized while the lesbian is covertly masculine, an equation he makes even as he recognizes that any simple gender reversal is inaccurate.[16] Homosexuality also becomes a primary symptom of the story gone out of control in the paranoid's megalomania, becoming not in itself psychotic, but a structural feature of psychosis.[17]

The debate about the cause of homosexuality is far from over. Each new productive cultural crisis spawns revivified versions of homosexual cause. The nineteen-eighties and nineties have returned to biology, to the "constitutional." The reappearance of nature as opposed to nurture signals a shift in the understanding of the relation between the family and production/reproduction. Now the victim of a degenerescence that has become cultural instead of familial, the family can no longer be held responsible for its homosexuals. Instead, in a culture whose reproductive laws have become increasingly unstable, homosexuality becomes a wild card in the social deck, chosen at random, and contained in the degenerate atmosphere of the Father's temporary decline. That homosexuality is not attributed to the pathology of the fatherless family (like juvenile crime) is interesting and suggests the exculpation of the family altogether from all forms of misfortune ascribed as natal. All has become environmental or at worst genetic. Homosexuality is genetic; its symptom in males is a smaller (or larger) hypothalamus. But appealing to genetics is finally another version of hopeful control. Although a genetic cause would seem to naturalize the category of the homosexual, removing it from the realm of voluntary aberration, genetics becomes a primary cause at a period of time when we are on the threshold of being able to control genes. Appealing thus to a genetic cause means the hope of a cure and the return of the healthy family.

Perhaps now more than ever, the homosexual has ironically become crucial to the productive script, which has increasingly shifted from production to simulation. The narrative place of the homosexual (both male and female) is a version of simulation; it is, however, a false simulation that can be penetrated to rediscover an authentic gender (production) thought to have been lost, simulation becoming the "same" to the "difference" represented by the authentic. The literalness of this cultural drama suggests that right now family narratives, in the pattern of the Name-of-the-Father, operate to cover over the family's instability where this instability is blamed on a loss of the authentic in the form of television, fast food, and working mothers—anything that interferes with the real stability of family dinner with paternal grace. Instigated by the public reemergence of a highly certain maternal relation that creates the possibility of an identity operating outside of paternal law, nostalgia for the nuclear family is the defensive ending to a story whose middle has begun to go another way.[18]

But if we understand the metaphor of patriarchy (giving the child the father's name to seal any doubts about paternity) to be undermined by nineteen-eighties access to quite literal proof of paternity (the father's identity can be discerned through DNA testing), then the emergence of the homosexual as a public category might also have to do not only with increasing political activism and commodity identification but also with the temporary threat to Law such de-metaphorization of the Father imports and that the homosexual already represents. The loss of the metaphor that sustains Law requires more vengeful stories of Law's return, which requires more overt reproductive villains such as homosexuals who have obligingly become more visible. This visibility and its commodity underpinnings seem liberating on one level, but they also contribute to the even more effective functioning of the reproductive heteronarrative.

What this all suggests finally is that the narrative distinctions between lesbian and gay male roles are completely intertwined with the narrative ideologies operating on the scale of culture. What this implies is not that narrative shapes or simply reflects culture but that narrative and ideology have coalesced, reflecting one another not only in content and disposition but in the very shape of the dynamic that defines categories, assigns them roles, and fashions the ever-reiterating story. But this also suggests that if we understand this interrelation, we might use narrative as a way of changing the story, of wrenching it from its familial house, battling its insistence on difference deployed in such paternally specific ways, by working to change the cultural conceptions of what a story is. Narrative is not a cause; it is, however, an entrée that might permit enough play for cultural shift especially now that the embattled reproductive narrative has enabled/required more visible, more definitive homosexual space.

CHAPTER FOUR

The Second Coming

To regard this group of people as a horrid sideshow of freaks is not only to miss
the point, but to confirm our wills and harden our hearts in an inveterate sin
of pride.
—T. S. Eliot, "Introduction" to *Nightwood*, p. xvi

How do the dynamics of the inadvertently lesbian moment produced
in cross-gender narratives translate into the narrative disposition of
deliberately lesbian characters? And how might lesbian writers either
profitably deploy this middle or explode it to shift narrative's ideology
from its insistent heterosexuality to broader, less binary possibilities?
While these questions have differing political stakes—the first tracking
the continued cultural disposition of the lesbian, the second suggesting
some agency to a lesbian locus and identity—the conventional answer
to both questions has generally been the simple appearance of an
acknowledged lesbian character. In relation to narrative foreclosure, this
politics of visibility seems to challenge narrative's more covert lesbian
metaphors, its tendency to limit the lesbian to the middle, and its disposal of her into a concluding heterosynthesis.

Appearing more frequently in mainstream popular culture since the nineteen-eighties, the deliberately lesbian character, like the gay male character, easily becomes a part of narrative's sideshow, conforming to the position of middling variety that an analysis of narrative anticipates.[1] Visibility does not necessarily signal a change in ideology or structure. This is true particularly in television narratives where lesbian characters appear fleetingly, usually in contrast to a primary female character as challenge and contrast both to her heterosexuality and her liberalism.[2] The difference, however, between narrative's production of lesbian sexuality as the sameness requisite to narrative function and the deliberate inclusion of a literal lesbian character is a difference that requires—invites—a more complex ideological negotiation.

COMING OUT

The quintessential lesbian narrative is the coming out story, not because there is something inherently lesbian about it, but because it is both ubiquitous and proclaimed as such by lesbians.[3] Even if the coming out story does not typify something essentially lesbian, its function as a ritual of self-identification, flirtation, and even erotic pleasure situates it as an emblem of later twentieth-century lesbian culture.[4] The coming out story, however, is not wielded only by a lesbian or gay male narrator; mainstream culture also employs it as a frame and pretext for including lesbian and gay characters. While for lesbian cultures the coming out story might be liberating, in a more inclusive cultural picture it limits the potential roles and functions of lesbian characters.

The fourteen coming out stories collected by the National Gay and Lesbian Survey archival project and published in *What a Lesbian Looks Like* illustrate the story's structure and functions. Kerrie Sutton-Spence, Women's Director and coeditor, details the care the project's field workers took collecting the book's widely representative series of anonymous anecdotes. Exemplifying the protagonists' diverse class, race, and age, all of the coming out stories in *What a Lesbian Looks Like* share the same narrative structure. Each narrative features a protagonist who somehow feels that she does not fit into the role typically assigned to women in the larger heterosexual cultural story. Sensing the disparity between her narrative and that which culture has written for her (an inner/outer dichotomy), the coming out protagonist locates herself in the place of difference (both within herself and between herself and patriarchal culture). The lesbian protagonist experiences an internalized struggle between her discomfiture with the known heterosexual part and an unknown, but intuited correct identity. She pretends to be straight, affects an unfelt stereotypical femininity, and feigns an interest in boys. Solving the conflict between inner and outer by aligning the inner lesbian with the ultimate truth of lesbian identity finally expressed in self-affirmation and visible "lesbian" behavior, the lesbian protagonist's assertion of lesbian difference becomes the victorious truth of lesbian identity and the end of the story.

As collected anecdotes, these coming out stories are folktales whose structure is remarkably like that of the folktales that form the basis for early structuralist analyses of narrative. The narrative sequence of the coming out story correlates with Vladimir Propp's understanding of the seven categories of folktale elements that comprise the folktale's plot.[5] Such Proppian components as "well-being prior to complication" (lesbian children are usually quite innocent), the imposition of an interdiction (you must be a good girl), the process of interrogation (Who am I? Are there other people like me? What is a lesbian?), the deceptive villain (the obligatory boyfriend, the suspicious mother), the conjunctive moment (adolescent fondling), the appearance of donors who transmit magical information (homosexual literature, the all-knowing friend), the unrecognized arrival (the first lesbian love perceived retrospectively), the difficult task (turning away the boyfriend, asking out the girl), the resolution of the task (boyfriend gone, girlfriend here), the recognition (I am a lesbian), and the final exposure (look Mom, I'm a lesbian) are as applicable to coming out stories as they are to Russian folktales. Although part of their similarity comes from the way in which we view and analyze narrative, the correlation between coming out stories and Propp's folktale categories suggests that heteronarrative structures the shape of lesbian affirmation despite the stories' countercultural purpose.

Narrative itself plays a significant—even determining—role in the coming out story, both as presented in *What a Lesbian Looks Like* and as generally manifested in lesbian communities, and provides the impetus for the reconciliation of inner and outer. The protagonist retrospectively renarrates her relations with other girls (the story of her life), seeks literature containing homosexual references, listens avidly to stories about homosexuals, and pays attention to those women supposed to be homosexual—i.e., the gym teacher, the tennis star Martina Navratilova, or the singer k. d. lang. Narrative also provides the means for experimentation before the inner/outer reconciliation, as the lesbian protagonist tries such different narrative roles as having some sort of proto-affair with a girlfriend, trying a sexual liaison with a gentle man, or surviving an encounter with an evil, repressed straight woman who experiments with her, then calls her a dyke. In reaction to this naming, which effects a kind of accidental conjoinder between inner and outer, the protagonist finally and defiantly assumes a lesbian identity as the synthesis between her cultural role and her underlying, natural, true emotional and sexual identity and self.

The product of the lesbian's coming out struggle is identity, produced as the knowledge effect of a heteronarrative that understands sexuality as an underlying cause. Terminal synthesis means certain identity and either the first meaningful relationship with another "real" lesbian or a new kind of loneliness.[6] The terminal synthesis among lesbian identity, role, and community is signaled by the protagonists' parting words in such narratives: "This was the start of learning and accepting my real identity from the inside, as it were, which changed my whole perspective" (42), or "I could finally imagine growing up to be someone I recognized as myself" (46). Like the scenes of sexual crisis in cross-gender narratives that produce a lesbian suggestion, the lesbians' role confusion and experimentation catalyze a final trajectory to the correct and productive synthesis between inner and outer that produces lesbian identity.

But what does this coincidence of folktale categories and lesbian coming out stories reveal except that coming out stories are folktales or that Propp's categories can be made to fit almost any story? Or is that exactly the point: that all stories that fit cultural ideologies of narrative do in fact fit into many of Propp's groupings because they all belong to the same logic of narrative. If the lesbian character's visibility is the end product of a narrative struggle between inner and outer that results in knowledge about sexual truth and identity, then coming out stories embody the same reproductive narrative trajectory as dominant cultural stories.

The coming out story is, thus, a story within a larger cultural story that locates a protagonist in a particular place in a lesbian narrative that parallels and, in fact, belongs to narrative heteroideology while simultaneously seeming to emphasize identity as difference from that narrative. Situating lesbians within narrative and culture as simultaneously productive (playing the story out) and as confirming their no difference homological function within a larger cultural story, the declaration of a lesbian identity removes the protagonist from the field of sexual availability (to men) and patriarchal reproduction. Coming out stories provide a way for the female who refuses her heterosexual role to nonetheless function in narrative and in the world; heteronarrative's emphasis on identity exhibits and contains her desire at the very moment the lesbian's self-affirmation would presumably free her from heterosexual expectations. The coming out story is, thus, a story of sequestration, comforting and exultant on one level, but robbed of or trading away its really disturbing potential to mess up heterosexual systems. Coming out's victory provides only a momentary and repeatable pleasure within its own frame of reference.

If the coming out story is a version of dominant culture's reproductive narrative, why does it command and please a lesbian cultural imagination? Perhaps part of its attractiveness is its familiarity; comforting because it fits into traditional story patterns, the coming out story seems both radical and liberatory because its conventional pattern has apparently been mustered in the service of something called a gay or lesbian identity. It is also doubly "natural," a traditional story in the pattern of the folktale or a bildungsroman that reaffirms what its narrator already knows. Its similarity to bildungsroman provides the suggestion that coming to a knowledge of sexuality is like coming to a knowledge of individual value or mission, equating the recognition of membership in a sexual category with other narratives of artistic development. This natural affirmation makes the coming out story seem positive, inevitable, and immensely satisfying. The narrative existence of a product called "lesbian identity" is a victory even if such identity is an effect of the heteronarrative and even if it is recuperated in the service of a larger story. But to see the coming out story as being any more valuable than that is to locate lesbian in a mirroring circle where a lesbian is a lesbian is a lesbian.

A FAMILY OUTING

While the lesbian-narrated coming out story suggests a vexed narrative liberation, popular culture's use of the coming out story more clearly contains the lesbian, enabling her apparently laudable visibility while restricting her to a secondary and often silly status in the larger drama of the capitalist nuclear family. One recent example is Nancy's coming out plot on the television show *Roseanne*.[7] In this prime time comedy, the star's, Rosanne Conner's, friend Nancy (Sandra Bernhard), who has been married to another of the Conners' friends, Arnie (who was Roseanne's real-life husband Tom Arnold), announces that she is a lesbian. At the opening of Roseanne's "loose meat" restaurant (which features an amorphous entrée Roseanne discovered in Iowa), business partner Nancy appears with her new girlfriend, Marla (Morgan Fairchild), and Roseanne and her sister Jackie (Laurie Metcalf) accept Nancy's "new" sexual identity. In the next episode, Nancy's estranged husband, who has been abducted by aliens, returns, is informed of Nancy's lesbian choice, sees it as a reflection of his manhood (the butt of his buddies' jokes), and tries to woo her back at a Kung Fu parlor where the women are learning self-defense. He doesn't succeed and Nancy's lesbian status remains intact; in fact, in one episode, it even seems to have a heavenly imprimatur as the Christmas show ends with Roseanne's *It's a Wonderful Life* quip that "Every time lesbians kiss, an angel gets her wings."

But does Nancy's highly public visibility as a sympathetic lesbian character signal a positive change in the heteronarrative? The inclusion of a lesbian subplot makes *Roseanne* look subversively liberal, as it continues Nancy's character, pokes fun at her husband and his masculine insecurities, and makes her sexuality "all right." Although in the history of television sitcom, a regularly appearing, sympathetic gay character is rare (and a sympathetic lesbian character is even rarer), the *Roseanne* show accounts for two gay characters, having already included the continuing story of Roseanne's gay boss, played by Martin Mull. Nancy's lesbianism is certainly an improvement on the usual media invisibility; and the mere fact of visibility seems a harbinger of better media times in the age of Clinton, of some general acceptance, or a kind of cultural normalization for lesbians and gays. On *Roseanne* the lesbians even openly and passionately kiss.

Visibility, however, is not all it seems to be; still the product of a typical coming out story, it has a narrative price whose payback is a spectacular recaptivation by the plot (to the same degree to which Nancy's coming out has been spectacular). The show's complex relation to both parody and an understated commonplace suggests several conflicting, but coexisting ways in which this lesbian character's appearance is not so much liberating as necessary to support a heterosexual, capitalist system. Looked at in one light, Nancy's coming out is simply another of the show's nonmarital subplots. In relation to the dominant Conner family saga, Nancy's lesbian persona is minor, proving more than anything else the Conner family's tolerance. The family's triumphs over fiscal challenges, in-law incursions, and offspring peccadillos constitute a repeated narrative of family productivity and survival. In relation to the family's struggle to continue, the divorced, the single, and the homosexual are colonized contributors to the Conners' familial reproductive narrative. The show's intrinsic comparison among these satellite beings situates them as a series of lesser choices whose subordinate relation to the nuclear family is a foregone conclusion and whose presence is permitted precisely because they are no threat at all; they are merely illustrative variations that show the ultimate desirability of the Conners' familial stability. And yet their presence is necessary to provide the homologous tension—the sameness, or same difference—by which heterosexuality and production are sustained.

The addition of the new episode of the lesbian in the 1992–93 season at a point in the series when the children are leaving home was necessary to fuel the continuing story of the Conner family. The show's narrative renews itself through the introduction of brands of sameness against which the fertile heterodifference of the nuclear family can perform, this time made necessary by the potential shift of Dan and Roseanne into obsolescence or adolescence as their eldest daughter is married and Roseanne's mother, Beverly (Estelle Getty), moves onto the scene. That Roseanne might be too like the mother and yet returned to the position of the daughter creates a production crisis in the Conner family to which only capitalism or reproduction—or both—are the answer.

The show's capitalist gesture is both a literal capitalism and a kind of character capitalism represented by putting the excess adolescence of Nancy and Roseanne's sister, Jackie (who falls in love with a much younger man who abuses her), to work. Using money given to them by Beverly, Roseanne, Jackie, Nancy, and Beverly (as silent partner) open a restaurant and, at the same time, find out that Nancy is gay. The connection between their venture and Nancy's sexual identity is precisely the connection between the need for a proliferation of multiple, non-(re)productive others on one hand and the reinstatement of a capitalist (even as they are working-class) nuclear family as the core model on the other. The family's capital venture, the "loose meat" restaurant (the term conjuring the prolix possibilities of some kind of reversed play on words having to do with the very nature of the women involved) figures and parallels the function of the multiple unmarried women on the show, including especially the newly lesbian Nancy as that undifferentiated ground against which the heterosexually productive family can play. More adolescents, more characters with "arrested development," more cultural "others," are necessary both to reinstate Dan and Roseanne's position as the true parents and to enable productive familial capitalism. The show's 1993–94 and 1994–95 seasons bear out the literal, perhaps overly compensatory reproductive impetus of all of this as sister Jackie has a son and Roseanne becomes pregnant.

This analysis suggests that the lesbian moment in the coming out story is mainly useful in sustaining heteronarrative and that its position is the inevitable locus of the sameness necessary for productive difference. But might not the show exploit this middle a bit? One of the trademarks of *Roseanne* is its self-conscious, self-reflective commentary on the shape of narrative and the absurdity of social roles within whitebread, Reaganite family ideology. This includes an overt consciousness of extranarrative elements such as the real lives of the show's performers or an intertextual awareness of television. Because of this extradiegetic consciousness, *Roseanne*'s characters never remain solely within the show's fictional world, slipping often into a joking meta-commentary and playing upon performers' reputations and identities as part of the show's humor. Sandra Bernhard can not come out as gay on this show without at the same time referencing her coming out elsewhere. And her coming out on the show is a joke insult to Roseanne's real-life husband, portrayed on the show as a self-pitying masculine victim who stupidly refers to every lesbian myth and stereotype. His inanity, so overdone as to point to the idiocy of the remarks and their utterance by a crass and completely ignorant character laboriously constructed as such, becomes a way of showing the absurdity and silliness of those who believe such stereotypes.

Sandra Bernhard potentially plays very well in this mix. Always mocking in her personal appearances, including her *Playboy* spread, Bernhard, whose lesbianism has been no secret for a while, loses nothing and can only gain by attempting to depict a "normal," well-adjusted lesbian character on a prime-time sitcom.[8] Perhaps this is why she plays the character straight, so straight as to be completely unlike her previous, highly burlesque performances of Nancy on the show. This sudden seriousness might indicate that Bernhard is taking narrative literally for the first time. The brave visibility of the lesbian character fools her into believing that narrative is somehow real and the heavy responsibility of depicting a real lesbian on prime time television tames her mockery in favor of a respectful and "realistic" portrayal. The foolery she performed around her courtship with Arnie—the body-wrap kisses, the slapping abuse, the outrageous clothing that pointed to all of the conventions of a kind of crazed heterosexuality—has disappeared in exchange for politeness, deference, and, frankly, boring new love. Perhaps because the show is being "liberal," it dare not be mocking at the same time. In fact, the *Roseanne* show's inclusion of the lesbian seems to belong to a completely different philosophy, one where narrative means what it says and one that takes seriously the responsible portrayal of minority cultures. Only the ridiculous ignorance of the Tom Arnold character presents the kind of narrative excess necessary to break apart narrative assumptions, and he is no longer on the show.

The apparent naturalness of all of this—the fact that we tend not to question *Roseanne*'s highly heterosexual impetus or the Conner family's liberal generosity—occurs in part because the show's main plot is the most mundane, literal version not only of its underlying narrative structure but also of the very ideology of joinder, synthesis, capitalist production, and reproduction that shapes our assumptions about narrative. It is, thus, difficult to separate aspects of the show's narrative constructions from either its apparent ideological investments or its specific content: they are the same. Because of this, Nancy's coming out appears to be an opening, a progressive rendition of a positive "role model," the recognition of what is simply another version of family. Her announcement creates no consternation, only comic insecurity in her husband; and it is this effect on the husband that positions the story as slightly subversive.

Its subversiveness is fleeting, however, because the Nancy story is necessarily transient; it is, in effect, already over, since its essence was the announcement of identity, the most literal moment of a homologous self-sameness. Unlike the pattern of most coming out stories, Nancy's announcement of her lesbian preference follows no visible struggle; in the show it provides an explanation for Arnie and Nancy's marital problems and on a metamedia level, refers to Sandra Bernhard's real-life pronouncements. Because Nancy's (Sandra's) sexual identity produces knowledge on a vertical scale, it momentarily gets great comic mileage, but it cannot go anywhere else. Anything that follows aligns with the synthetic reproductive trajectory of the narrative, and Nancy and Marcy can only reiterate the heterosexual model or break up. And in fact they do, quite quickly, as Nancy, in one 1993 episode is revealed as the quintessential narcissist (whom the lovable Dan despises), performing a displaced critique of homonarcissism at the moment she is fading. But like the lesbian's position in heteronarrative, Nancy reverts to men when the characters become newly productive as Jackie has a child, Dan gets a regular job, Jackie gets married, the Conners take in Darlene's boyfriend as their new adolescent, and Roseanne gets pregnant. In this mass movement toward synthesis, Nancy's role diminishes. She reverts to an apparent heterosexuality without much explanation.

Within the naturalized heteroideology of both narrative and sexuality, lesbian identity becomes the productive limitation of the lesbian story—a self-contained victory in its pronouncement, but an inevitable self-containment and deadly homology. If we understand the sexual impetus of narrative to be not only joinder or synthesis but also the ensuing (re)production—of people, of goods, of more narrative—then the lesbian fix on identity can be only self-productive, a kind of Escher paradox of a self-same, perpetually reiterative identification. This is the case in the *Roseanne* narrative; the show's emphasis is on Nancy and Marla's lesbian status and not on their relationship. When informed, for example, that his wife's lover is the cosmetic counter girl, Arnie exclaims, "she must be a lesbian, too." Fixed on identity, the lesbian is perpetually coming out but going no where in the heteronarrative, existing in the no-where land of sexuality without context enjoyed by the show's adolescents who are just discovering (and announcing) their heterosexuality, by its infantilized old people who are rediscovering (and announcing) theirs, and by the show's 1994–95 season's obsession with the details of the adolescent D. J.'s sexual development.[9]

Does Nancy's coming out story function only as a sacrificial dead end in a narrative that is as specifically as well as implicitly heterosexual as *Roseanne*? The lesbian story produced by this heterosexual narrative exigency translates sexual identity as catharsis, production as self-production in a kind of sexual short circuit necessary for the uninterrupted continuation of heterosexual (re)production. The problem is the structure of the story itself and its ingrained logic, which rests not so much on superficial oppositions but on heterology: the constant maintenance of differences as a fact of narrative structure. In these popular cultural renditions, both female and male homosexuality are figuratively associated with homology, stasis, and death that appear in narrative as communism, totalitarianism, Nazism, vampirism, disease, and death, whatever poses a threat or represents an anxiety in relation to cultural production. Even the evocation of the stylish gay male or lesbian is contained as emblematic of the simulation economy of the story that goes nowhere. These positions are the necessary antagonists, just as the rival male or female is in the love story. Seeming to block, they make the story go but at the price of their own destruction. So we have lesbian vampires, lesbian murderers, lesbian prostitutes, lesbian anything that gets in the way of reproduction by substituting some false sex for the real thing. In this way the lesbian's alignment with stasis or sameness arrives at the kinds of literal roles lesbians tend to play in mainstream narratives.

A DUBIOUS OUTCOME

We can easily run through the archetypes of the lesbian in popular narrative: pretend and ultimately failed man, immature sexual explorer (as in porn), prostitute, feminist, vampire, murderer. Because analyzing these lesbian roles would comprise a book, all I want to do here is run through a brief analysis of how these roles work within heteronarrative to demonstrate how the ideologies that underwrite narrative's contemporary shape are also manifested in characters and roles explicitly defined as lesbian.

While the pretend man, sexual explorer, and prostitute serve the heterosexual imperative I have already outlined by simply acting as a sidetracked variation on the road to a happy heterosexual reproductive end, the last three roles—feminist, vampire, and murderer—are interconnected and depicted as deadly. Embodying the sameness that provides narrative's threat in the microdynamics of stories, on a larger scale their menace of sameness is directed toward the father they wish to supplant. They become the villainous stasis reproductive heroes must overcome. But while their presence manifestly threatens figurative fathers, their more extreme menace and means of recuperation is their threat to expose the emptiness allayed by the Law-of-the-Name-of-the-Father, the metaphor that secures a paternal aegis where there is none.[10] The murderous lesbian recalls the oedipal son, inscribing a pseudomale in the place of the woman whose envy reinforces the paternal game and whose threat of no difference imperils the stability of paternal law. The lesbian figure simultaneously threatens a lack of differentiation (often signified by the threat of alien species), an inability to discern difference (who is the alien, murderer?), and the demise of human power (signified by the deaths of fathers).

Manhattan, Woody Allen's 1979 film about a man grappling with art and the meaning of life employs a lesbian character as the struggling artist's castrating nemesis. Television writer Isaac Davis's (Woody Allen) ex-wife (Meryl Streep) left him, as he says, "for another woman," and has compounded the injury by writing a book about their marriage in which all of Davis's failures and foibles are exposed. Doubly castrating (like Davis's castrating Zionist mother), the ex-wife functions as the perfect inscription of Davis's insecurities, which are posed more as problems of gender than of reproduction, even though reproduction (both artistic and human) is at the core of the film. Davis is afraid he cannot write, isn't a good father, isn't a sexually desirable man; his ex-wife writes a best-seller, leaves for a woman who is more sexually inspiring—more "man" than he—and who is a great "father."

But the film contains the lesbian's threat in several ways. First, Davis's rantings about his ex-wife function to reveal the nature of his own insecurities; the character is threatened by her, but the film is not. In a sense the film's self-consciousness reveals the nature of the lesbian ex-wife's threat for what it is. But while this seems very liberated, using the lesbian ex-wife to expose Davis's insecurities works on another level to reify the gender symmetry by which those threats are defused. His ex-wife coupled with another "man," his son has two "fathers," (himself and his wife's girlfriend), his wife's writing simply makes a comparison between the neuroses of her ex-husband and the qualities of her new man-woman. On a third level, this recuperated gender symmetry finally functions to extol the existentialistic but humorous struggle of the pathetic clown protagonist, whose lack of comprehension of his friends' illogical pairings (pairings that are unproductive and antireproductive) fuels his own artistic production, which subsequently emerges at a higher level—the level of meaning, creation, the wisdom of self-parody, the film itself.

While Allen defuses the lesbian menace by using her threat to certify his creativity, the figure of the lesbian vampire represents a more extreme version of mortal threat to reproductive systems. Constituting a species of unauthorized reproduction whose main selling point is a fraudulent offer of immortality, the connection between vampires and lesbians in such films as *Daughters of Darkness* (1971) and *The Hunger* (1983) exposes the nature of the threat posed by the woman who eschews phallic hegemony. Projected as an alternate and parasitical reproduction, the vampire lesbian disrupts and derails normal biological reproduction and the nominal immortality of paternal aegis. Although *The Hunger* is an ironic film, ending with an apparent vampire victory in the heroine, Sarah's ascension to the vampire, Miriam's role (and in this sense it is different from lesbian vampire films in which the vampires are destroyed), its emphasis on immortality reveals to some extent why the lesbian vampire is such a threat.

In *The Hunger* Miriam (Catherine Deneuve) seduces a series of lovers, who, after enjoying a greatly prolonged youth, suddenly succumb to the accelerated ravages of old age. After watching her male companion, John (David Bowie), age in two days, Miriam seduces Sarah Roberts (Susan Sarandon), a medical researcher whose work on aging brings her to the vampires' attention. The desperation of the vampire—her inability ever to escape from exile in a horrible death-dealing life—enables her to employ supernatural powers of suggestion, telepathy, and mesmerism to secure her companions and her victims. Seducing Sarah, the monstrous Miriam infects her with vampire blood, which forces Sarah to seek Miriam in order to learn to kill and survive. The association of bloodletting, supernatural seduction, and lesbian lovemaking defines the very terms of the lesbian threat to heterology. Beyond the understanding and control of patriarchy, the loving lesbian commingling of bodily fluids creates an evil hunger for death—the death of patriarchy and the death of heterology in a scenario of lusty enslavement and selfish homicide. And as might be expected, poor Sarah is merely an innocent victim in this seduction; she fights back by refusing the vampire's gift, committing suicide instead. Her premature cessation (she is not dead, but only eternally vegetating) arouses the living corpses of Miriam's last twenty lovers whose decomposing corporeal ardor forces Miriam to fall to her destruction. But Miriam is not really annihilated; her blood lives on in the still-youthful Sarah who continues the vampire's seduction in the film's ironic last scene.

The connection of the lesbian to both death and unnatural reproduction has to do with unauthorized reproduction—the irresistible
theft and separation of immortality from human reproduction. Just like
the lesbian in the family romance, the lesbian vampire makes the mistake of taking things too literally; while the name of the father enables
continuity through identified generations—through metaphor, the lesbian vampire—in fact all vampires—make immortality literal in the
body rather than in the vampire's name, an immortality made possible
only by its feeding upon humans in a parasitical dependence upon
patriarchy. But the lesbian vampire's immortality exposes the lie of the
father and of the ideologized necessity of heterosexuality; this exposure
threatens to import the reign of desire instead of obedience, of illimit
instead of boundary that promises societal chaos. The vampire's promise
of immortality must itself be exposed as fraud to suture and sustain
patriarchal reproduction by providing a suitable and equally immortal
foe to defeat.

The other half of lesbian vampire villainy is a direct murderous threat
to males who are synecdochal of a heterosexual heterology. The lesbian's rejection of the phallus (both big and little "p") suggests that
phallic hegemony might also be artificial. If lesbian vampires can live,
reproduce, and conquer "normal" hetero people, then the paternal
order must be weak. The threat of this weakness provokes patriarchal
pyrotechnics in the hunting and killing of vampires. But while straight
vampires are vanquished with a phallic stake in the heart, lesbian vampires continue to live defiantly through continued generation. Unlike
the heterosexual vampires who simply threaten an alternative patriarchy (on an overtly polygamous model), the lesbian vampire constitutes the threat of a thriving lack of differentiation. For this reason the
lesbian is sustained as the perpetual menace that proves the phallic
power of human reproduction over the specter of a different feminized
order in a potentially unending narrative battle.[11]

Basic Instinct, Paul Verhoeven's 1992 much-publicized, presumably
homophobic film, cleverly reads and uses the narrative jeopardy of the
lesbian archetype. The film's obsessive connection of lesbian characters
with murder (there are four) invites a homophobic critique based on a
notion of film narrative as both realistic and morally prescriptive. But
the film is smarter than this (though identity-bound audiences might
not be). On one level the film is about narrative (re)production and
who can wield it. The murdering lesbian antagonist writes books in

which men are murdered. A murder similar to that described in one of her books is committed. Through a tangled Verhoevian web of intrigue, the murderer (or the film) manages to fabricate a series of narratives that, working on a specific paranoia about the lesbian as murderer configuration, implicate several other women as both lesbians and murderers with the proof that they are murderers residing in the fact that they are lesbians. While the author's friends are lesbianized, the author herself is gradually heterosexualized, though she is still cold and calculating and, more important, continues to use sex with men as research for her own literary productivity. She must therefore be lesbianized since she defies heterology for a kind of self-production.

The point here is not that all lesbians are murderers but rather that the author (or film) can easily use the fear represented by the lesbian murderer archetype to drive the series of narrative solutions and misapprehensions that kill off a rock star and two cops, all heterosexual males. A large element of this fear o' lesbian lies precisely in a fear of homology or sameness represented by the fact that the four lesbian villains either look alike or deliberately masquerade as one another. This sameness not only enables a mistaken identity plot but brings the identity of all of the women into question—both their literal identities and their sexual ones. The fear that women might really all be lesbians brings male heterosexuality and narrative heterology into jeopardy. The real anxiety of this film is a fear of sinking into a realm of homogeneity that paralyzes action, mastery, and reproduction. Hence, the protagonist cop must obsessively reiterate the counternarrative by which he hopes to fend off defeat: he and the antagonist will "fuck like minks" and produce a "batch of rug rats."[12]

The film's overt fix on narrative-making, in the novelist's life and in the mystery that grows around her, divulges the inextricable relation between narrative, reproduction, and the lesbian archetype's role. What is at war here are two versions of reproduction: that of the female author (necessarily lesbian) who reproduces self at the expense of heterosexual males, and that of the nuclear family. While lesbian murderers have terminated specific nuclear families (both of the author's friends have done away with their nuclear units or parts of them), the lesbian author is the greater threat since her production means the destruction both of individual males and of the heterology necessary for nuclear reproduction. She takes things too literally. But even though the reproductive villains here are all lesbians, the film is finally more misogynistic than homophobic (a grim contest). The problem is that the woman writes and her continued production is at the cost of reproduction. And on top of this (the lesbian author is almost always on top), the very possibility of an underlying lesbian proclivity throws the whole binary heterologic into a spasm; the gender organization that enables heterology and reproduction is at risk because you'll never know when the woman you're fucking will wield the deadly ice-pick phallus herself.

The end of the film is predictably synthetic (almost a parody of synthesis) as the male protagonist and the female author end up in bed together. But like lesbian vampire figures, the threat of the author's independent production is not quite allayed. Instead, the ice pick looms under the bed waiting to be wielded by that unauthorized productress, the mystery we thought was solved continues driven by a lack of resolution about the female author's sexuality. Her apparent bisexuality covers over the threat of her lesbianism.

The role of the overt lesbian in these mainstream narratives is not primarily a moral lesson aimed at lesbians; as we all know, lesbians tend vehemently to deny any identification attempted on that score. The lesbian objection to such roles arises because of a feared confusion between the lesbian of the narrative and real lesbians that threatens to transform these suturing narratives into prescriptions for social action. The function of these visibly mainstream lesbian roles, however, is not to discipline real lesbians, destroy tropes of lesbian identification, or enact narrative chastisement; rather, these narratives use the lesbian to signify reproduction gone wrong by employing the lesbian as the displaced locus of what is wrong with the father: he—like the lesbian stereotype—is always a pretend man. To create narrative conflict, the lesbian character must provide a counterthreat of immortality as a huge challenge to the paternal brand of reproductive immortality that provides a context for the continued exhibition of paternal potency. Only by vanquishing, but not killing the lesbian does the father succeed in reasserting his immortal power over the other. Actually killing the lesbian would reduce the whole world to literal mortality, thus also literalizing any reproductive claims for familial immortality via generation and making apparent the paternal weakness the lesbian evokes. The lesbian, like the oedipal son, is only valuable if she can sustain the threat of the vanquished that perpetuates the display of paternal power. Hence, the lesbian vampire is the perfect foil: she is vanquishable, but she never dies. But any lesbian character who is not killed becomes both a valuable threat to and a catalyst of (re)production.

The film's reception—its popularity and the gay outrage it piqued—raises interesting questions then about the identificatory confusions that attend analyses of characters as sex-role stereotypes. Does anyone ever take these characters literally or are they always already inscribed within a narrative unconscious that permits both belief and disavowal? If that is the case, might we not play upon this disavowal to enable a rescripting of this imaginary, not by providing positive models but by effecting a restructuration of the entire system's dependence upon homology and false differentiation by playing up that reliance? If narrative is always about narrative and if the production of narrative is linked to insecurities about reproduction, might we not change the structure and understanding of narrative by exposing the very insecurities upon which its shape now depends? After all, the basic instinct of *Basic Instinct* is that in the wrong hands narrative kills. If this is the case, should we condemn narrative to death or merely life imprisonment in perpetual critique, or, like the J'nnai, subject it to psychotechnical reconfiguration that inscribes a new notion of differences freed from the necessity of supporting the failing paternal law? Or, like the secret woman, should we just mask ourselves and go to the ball?

COMING INTO THEIR OWN

If popular narrative presents visible lesbian characters to sustain some nuclear family imperative and to personify to-be-conquered threats to patriarchy and narrative, is it possible to have a narrative with a lesbian protagonist that can avoid this narrative restriction? Can a lesbian character occupy the protagonist position without somehow propagating heteroideology? Could we fashion such a story and still have a narrative recognizable as a narrative? These questions assume that a lesbian category exists outside of heteroideology and reflect a wish for a lesbian narrative agency—that somehow tinkering with narrative content or characters might change the cultural story. But if the intertwined ideologies of narrative and sexuality produce the metaphorical position of lesbian, narrative might not be the best venue for trying to change cultural ideas about actual lesbian people.

Even so, the pleasures of narrative, thought to be more available if one can identify with the protagonist, also belong to the lesbian reader. Lesbians write stories with lesbian characters, often in a more or less realist mode, depicting the triumphs and quandaries of lesbian life and normalizing a specifically lesbian existence.[13] Although many such narratives de-eroticize and de-exoticize lesbian characters, insofar as lesbian is a sexual category enjoying a specific sexual oppression, the lesbian protagonist's concluding triumph in these narratives still effects a kind of victory appended to a sexual identity. If a lesbian protagonist triumphs, even over other lesbian characters, the category *lesbian* also prevails, having occupied the productive narrative position by showing that lesbians can produce and therefore are not death, stasis, or adolescence and demonstrating that they have escaped their medial imprisonment. It would seem that this triumphant lesbian repositioning might undercut heteronarrative's heterosexual alignments by inserting a different sexual paradigm in their place.

Following the girl-loves-girl gender logic by which lesbian sexuality is often represented and interpreted, lesbian narratives situate lesbian characters in more than one narrative role, creating the "difference" necessary to narrative by marking the lesbian characters as different from one another, frequently by recourse to differences in race, nationality, age, or gender (masculine or feminine, butch or femme). While the evocation of surface differences preserves a veneer of heterology, the fact of two women engaged in a trajectory toward "joinder" seems to run against narrative's reproductive logic, producing something that is potentially beyond or outside of the heterosexual. One might expect, therefore, to find the most direct challenge to narrative in a lesbian sex story, especially if the most literal sexual story is the most overtly metaphorical version of heteronarrative. If the terms of narrative are metaphorically like the differences that come together in heterosexual coitus, then the narration of lesbian sex might force in narrative another direction or make visible narrative's heteroideology unless that heteroideology is sustained in other ways. And if it is, what, if any, is the relation between a lesbian heterology and the heteroideology that sustains the heteronarrative?

Let us look again at narratives of lesbian sex. Here is the passage from *She Came Too Late*, which I cited at the beginning of chapter 1:

> She leaned over me and put her mouth on mine. I felt her exploring my mouth, taking it, drawing me into her. I would have been afraid except that I felt her warm hand on my back reassuring me. Then her hand found my breasts and began to find all my reactions. I couldn't stop a funny squeaking sound from escaping. She

had my hands clasped over my head with one strong arm and her other hand went further and further pursuing all the boundaries, taking me so far along in the excitement it was nearly pain. And she went on and on, almost methodically except that I felt her own breath rising in response. I fought with the passivity but it was only fun to fight it. I let her go wherever she wanted. I let her find things I didn't know were there. I was so wet, with her hand between my legs. Her finger slipped inside me and my body rose. She held me for two minutes or ten minutes. Then it was my turn.   *(67)*

Featuring two women, this sequence is recounted from the point of view of the "passive woman," a ploy that tends to emphasize the female-ness of both lovers. Using the voice from a "stereotypically" feminine position to describe the actions of another woman, the more active woman's womanliness is emphasized rather than elided into the "mas-culine" position that accompanies stereotypical assumptions about the identity of voice and activity. In addition, the passage's penultimate emphasis on an indefinite period of afterglow ("two minutes or ten minutes") subordinates the already indirect image of climax ("my body rose"), shifting the narrative's trajectory from an emphasis on joinder to the calm that presages the story to come. In this way, Wings counteracts the active/passive structure she otherwise inscribes (and that via gender is typically associated with sex), confusing the lovers' and the reader's positions and suggesting different, less direct, ways of reading synthesis and closure.

Wings's heterologies, produced by the dislocated oppositions be-tween active and passive and cause and effect, appear to remove this coming story from the metaphorically heterosexual. Even so, these dis-locations are effects of style (even if they might be components of a specifically lesbian sexuality), and the passage's disjunctures between the lovers and their actions do not destroy differences altogether. Instead, the story relocates oppositional differences into the registers of sound and reaction instead of vision and action. The map of the body—lips, back, breasts, crotch, site of penetration—provides a literally descending order that marks progress through time, carefully tracking the narrative steps of the somewhat disembodied hand as it evokes certain responses: kiss-ing causing fear, hand on back providing reassurance, hand on breasts inviting a funny squeaking sound, slight bondage and further manual exploration bringing excitement close to pain, hand between legs precipitating wetness, finger inside inducing rising/coming.

Despite the differing emphases of Wings's passage above, its organization as a hierarchical series of cause-and-effect events recaptures its redistribution of passive and active positions and directs its general coital direction. The passage's insistence on passivity and a kind of detachment makes this narrative seem a subjective tracking of response, a kind of one-sided deal. As the story of the done-to, it emphasizes a cause-and-effect trajectory to climax, even though the narrator appears to both know and not know the story. The remarkable absence of reaction in the owner of the hand (except for the narrator's observation that she felt the other's "own breath rising in response") perhaps paradoxically emphasizes the cause/effect opposition by shifting attention from the more traditional opposition between actors to a tension between actors and their acts. The clear product of these binaries, the climax of the sequence is itself productive, not of a child but of another narrative, the missing story of the narrator's turn to be the cause.

But does the nature of these differences change the understanding or shape of the joinder that configures this episode? Might not indirection and dislocation at least show up the more normatively heterosexual metaphors of narrative? Rather than exposing any terms or patterns clearly, this passage actually blurs differences through its indirection, enacting a kind of perverse multiple sameness in the place of lesbian sex. This sameness or no difference, reminiscent of the multiple female erotics suggested by Luce Irigaray, seems both laudable and liberatory, distinguishing narratives of lesbian sex from the more distinct binaries that characterize heterosexual narratives. But while its lack of direct description might undermine a straightforward trajectory, the passage also produces a dynamic of desire that itself results from flirtatious indirection—a kind of planned perversity. This dynamic, while pleasurable, is already culturally and ideologically linked to the lesbian and to the specifically lesbian site of no difference in heteronarrative. Thus, while appearing to render some lesbian experience, the passage fits right back into the hetero scheme. Although the register of the anxiety this no difference represents may have changed from threat to pleasurable interlude, lesbian no difference still leads to a binary, reproductive terminus.

No matter how realistic, pleasurable, provocative, or even disconcerting it might seem, this narrative peopled by lesbians still doesn't inscribe a different narrative or express a "non"-heterosexual experience in a "non"-heterosexual metaphor. This may be because the narrative of lesbian sex always occurs in relation to its "other," the heterosex of narrative and dominant culture, or because we read sex through that heterosexual matrix, or even because we have difficulty making sense of same-gendered sex because sex is already heteronarrative. Even if we claim that an orgasm is not already narrativized but is, rather, a real-life, measurable physiological effect produced by specific physiological causes; and that narratives of coming transparently represent the cause-and-effect order of this physiological phenomenon; and that lesbian scenarios therefore cannot be shaped any other way, the selection of this moment from all others and its specific determination of cause and effect defines its position within a heterologic. Coming stories, even lesbian ones, are already the effect of a particular way of understanding a) that there should be cause and effect at all; b) that cause precedes effect; and c) that cause/effect relations ultimately produce something beyond themselves: pleasure, ending, reproduction, death.

Perhaps Mary Wings's description is not a typical example, and other descriptions of lesbian sexual activity employ a different kind of narrative. Looking for other examples, I found a collection called *The Erotic Naiad*; from its title I assumed that it would contain a number of coming sequences and that the stories included would indicate what the collection's editors, Katherine Forrest and Barbara Grier, thought about what kinds of narratives constitute lesbian erotica. As I might have anticipated, all of the volume's nineteen stories except one follow the same pattern Wings's story does, overtly establishing differences between the women, creating a series of cause/effect events that lead to a synthesis usually figured by orgasm; the one exception ends with the discovery that both partners are wearing men's silk underwear (an interesting "inner").

The differences among women in the *Naiad* stories tend to be defined in terms of power and stereotypical sexual role, while other differences among women such as race and ethnicity seem to make little if any difference, though few racial or ethnic differences are represented. The only story in the collection by a woman of color is the first, "Getting to Yes," by African-American author Nikki Baker; it is perhaps the most insightful example of the connections among the narrative of sex, the sexuality of narrative, and capitalist ideologies constructed in the same terms. In this story, two acquaintances, Thalia, an assistant school superintendent, and Ann, a teacher, meet on opposite sides of a negotiating table during a teachers' strike. When negotiations, which are the pretext for mental foreplay, stall, Thalia goes to Ann's house and the two make love:

> Ann kissed her with a mouth that did not want to rest, pressed down over the length of her body, mouth to mouth, grinding hip to thigh. She worked her way down from Thalia's throat to the paunch that sat below her belly as if she walked a well worn path fondly, stopping for memories. She went with her fingers firmly into places that Thalia thought she had forgotten. Her body sucked and caught Ann's fingers as they came and went deeper at each return. Their motion smacked softly like a closed-mouth kiss and Ann gasped as if she herself were being penetrated. Thalia heard her own pleasure as if it came from someone else. The sound fed itself on the rhythm of Ann's fingers; it built like a distant train and stopped with a catch of breath and a sigh of completion.   *(11–12)*

This passage, like Mary Wings's, follows a body map from top to bottom and, like Wings's description, curiously detaches the lovers from their responses—"as if it came from someone else"—in this passage perhaps even more distanced because of the use of a third- rather than first-person narrator. Even this third-person narrator plays with its omniscience as it shifts quickly from one lover's actions to the other's response in such a way as to remove the distance between them while retaining a passive/active model. Ann's kisses and fingers make "smack," Ann "gasps," the sound itself feeding "on the rhythm of Ann's fingers," finally building with a comparison to the sound of a "distant train" and ending in a "sigh of completion." In relying as much on evocations of sound as on detailed descriptions of action, Baker's narrator adds a second dimension to cause and effect. Focusing on acoustic signifiers of pleasure emphasizes the response and distributes the effects between characters, leveling out their passive/active positions.

The primacy of sound in this passage displaces cause/effect slightly from its role describing a physical process to a signifier that extends beyond the body; in this sense the description is poetical and indirect. But the shape of this narrative is like that of Mary Wings's description: moving from the head to the genitals, building in intensity and wetness, the process ends in completion. In Baker's story the product of this sex

is an end to negotiation stalemate, the joinder of the women changing
the receptivity of the men. In this sense, lesbian sexuality is positioned
as a positive force, one that creates peace and open-mindedness; ideologically that is a good thing. But this occurs because the women's sexuality is located and described in the terms of a narrative heteroideology that is above all things productive.

Both of these narratives of lesbian sex, we might say, do shift the het-
erostory, at least on the surface, but their inscription as a coming
together of passive/active or labor/supervisor opposites that leads to a
climax and the production of something is still situated within narrative heteroideology. It is not finally what is done, or who is doing it, but
the insistently binary terms of its narration that expose its underlying
alignment with a reproductive ideology. Even though I do not want to
underestimate the positive potential of this use of the heteronarrative
despite the fact that heteroideology itself may in the end produce and
perpetuate the oppression of lesbians, its prevalence in lesbian erotica
indicates another problem. Perhaps I (and Katherine Forrest and Barbara
Grier) chose these stories because they already conform to the ideology of narrative. Maybe my ability to even identify what is a sex scene
at all depends not on the penetration that Marilyn Frye suggests defines
sexuality in Western culture but on my identification of this narrative
pattern of opposition and synthesis whose dynamic is culturally understood as sexual and heterosexual.[14] If this is the case, could I possibly
identify sex scenes as such that were not written in this heterostructure?
Or why might it be important to do so? Might it not be, as I suggested
earlier, a liberating gesture to take over these heterosexual stories and
people them with lesbians? Might that not demonstrate that lesbians
can be productive members of society, that they are not "abnormal"?

Mary Wings's novel, *She Came Too Late*, tries this ploy to the limits of
the literal imagination. A mystery story featuring Women's Hotline
detective Emma Victor (note even the name), the novel traces Emma's
attempts to solve the murder of one of her callers, a caller whose murder she was "too late" to prevent. In her investigations, Emma meets
Frances Cohen, a physician and researcher at the Women's Clinic, with
whom she has a pleasant but somewhat enigmatic affair. While Emma
tracks down wealthy philanthropists, union busters, and feminist man-
agers, always somehow coming too late to prevent disaster, Frances
works overtime completing some mystery research that, at the end of
the novel, is revealed to have been a successful attempt to spawn tad-

poles from two female frogs. The end of the novel indeed proves that two females together can reproduce, that the lesbian story can quite literally take its place in the production of succession and generation as Frances proves the reproductive capabilities of girl amphibians and Emma solves the mystery.

As a lesbian story, *She Came Too Late* is oddly preoccupied with the issue of reproduction. This does not signal an anxiety about reproduction or Eros as we might suspect—or even a triumphant assertion of lesbian productivity; rather, it portends an uneasiness about gender and the maintenance of difference. For example, one of the fears of the head of the women's clinic is that the more reproduction becomes technological, the more men will use it to reproduce only males, thus creating a male homoculture in which women become obsolete. With either frogs or bottle babies, same-sex reproduction displaces the joinder of differences as the direct cause of reproduction, replacing it with a repressive, same-sex culture of homology. In narrative's reproductive heterologic, the displacement of difference as the precursor and stage for synthesis potentially changes the position of reproduction in the heteronarrative, making reproduction not an end but a by-product, not a synthesis but a magic act. While this appears to change the reproductive narrative by altering cause, what it really does is play out in gendered terms an extreme version of the same old story of patriarchy where production, reproduction, identity, immortality, and knowledge are perpetuated in the name of the father and at the expense of the mother. It also extends fearsome homology into the realm of technology, making technology another signifier of stasis or death.

The novel's anxieties about the disappearance of gender obscure the fear of homology the novel's lesbians might otherwise represent. The novel shifts homology onto men in a gynocentric and somewhat self-contradictory logic. If reproduction is removed from its heterosexual cause, then women will be eliminated; but if reproduction is controlled by women, though it is removed from heterosexuality altogether, the possibility is liberating and utopian within the terms of this novel. Such logic is plausible because in this novel, productive differences exist among women, while men are often depicted as homologous to one another and, thus, as the enemies to women's joinder and productivity. The fear here finally is not a fear of patriarchy but a fear that the narrative will in fact change, that the enemy homology, now figured as male, will take over and end the story before the story can end, before lesbian culture can come into its own as a productive universe. The anxiety about the disappearance of narrative linked directly to the dreaded triumph of homology is screened by an apparently more immediate anxiety about the literal disappearance of women, the odd, but perhaps logical effect of an emphasis on homology *as the enemy*—as patriarchy—that might win out over the narrative of productive differences the novel locates in the lesbian community.

Shifting the place of homology to patriarchy in an attempt to recoup the story—what is in fact the same old reproductive narrative—reiterates and emphasizes the narrative dangers of homology itself. While Wings's attempt to associate homology with patriarchy may be a bid to extricate lesbians from their limited, middle-narrative position, it also emphasizes homology, reinscribing, in perhaps more adamant terms, a literally reproductive narrative. Even if the possibility of intralesbian reproduction is utopian for lesbians, what it does unfortunately is valorize the same cause/effect relationship between difference, conflict, and productive joinder as does the heteronarrative. The relation between difference and production becomes the problem, because this cause/effect connection sustains the repressive structure that produces and opposes homology to heterology even if the lesbian story tries to displace homology onto patriarchy. The lesbian dream of following this reproductive narrative through in literal terms thus also carries the danger of narrative (and lesbian) extinction, since homology plays the same narrative part. The effect of trying to change the story may just as easily be death as emancipation, elimination as production.

Making the lesbian a protagonist is thus not so simple; rather, it involves a complex rebalancing, a shifting and displacement of the terms of narrative in such a way that the narrative status quo is maintained not only so the story is recognizable and pleasurable in cultural terms but so as to preserve the very mechanism by which narrative change is believed to occur. The paradox of lesbian narrative is that in this form and practice it must at the same time perform the contradictory processes of challenging narrative and perpetuating its terms. The problem with this is that because of the ideological sexual constructs that underpin narrative, sexual identity and narrative position are not as extricable as we might believe (in fact as the triumphant lesbian identity narrative might lead us to believe). Instead, entangled in the heteroideology constituting narrative, the sexual persona of a character and that character's narrative function are interwoven in a self-compensatory structure that resists change as it is made; for this reason, simply making the lesbian a protagonist does not work to change narrative at all. In a narrative ideology aimed toward metaphorical reproduction, gender governs the disposition of differences where the sexual is at issue; as by definition demonstrating no difference, lesbians usually end up alone, disappointed, having produced only identity, the lesbian's true progeny. The point is that without changing the very logic of the story, we will always end up in the same place, even (and especially) when we think we are fabricating a triumphantly lesbian story.

COMING TO NO GOOD END

The coming out story with its stake in knowledge, identity, and visibility is a version of the heteronarrative that relocates the lesbian within a larger heterosexual system where she becomes again the narrative villain, the representative of stasis, the destroyer of the heterosexual family, the murderer, the vampire, the feminist, the bitch—in fact, the representative of the dangerous sameness against which the production of narrative differences functions.[15] As a protagonist, the lesbian plays out the fearsome anxieties about sameness that might adjust but that do not change narrative's heteroideology, providing an oblique, but still dominant representation of the same heterosystem. Is it possible to escape at all the hegemony of a structure that posits heteroideology as a basic truth underlying the operation of language (as does Greimas) or shapes the very way we think about things, including the constitution of the category *homosexual* itself? Are attempts to alter whatever sustains the lesbian's apparent narrative impossibility thus inherently "experimental"?[16] Can we rethink narrative outside of narrative or sexuality outside of sex? Or might we explode the system by playing on, exaggerating, parodying, or performing its own elements in what Elaine Marks has called a subversion through excess or what Judith Butler calls the politics of performance or what Teresa de Lauretis calls "Oedipus with a vengeance"?[17] If so, we must be careful, since such forms of performative excess as drag and butch/femme tend not to work systemically; that is, they are conventional, sometimes assuming parts in narrative without showing up the system.

Exploiting the possibility that the place of homology is in fact a disturbing, confusing, or threatening interlude, authors such as Monique

Wittig and Nicole Brossard enact narrative insurrections, refusing clear cause-and-effect relations, binary oppositions, and culminating joinders, redefining what the lesbian and lesbian sexuality might be. The effect of this is an alternative rendering of both narrative and sexuality; narrative acquires a different emphasis and sexuality becomes more pervasive, linked to desire instead of orgasm. Their differing renditions of this strategy (sometimes in addition to a more traditional use of a lesbian protagonist) require tactics that disenable some of what we traditionally identify as pleasurable in narrative: mastery through clear or easy identification with characters, predictable and normative cause/effect relations, stylistic transparency, and a libidinally rewarding structure. At the same time, Wittig's and Brossard's candid alignment of the lesbian with a different narrative structure might again recontain the lesbian in the middling proposition the lesbian already occupies, precisely because their expansion of and/or emphasis on an indeterminate form and their failure to provide resounding coital-like conclusions looks like an elaborated middle in relation to a larger, still omnipresent narrative ideology. Even so, the intersection of the runaway lesbian middle with postmodern narrative practice works to divulge narrative ideology, heterosexual investment, our pleasure in certainty and closure and, at the same time, inscribes the lesbian as a moment of perpetual play defying closure and the ideological investments such closure certifies.[18]

Despite the more literal lesbian identifications of Wittig's and Brossard's work, their strategies take advantage of a *metaphorically* lesbian narrative position, a position shared by other categories also attached to the ideological position of stasis. These other narratives employ similar tactics, not because they want to be lesbian but because a postmodern loss of mastery metanarratives shifts emphasis from the satisfying end to a more indeterminate middle—hence a postmodernism that is sometimes confused with the lesbian, hence the way such forms are received in a culture that is narratively fixed.[19] Rather than effecting a large-scale lesbianization of narrative, postmodern narrative strategies tend to employ indeterminacy, stylistic self-consciousness, and multiple variants to secure an even more knowing mastery someplace else. The difference between the lesbian and the postmodern is finally more a matter of control and perspective than style, but control and its identifiable locus make all the difference between the two. If the postmodern can be seen as a frustration of identity, certainty, and control, and the relocation of mastery to the place where one knows one cannot know, the deliberately lesbian efforts of Wittig and Brossard, insofar as they attribute style to sexuality and/or identity, defer control in favor of a perpetual play whose valorization disarms confusion's threat or fears of a lack of mastery.

Monique Wittig's novels, *Les Guerillères* (1969), *L'Opoponax*, and *The Lesbian Body* (1973), and her *Lesbian Peoples: Material for a Dictionary* (1978) with Sande Zeig, all challenge the notion of a speaking subject organized under the aegis of heterosexuality, enact a broad intertextuality, and recast narrative. In her essay on "Lesbian Intertextuality," Elaine Marks attributes Wittig with revolutionary accomplishment, declaring Wittig's "J/e" "the most powerful lesbian in literature . . . the only true anti-Christ" (376) and crediting Wittig with effecting an escape from "male literary culture" (375). Namascar Shaktini claims that Wittig accomplishes an "epistemological shift" away from phallocentrism through her "reorganization of metaphor around the lesbian body" (29). Marilyn Farwell believes that Wittig's textual practice "undercuts dualism" in its creation of a "lesbian narrative space" (98). Diane Griffith Crowder, equating the lesbian with a political position, sees Wittig's work as having already eluded a phallocentric *weltanschauung* by virtue of its lesbian standpoint: " 'lesbian writing' restructures the meanings of words and of literary forms because it is written from a social position in which masculinist thought has been nullified."[20]

Wittig's critics, perceiving the narrative revolution her work proposes, all locate that revolt in the persona of the lesbian. At the same time they understand this lesbian position as a part of a binary opposed to the male, the masculine, or the heterosexual, positioning Wittig's work in the place of the successful adversary confrontation of identity, truth, power, and knowledge as those are constructed within a heterosexual system. In other words, defining Wittig's works as a challenge to patriarchy, critics situate it squarely within the metaphorically lesbian position in heteronarrative, thus inadvertently reinscribing the project within the same old story.[21]

Despite this resoundingly modernist critical understanding, Wittig brings the very categories by which the lesbian can be known into question, creating a species of lesbian postmodern operating in the realm of a materialized language. Characterizing the relation between language and materiality as a gender struggle, Wittig sees language as a material means of effecting structural and ideological change. In her

essay "One Is Not Born a Woman" (1980), Wittig insists on the material basis for any challenge to gender oppression, locating the lesbian at
the point of that challenge. Perceiving the oppressiveness of the gender
system as a system and challenging the epistemological basis of naturalized gender categories, Wittig pits the material experience of lesbians
against a heterosexual hegemony: "Lesbian is the only concept I know
of which is beyond the categories of sex (woman and man), because the
designated subject (lesbian) is *not* a woman, either economically, or
politically, or ideologically" (53).

Wittig's deft transition from materiality to a categorical confrontation with gender skips over one of her problematic underlying assumptions: that language can transparently represent experience and can thus
directly transform ideology. By eliding the practical difficulty of getting
from imagined materiality to representation, Wittig can offer the act of
rejecting gender as a way of surmounting it. This utopian gap in Wittig's
otherwise perceptive critique of the ideology of gender exposes her
very traditional reliance upon the originary existence of a subject outside of ideology, assuming as Judith Butler observes, a "pre-social ontology of unified and equal persons" (115). Wittig's notions of gender and
sexuality rely upon what Butler calls "the systemic integrity" of both
heterosexuality and homosexuality, where homosexuality is "conceived
as radically unconditioned by heterosexual norms" (121).

Although Wittig's writing *looks* postmodern (it would fit nicely into
Ihab Hassan's list of postmodern traits), its covert reliance upon the very
categories it rejects, its appeal to a preexistent nongendered, lesbian
identity, and its uncritical belief in the power of language are, as Butler
suggests, "a modernist" practice; despite appearances, Wittig is as her
critics define her.[22] The figure of the lesbian in Wittig's oeuvre moors
and stabilizes challenges to gender, resulting in the celebration of a lesbian persona liberated from the hegemony of heterosexuality—a persona fixed in her fluid subjectivity, interpenetration, and capacity to
wield the language of desire and ferocity.[23]

That lesbian position, as we have already seen, is constructed by and
exists already within the heteronarrative; declaring Wittig's works as lesbian or challenging patriarchy on that basis recontains them in the same
old story. It is, rather, Wittig's attempt, in the name of the more
metaphorical lesbian, to change the shape of the story itself that inti-
mates a possible revolution. *The Lesbian Body*, for example, is a fragmented, metaphorically corporeal narrative of the relations among

bodies, loosely identified as lesbian, though with none of the traditional cultural markers—masculinity, adolescence—thereof. With no immediately apparent narrative trajectory and with no suggestion of one to be easily devised, *The Lesbian Body* appears to focus on a microprocess of relating, not in terms of discrete wholes but as parts intermingling. Cause and effect therefore are not always clearly defined; the doer and the done-to commingle. Neither are the characters clearly situated in roles in relation to any equilibrium-disequilibrium-equilibrium (to use Todorov's model) trajectory, though that trajectory sometimes does play out in the smaller segments that make up the novel:

> *I* wrench out your teeth, one by one, your minuscule short and square incisors your well-developed pointed canines your premolars *I* arrange them in front of m/e, one by one *I* see them gleaming, they are removed with their roots, to whom should *I* offer them if not to Sappho the most distant telling her that reassembled they constitute the most living necklace ever to be seen by female eyes. *I* ask you which of us shall wear it, you part your lips m/y mutilated on over your blood-stained gums, *I* insert m/y tongue into each socket in succession, *I* probe your wounds, m/y lips m/y fingers receive your blood, with m/y mouth with m/y hands *I* make red marks and traces on your body, your mouth bleeds without stopping, you do not complain m/y so silent one, you regard m/e fixedly while in great haste *I* cover your body with great signs, while *I* am all gooseflesh, while *I* seize the small shreds of your ripped flesh between m/y intact teeth, while you smile horribly at m/e you most beautiful of all women.   *(125)*

Proceeding from a preextraction equilibrium through a middling intermingling to a resolutionary smile, the passage reproduces a traditional narrative pattern on one level. But its series of events in which an "*I*" takes out the teeth of a "you," arranges them, makes a necklace, asks who shall wear it, probes the mouth of "you," they look at one another, the "*I*" bites the "you"'s body and the "you" smiles "horribly" at her is hardly typical of the more socially defined terms of a traditional narrative.

But more than its uncommon subject matter disturbs what could be seen as a traditional narrative trajectory. The cause-and-effect rationale for this sequence, is, according to the tender and respectful tone of the narrator, some deeply felt relation, an intimacy that goes beyond the surface. And it is only with some difficulty that the "*I*" and the "you," both women, can be fixed as opposite players. Even though the one takes out the teeth of the other, such dentistry is posed as something beyond violence. The matter-of-fact description of the processes suggests ritual rather than horror, intimacy rather than invasion. In this context, opposition and joinder have no meaning; actions (probing the wounds with tongue) revisit actions (the tearing out of teeth); a repetition with a difference reigns. Progress through time is slow, sometimes indiscernible except through the play of words on the page. The body parts and their dispersion seem to be metaphors of a relation that exceeds the individual and the binary, multiplying and mingling where the two are not lost, but their opposition is annulled.

The entire novel is comprised of similar passages, all reminiscent of a narrative we remember, but instead of building themselves into the same pattern, the passages repeat with differences, interspersed with lists of body parts, moving not to any consummation (as the book's promotional language suggests, "the epic consummation of a profoundly physical love") but to a sense of radiance, exchange, proliferation, and ubiquity. This ubiquity and sense of the omnipresence of all works against any connotation of production or reproduction, referring instead to a kind of painstaking nostalgia, transmutation, a pleasure in the infinite invention of the moment that springs neither from joinder nor opposition, but from the self-generating fecundity of multiplicity itself. The exchange that figures the above passage implies two, and the two are there, over-written by the insistent multiplicity of their pieces whose exchange enacts a permeation and trading of discrete boundaries even as they are preserved in the passage's tortured pronouns. Structured by repetition and variation, *The Lesbian Body* inscribes an economy of nonculmination whose pleasure is in presence rather than anticipation and for which mastery itself is no longer relevant.

Wittig's lack of character definition and the novel's refusal of more traditional narrative terms in favor of what might be seen as a multilayered excursus infinitely repeated in a different cadence disallows the very position of homology within the novel by deploying difference and sameness, insofar as such concepts remain meaningful, in a different way. Sameness and difference exist and play importantly in the prose poetry, but the distinction between one person and another lacks propriety; "*I*" and "you" as belonging to no one, as not objectively fixed, thus constitute neither difference nor sameness. The sameness/difference interplay, instead, occurs on the level of language metaphorically appended to anatomies, where in contrast to the "*I*"/"you" of the apparent actor/actants, sameness/difference and propriety/commonality intermingle in the scattered sorting of a morphological passion. The interplay of these two levels confuses rather than negates difference, at the same time denying rather than reifying sameness. The effect is that sameness and difference, though sometimes discernible, become meaningless as structural categories.

If the categories *sameness* and *difference* produce and are produced by narrative, and if, in turn, they reproduce narrative, Wittig's novel stymies both the production and reproduction of narrative and the relative positions upon which its production depends. In this sense Wittig explodes the dominant narrative metaphor of the lesbian and, curiously, also shatters the dynamic of desire insofar as its dynamic is dependent upon a sameness/difference narrative economy. Wittig replaces it with a more ubiquitous longing that seems not unlike the Aristophanic desire for the recovery of previously whole beings Freud evokes as the underlying rationale for Eros. In part, this nostalgia is produced by the novel's overt appeal to fragmented bodies; in part, it has to do with the narrative relation of those bodies, which, neither oppositional not complementary, is always ever partial, never complete, constantly craving.

The character of this craving also seems to recall what appears to be a pre-oedipal dynamic, a lack of differentiation from the Other (Mother). The similarity between Wittig's writing and the pre-oedipal, however, is formal rather than essential; *The Lesbian Body*'s world is beyond the trajectory of the temporal narrative that locates the pre-oedipal in the first place. While this pre-oedipal evocation explains the resonance between Wittig's body imagery and Luce Irigaray's explorations of feminine sexuality in "This Sex Which Is Not One" (which also evokes but is not the pre-oedipal), *The Lesbian Body* is distinctly postoedipal, not just in a developmental narrative, but in a narrative that is beyond the need for Oedipus at all. The cultural confusion among the interrelation of women, the pre-oedipal, and lesbian sexuality is another version of the narratively inflected understanding of women together (sameness) as immature, as precisely not arrived at the oedipal at all.[24] But the self/other distinction of Wittig's text belies the self/other confusion of the pre-oedipal; its politic of mingling is deliberate rather than infantile, the result of the irrelevance of oedipal rules of separation rather than their not yet having come into play.

The dynamic of Wittig's narrative fine-tunes what in a larger frame appears to be a homology. Challenging narrative, securing a place for something in addition to, the novel's title simultaneously relocates the novel in the larger cultural narrative; its challenge to narrative becomes a difficulty to the "normal" reader, and the project of shifting narrative is practically lost. While we read the text carefully enough to discern its different interplay, not everyone reads it that way (if they read it at all) and it is just as likely to annoy those invested in traditional narrative as it is to install a different way of thinking about narrative altogether.[25] This is not the problem of lesbian narrative challenge, but of any attempt to alter the pleasurable dynamic expected from narrative literature.

Nicole Brossard's *Picture Theory* also takes up issues of language, narrative, and genre, forging a writing and aesthetic that, like Wittig's work, creates a challenge to any narrative heteroideology. And like Wittig's writing, Brossard's work is not posited as an alternative to or a practice against heteronarrative; instead, it posits a narrative that works another way. Where Wittig employs a body/language matrix as the basis for a different ordering of meaning, Brossard employs a dynamic of desire played through the overtly self-conscious field of reading and writing where an identity between text and psyche embodies the kind of self-conscious performative strategies often attributed to postmodern texts. Seeming to equate textuality with sexuality, Brossard inscribes desire as a function of language whose trajectory shuns clear temporal, character, and cause/effect relations, appearing instead to be organized in sets of associations premised upon an impression-based metonymy.

Picture Theory itself has two different meanings metonymically connected through the word *theory*, meanings that radically shift the project of narrative. "Picture theory," the narrator decrees, "there are islands above Arizona" (23). The picture of theory is improbable, lyrical, aerial; "luminous 'an image is a stop the mind makes between uncertainties',", the narrator quotes *Nightwood* (23). "Theory above the cliffs like islands overhanging the desert, the reality of synchronous women modifies the horizon, the streets of the glass city, reflexion made, mental space for a contemporary vision" (171). Or "Picture theory," the theory of pictures, the hologrammatic return, overtraced resonance of the once-seen, almost-seen, soon-to-be-seen. While "language is a spectacle of what we cannot think as *such (women)*" (163), "every image hides subliminal, formal fire, or (O liquid) accessory skull anchored at the bottom of the sea with no secret" (102). "Studious girls, we will divert the course of fiction, dragging with us words turn and turn about, igneous spiral, picture theory an existence in those terms" (93).

"There are two scenes" (21) to *Picture Theory*, the prose/poem/return/hologram metanarrative neonarrative of the insistence of narrative and its sometimes failure to hold course, the line of the ground, becoming aerial, spiral, turning back the image with its "subliminal formal fire." Two scenes: "the book scene and the rug scene," "picture theory and picture theory," "the white scene and the book scene," "the love scene and the writing scene," Curacao and Montreal, New York and Martha's Vineyard. "Riveted to each other as though held in suspense by writing, we exist in the laborious creation of desire of which we can conceive no idea" (21).

Two scenes, the two necessary to narrative, but nondichotomous, nonoppositional, two scenes multiplied, but nonalignable or orderable, instead transmuting, spiraling, "skin/screen," she says, containing, revealing, becoming one another, passing through, referring, reminding, but only vaguely, confronting. Two scenes, never the same two, flirting through time, with time, confounding, distracting, refracting the same old narrative, the narrative of Propp, Lévi-Strauss, Todorov, Greimas, Barthes, Disney, the narrative of joinder and (re)production, where opposites attract, join, produce, recognize, die, the narrative of birth life death told always in a single register, two scenes disenabling by displacing and disaligning its parts, fracturing, losing structure, now remnants, barely recognizable, but recognized for the artifacts they are.

The old story, those nods to the old story, the end coming now displaced as the vortex admitted in the felicitous disposal of its perpetual return. She announces that culmination, now somewhere just before the middle: "I know that the amorous scene has already been viewed and consumed in several of its strategies, I know that, I know that, repeated, it determines the opening and vanishing point of all affirmation" (41). "The opening and vanishing point," the "Idea" pictured, not of culmination, a coming to enjoy, raison d'etre of all narrative foreplay, but the picture of an alien theory of narration, based—oh maybe—on the same old model of conjoinder, but a conjoinder removed from its productive impetus, a conjoinder redefining conjoinder. "Responding to certain signs, with complete fluidity, our bodies interlaced m'urged to fuse in astonishment or fascination.

Literally thin film of skin for each other at the heart of radical motivation" (31).

There is a story, of course, or rather many, including the roughly traced story of the book itself, deciphered from the body whose theory it pictures. There are no borders nor even the idea of them, but there are vague beginnings evoked in the beginning of the end in time's trace on the spiral passage. "By beginning with the word woman in connection with Utopic, M.V. had chosen to concentrate on an abstraction of which she has an inkling" (153). This word, like words whose "hyperrealism" transforms our ideas of bodies and language, our dreams of their separation and orderly intrication, is a sign that radiates outward like a light from a translucent center that, never there, keeps moving (157). And in this story of writing where "time becomes a process in ultraviolet," the writerly "I" performs rites of light and language where words weave a screen at the end of a "patriarchal night" (155).

But this story of the story is not just the story of an "I," "it was epidemic this will for serial circulation of spatial gestures which the letter had initiated" (155). The skin is communal, osmotic, which obviates the work of meaning, which eventually commits a "breach of law" that sunders sense, invites memory (124). The "breach of law," the word already a breach, the sentence in its orderly grammar, the grammar of Greimassian narrative, already breached in its ulterior origin, its aerial spiral. "She is born from a phrase skin language surrounds her a woman expresses herself in her body it's a sensation not forgotten in the representation of space when the idea sees the day s/lash in the brain the metaphors where the heart is catch fire the effect of coherent light the ash" (182–183).

The body written, writes its idea, the word, letter, not Lacan's insistent letter but an uncertain one, many, whose appearance is culled from the idea and the body and the picture of bodies in reflexive intercourse past. This is not Cixous's writing from the body; this body already reckons its idealization, the absent boundary already spoken for in the form already spoken of and more, in the fiction, that like the book here speaks itself in excess, always more and less than it is. "Basically you say each time that you control yourself to stop *the words escaping you*. Fiction then foils illysybility in the sense that it always insinuates something more which forces you to imagine, to double. To come back to it again" (27). "In writing," fiction, "I would have everything for imagining an abstract woman who would slip into my text, crying the fiction so far that from afar, this woman participant in words, must be seen coming, virtual to infinity, form-elle in every dimension of understanding, method and memory. I would not have to invent her in the fiction. The fiction would be the finishing line of her thought" (153).

This fiction, purveyor of a pleasure that evades all ending, escapes the kind of definition that would fix it into the readable object, this "pleasure inscribed in language is the one that *amazes* at the very moment when pleasure con-verges" (167). Pleasure, like desire, there at every turn, and not trappable, fixable, here is pleasure and here is desire, but sliding through the idea and the breach, the white scene and the scene of the book. And pleasure and desire in the narrative now not any narrative we know and we have always known, pictured in this theory—this vision, this writing—of what else can be.

Brossard's narrative through suggestion, through a metonymy not only with the sensory associations of sex/text but also with a narrative sense, evoked, lost, forgotten, avoids the oppositional challenge that would locate its praxis in a recuperable sameness/difference dichotomy. Its evocation of narrative while forgetting it works to situate its other narrative in metonymic relation to dominant narrative so that the novel pictures its own relation to tradition as part of the desire it evokes. Its suggestion of narrative works to dislocate heteronarrative; but *Picture Theory* is not completely other. It is, rather, appended to, a side, playing through heteronarrative a writing that dissolves it. In this way Brossard performs a writing desire economy that might be understood as lesbian insofar as the writings' personae are all female. But of course, that understanding of the lesbian returns to the gendered heterosexually dependent definition of lesbian whereby the lesbian is already culturally located as confused, medial no difference. But Brossard avoids this return to a cultural fixation; the gender of the characters becomes less relevant than their interrelations, their histories, memories, and associations, and their connection to the atmosphere.

If, as Peter Brooks suggests in "Freud's Masterplot," narrative proceeds mainly through metaphor, Brossard's use of metonymy deranges the play of sameness and difference upon which metaphor depends. Its wholesale slippage is pleasure and desire, not ordered as desire then pleasure but as one and the same, typifying the short circuit Brooks fears will end narrative in its tracks. The circularity and circulation of Brossard's text denies any ending, or even its idea in favor of an "always been," a presence whose relation to the deadly foundations of traditional narrative is also a metonymy, for contiguous to death as the end of desire is the desire coterminous with pleasure.

Brossard's challenges to the relation between cause and effect and the identity-mastery of narrative both expose the investments of heteronarrative and point the way to a different concept of narrative, which is nonetheless still dependent upon the continued coexistence of dominant narrative ideology. Brossard's confusion of point of view, *Picture Theory*'s performative cast, and its wedding of text and space bring into question the politics of visibility that underlies some of the belief in the practical effect of a lesbian protagonist. Visibility as the triumphant culmination of the coming out story inevitably refers to the heteronarrative. Brossard's treatment of visibility—all is there and nothing is clearly "seen" but images—frustrates and displaces visibility as any hallmark of self-affirmation, replacing image with process, mastery with desire.

Wittig's and Brossard's narrative maneuvers may in some ways avoid the oppositional economy by which lesbian and even its concept are culturally located. Made more viable by a postmodern aegis, their writings offer disturbing narrative alternatives. But even if their strategies have dissimilar purposes and finally work differently than other postmodern projects, their surface similarity to the postmodern threatens to relegate lesbian narrative experiments to the same intellectualized and generally popularly rejected group of narratives as the literary postmodern. The potential association between a lesbian narrative praxis and one perceived as effete jeopardizes the possibilities for cultural change any lesbian practice might introduce. For this reason as well as for the many reasons that already inscribe a particular cultural pleasure in narrative structurally understood, Wittig's and Brossard's understanding of the power of narrative itself unfortunately promises little but very slow change.

SO LONG COMING TO

Now wait a minute! It's all of a certain night that I'm coming to, that I take so long in coming to," he said, "a night in the branchy pitch of fall—the particular night you want to know about—for I'm a fisher of men and my gimp is doing a *salterello* over

every body of water to fetch up what it may. I have a narrative, but you will be put to
it to find it.
—Djuna Barnes, *Nightwood*, p. 97

If, at this point in history, the narrative challenge of "experimental" writing is of limited use, how else might we alter narrative and its heteroideology to allow the expression of something else? Do we avoid directly narrating at all and instead rely upon suggestion, indirection, encoding, or playing out the politics of invisibility that have typified the representation and reading of the lesbian for so long? Do we simply follow the "perverse" narrative, Freud's residual streams, always there and only used when the main channel is blocked through some trauma or repression? Do we mount a challenge from the site of this perverse, this queerness lumped together as a more populated and hence more powerful opposition to the hetero powers that be? Understanding the perverse as an opposition to the hetero normal is already a problem, the same old problem of fitting into the structure heteronarrative already provides. And seeing the perverse as a set of groupable differences misreads the crucial differences among lesbians, gay males, and others in Western culture, situated differently in narrative and ideology and posing different challenges. Power in numbers is the old logic of visibility. Denial of differences is the old logic of sameness by which all that threatens reproductive patriarchy is relegated to the same necessary but overcome position.

Linking the lesbian to the "monster," Bertha Harris situates the lesbian as synecdochal of this perversity, reading Barnes's *Nightwood* as experimental and monstrous.[26] But even in *Nightwood* what appears to be specifically lesbian—the relations among Robin Vote, Nora Flood, and Jenny Petherbridge—is only one in a variety of the "perversities" that people the novel. Insofar as the figure of the grotesque or monstrous refers to Barnes's characters, the novel could still retain a most traditional narrative. But if, in addition to these characters, Barnes deploys the novel's narratives in a way synonymous with Freud's residual perverse streams, there might be a promise of some greater-than-the-lesbian narrative perversity that provides another means for unseating narrative heteroideology.

As I have discussed earlier, *Nightwood* is ironically and self-consciously narrative from its auspicious birthroom beginning. Replete with the telling of stories, especially those of the long-winded Dr.

Matthew O'Connor, *Nightwood* is a novel about narrating in which the narratives the doctor produces do not quite match nor even really articulate with the narratives of the characters conveyed by the novel's third person narrator. O'Connor's narratives do articulate, however, a certain wisdom about telling. "Life is not to be told," the doctor says, "call it as loud as you like, it will not tell itself" (129). Matthew's commentary is more about the nature and style of the text itself; it is akin to Barthes's *The Pleasure of the Text*, a guide for and an integral part of the text's pleasure and bliss that exist in a perverse relation to the novel's framing narratives of pathetic reproduction, misaligned romance, and the decline of meaning.

The characters upon whom both Matthew and the novel's narrator focus are associated not by some essential allure (like Freud's magical attraction between the sexes) that we anticipate in a traditional heteronarrative but rather by coincidence (contiguous seats at a circus), Matthew's perverse design (taking Felix with him to see Robin), and a logic of pathological identification (Jenny Petherbridge's "squatting"). Robin's serial couplings denote diversions rather than any logic of joinder. While we might understand that absence of magical attraction as a feature of the characters' homosexuality, rationalizing oppositions still exist between Robin and any of her partners (male/female, blond/brunette, young/old). None of these oppositions governs the novel's relationships, which are typified by projection (what each of them wishes or takes Robin to be) rather than by either partner's desire (or aversion) to coupling. Within their fantasies, each submits to Robin's will, which is the perverse will to deviate, to play out the unproprietary where propriety and property have no place. Joinder is prevented by a kind of wandering of attention; *Nightwood*'s characters, as Elizabeth Meese observes, "refus[e] any identification or transference."[27]

As the primary productions of the text, narrative and narrating are disjointed, not only within the doctor's stories of erratic and perverse night denizens but in the relation among Matthew's commentary, the character's narratives, and the novel's sad little story of Volkbein reproduction. This is not so much a destabilization of "the nature of narrative itself" as Donna Gerstenberger concludes, caused by the novel's undermining of the "grounds for categorization."[28] Rather, narrative is both there and disjointed, dislocated from categorical binaries that continue to exist but that have become irrelevant. This disjuncture among

the novel's narratives, seemingly natural because it is perverse, discon-
nects the literal cause/effect relation between narrative and production
(narrating produces a coherent story where parts relate to the whole)
and the more metaphorical relation between narrative and (re)produc-
tion as that is figured in the joinder of opposites, a return to equilibrium, the production of knowledge, insight, or in death.[29] This lack of
connection exists not only because the novel avoids the productive
alignment of sameness and difference but also because it arrays the perverse, including three lesbian characters, not as against the hetero but in
relation to the larger fabrications of cosmic/psychological meaning or
lack thereof the doctor fabricates. And because his wisdom is a logic of
the perverse—of the ways the stream doesn't flow or the flowing of
errant streams—the perverse plays with and within the novel's larger
parody of reproduction and meaning, not as its opposite but as the
now-revealed alternative that underlies and sustains any heteronarrative. Bringing this relation between the heteronarrative and the perverse into stark relief, *Nightwood* dismantles heteronarrative. Pulling it
into its parts, not completely but as narrative might function as a productive agency, *Nightwood* detaches heterosexuality from its ideological
supports and looses it as one perversity among many whose telling generates something other than the story we expect.

Nightwood, thus, performs not a different narrative but an analysis of
the relations among narrative, sexuality, and ideology and in so doing
links that analysis to a blissful style. But as Meese has pointed out, the
novel's reception as even a lesbian text has been reluctant (44–45).
While exploiting the perverse might be a way to show narrative up, it
probably cannot force its alteration or demise. And while *Nightwood* is
a text that writes its pleasure and is overcome with bliss, it is neither the
repository of the monstrous Bertha Harris would wish it to be nor the
sustained challenge (lesbian or not) to dominant culture I might wish
it to be.

It does, however, suggest a beginning, a way of displacing the heteronarrative, which in its analytic performance reveals the terms of culture while emphasizing a different pleasure in reading. *Nightwood*'s
digressions, ruminations, and texture of language furnish a substitute for
the more oedipal narrative gratification of mastery and totalized meaning. If other modes of organizing language can be recognized as meaningful in a way similar to the way *Nightwood* compels a recognition of
its imagistic metonymies and wandering associations, then the hege-

mony of heteronarrative might be loosened, making it, like Felix's marriage, only one in a number of possible modes of relation, of meaning,
suggestion, and bliss. By providing competing, compatible, and otherwise differing arrangements of language, pattern, and repetition, the
heteronarrative might take its place among them rather than dominat-
ing and organizing their deployment. And while displacing heteronarrative does not automatically decenter its intertwined ideologies, perhaps by enabling other arrangements, heteroideology might be decen-
tered if not dethroned.

As the work of Wittig, Brossard, and Barnes might indicate, narrative is difficult to displace in any politically efficacious way, but any
sense of failure around narrative comes from the oppositional structure
of narrative itself that dictates that narrative's disimbrication from heteroideology must be total, if it is to be disimbricated at all. The
moments of disarticulation, catachresis, and bliss produced as the perverse in much writing could provide another kind of narrative if
somehow we could only dismiss the ideology of narrative totality from
our perceptions. In a way that is what each of these three novels
does—but of course, it is the ideology of narrative totality that has
always been the problem. In a culture where (re)production bestows
meaning, moments of bliss seem to have very little power and yet for
the moment they are powerful indeed.

CHAPTER FIVE

Come As You Are

1

Nothing in man—not even his body—is sufficiently stable to serve as the basis for self-recognition or for understanding other men. The traditional devices for constructing a comprehensive view of history and for retracing the past as a patient and continuous development must be systematically dismantled.
—Michel Foucault, "Nietzsche, Genealogy, History," p. 153

I began the previous two chapters hoping to be able to say something optimistic about "positive" portrayals of lesbian characters in popular culture and in the writings of lesbian authors. I find myself instead weighing the virtues of narrative visibility—the idea that a lesbian protagonist or good role model will alter public perceptions—against a firmly implanted heteronarrative ideology. Although instances of sudden lesbian visibility in narrative catalyze heterosexual closure (as in *Switch*, for example), casting the lesbian as a protagonist or sympathetic character seemingly portends a lesbian victory, especially in the narrative logic by which visibility and identity stand as the masterful rejoinders to conflict or disequilibrium. The sense of social enfranchisement occasioned by the mainstream appearance of sympathetic lesbian characters reflects a politics of visibility understood as an effective beginning to socio-political gains by lesbians and gay men.

This chapter examines how heteronarrative informs the choice and deployment of political strategies, particularly those linked to identity, identification, and visibility. While these processes belong to the registers of the Imaginary and the visible, they are also completely bound up with narrative, existing as narrative products, attached to a particular narrative shape and set of assumptions, and inflected by narrative heteroideology. In fact, visibility and identification only exist as political possibilities because of their narrative situation and they only work within a generally unacknowledged, but intrinsic narrative frame. Beginning with visibility politics' narrative environment, this penultimate chapter examines outing, role models, identification, and identity as they captivate the political imagination; because of their heteronarrative engagement, they generally work against the very aims they set out to assure. The point is to discern how, if we understand narrative's heteroideology, we can make narrative work for positive cultural change.

Coming Into View

Stressing the efficacy of visibility per se, proponents of outing vaunt visibility as politically necessary, arguing that outing will make visible an already-visible personality's sexuality, will provide "role models," furnish "magnets" to attract others to the movement, refute the internalized homophobia and self-limitation incident to secrecy, produce a more politically threatening group by swelling the number of visible gays and lesbians, and send the message that gays and lesbians are everywhere and therefore can neither be stereotyped nor denied access to places they have long inhabited.[1] Given contemporary society's penchant for media, modern culture's ideological bias toward the visual, and the trope of visibility inherent to the closet metaphor itself, a reliance on visibility might seem both a natural and a canny political ploy.

Certainly visibility as attached to role models and cultural perception seems to have helped the struggles of racial minorities and women. There is an important difference, however, between categories constructed through visible difference such as race, and the categories of sexuality whose primary construction is in relation to the heteronarrative rather than to the visual. While visibility might logically work to challenge precisely the conditions by which such racial and gender differences are perceived, for lesbians and gay males, visibility is linked to identity instead of to the constitution of sexual categories. For gay males and lesbians, visibility thus leads to identity rather than to any deconstructive consciousness of the constructedness of the category *gay*. Even imagining visibility as a politically effective ploy for the establishment of gay male and lesbian rights and recognition means understanding visibility (whether simply affirmative [coming out] or politically aggressive [outing]) as bound up with a knowledge of identity.

Posed by outing advocates as an all-purpose answer, visibility obscures the nature of the oppressions it presumably alleviates. The political problem for which visibility is posited as an answer is not so much homophobia but rather, as Larry Gross suggests, the invisibility of both the quantity and type of examples that might allay the fear that founds homophobia and that renders gays and lesbians ineffectual as a perceived community. In other words, if the world knew what we were really like, they wouldn't be afraid of us and even if they were, our sheer numbers and influence would protect us. Oppressive invisibility is the product of both the closeted secrecy of many gays and lesbians and of media "inning," or active suppression of information about any homosexual way of life. Rather than being intrinsic to lesbian- or gay maleness, the argument goes, invisibility is thrust upon gay males and lesbians as the deliberate suppression of correct information. As the prime site of cultural visibility, the media becomes the setting for political action to correct this invisibility; correction proceeds according to a victory narrative where visibility performs the overdetermined counter to homophobic acts of suppression and supplies a resolution to the misalignment of the "inner" truth that numerous well-adjusted and successful lesbians and gay men exist and the outer appearance that only a few culturally challenging "queers" do.

Predictably, the problem visibility appears to resolve, then, is invisibility—which is a product of the very same logic that produces visibility as an answer. Like visibility, invisibility really stands for knowledge; in this narrative, invisibility represents a misleading knowledge that contradicts the true state of affairs—that there are more and better lesbians and gay males than we are able to see. Together, visibility and invisibility refer obsessively to a knowledge of sexuality that performs a disciplinary function. When visibility is the privileged register of knowledge's proliferation and consumption, it conceals even the telling asymmetry that the sexual identities in question are the only sexual identities that must be rendered visible in the first place.[2] It must also skew the dynamic in which the possibility of a lack of visible corporeal markers is a part of gay or lesbian erotics.

And such visible identity doesn't simply shine like some seductive queer beacon; it, too, masks a complex narrative of knowledge and identification by which identity is significant in the first place. Recognizing that in relation to issues of sexuality visibility is really a metaphor of knowledge about identity acknowledges the more complex narrative status of the political staging of visibility that seems (in a logic by which surfaces reflect essences) to have been superficial in the first place. The controversy over the ethics of outing, attentive as it is to questions of morality and privacy, rarely questions the efficacy of visibility itself, worrying not about the logic by which visibility is posed as an answer (and in like fashion, invisibility posed as the problem) but rather about how to balance questions about the "violation of journalistic and human ethics" with the idea that outing is "a necessary political weapon of an oppressed minority whose pervasive invisibility fuels their oppression" (Gross 353). Because of its emphasis on visibility as both problem and answer, outing, though a spectacular, media-invested, arguably pragmatic praxis, misses the point, falling instead for the lure of mastery offered by the heteronarrative positioning of visibility as a proper end and, ironically, playing the proper part of the homo in the story. Visibility provides the illusion of progress in an entirely retrospective dynamic, an illusion that, if taken literally, furnishes additional justification for sticking to visibility as political praxis.

Visibility's implicit heteronarrative, however, undoes its political efficacy for gay males and lesbians from the start. At the beginning of the heteronarrative, what is first visible (i.e., a lesbian posing as straight) represents a posture that becomes retrospectively false in relation to the knowledge produced by the narrative of correct identity (she is a lesbian). What this means, however, is that this visible lesbian identity, even if it seems to be the story's end product, in fact defines the narrative's disequilibrium in the first place (she was a lesbian and didn't show it). Terminal visibility, as the metaphor of public knowledge, is thus produced by inviting or forcing a joinder between appearances and a preexisting "private" or closet knowledge about the quantity and "quality" of lesbians and gay males. As the end product of this heteronarrative, knowledge exists in a temporal paradox, preceding and engendering its own production, a paradox hidden by the fact that what the story seems to produce is not knowledge, since knowledge is transformed from private gay knowledge to public recognition, but visibility as the condition of knowledge's recognition and proliferation. The heteronarrative represents simultaneous and contradictory takes on a politics of visibility both as the amalgamation of knowledge and visibility that will engender cultural change and as the revelation of sexual identity that promotes the status quo.

The very spectacle of visibility (such as that enjoyed by media stars) calls out for the revelation of politically relevant identity as the proper end to its story. And proper ends produce more stories as the narrative of visibility proliferates itself through culture. Visibility becomes an end in itself, depending upon role modeling, emulation, and the production of many lesbian and gay male protagonists (more versions of the same visibility narrative) for its effectiveness. Like lesbian authors who try to shift public perceptions by making lesbians protagonists, visibility politics tries to strong-arm opinion by changing the image of an identity within the same logic that produced that identity, instead of trying to identify and alter the process by which identities are produced and situated and by which visibility/invisibility itself becomes the problem.

A Narrative Come-Uppance

The seeming paradoxes of arguments about the value of visibility—that invisibility is oppressive and that attempts to eliminate oppression through visibility reiterate oppressive ideology—are not so paradoxical if we trace the assumptions that sustain credence in the mechanism of visibility/identity. The political value of visibility for lesbians and gay males depends upon two underlying (and generally unrecognized) convictions: 1) a belief in the social and ideological efficacy of narrative as a transformative agency; and 2) faith in the social and ideological agency of identifications. The first assumption reflects the pervasiveness of narrative's transformative dynamic that constantly converts disorder into order and mastery. A belief in narrative's transformative power is a product of narrative's trajectory toward mastery. And although narrative seems mainly to organize or recount past events, we increasingly perceive it as an available mode of real-life transformation—something always in progress in which we might participate. One obvious example of narrative's cultural shift to the present (even future) tense is the way lotteries and other commercial come-ons (Ed McMahon, for example) invite consumers to live out their own transforming story by situating each of us in the position of winning protagonist. Despite the fact that for 9,999,999 out of 10 million people this narrative is a dream, participation in contests and lotteries is a narratively induced real-life attempt at a very-narratively defined transformation that inveigles some of us to act according to our narrative role and buy lottery tickets or affix stickers to and send back Publisher's Clearing House Sweepstakes entries. Our belief in narrative's transformative power, then, comes not only from its provision of an example of mastery, but also from situating narrative as an effective mode of change.

While simply being there to be seen (the first logic of visibility) seems to represent the victory of some larger unseen struggle against invisibility, media visibility as the goal of outing or the aim of a more docile liberationist tactic supports a second logic in which visibility generates counternormative understandings that will eventually result in wider cultural acceptance of lesbians and gay men. This second logic represents another version of the same heteroideological narrative; correct knowledge meets incorrect knowledge and produces a corrected knowledge in the form of visible social change. Although this is a very nice story, as a foundation for any kind of political action it presents the problem of how the confrontation of correct and incorrect necessarily effects change, especially when *correct* and *incorrect* are already ideologically defined. The transformation from knowledge to change occurs magically; the metamorphosis reveals neither the operation of reason or justice (except in so far as we might optimistically believe that right makes might) nor the processes of heteroideological conjoinder of correct and incorrect into some rectified progeny. Rather, the presentation of confrontation requires another more covert and oblique narrative of identification and empathy with the lesbian and gay personae who embody positive and visible lesbian or gay male identity. Visibility, thus, stands in the place of transformation itself.

In this second logic, visibility presumes identification and identification is presumably made through the register of the visible. Both visibility and identification depend on an emphasis on character whose correct identity or identification occupies the place of narrative mastery. Combined with a belief in narrative's transformative power as well as an increasing emphasis on protagonists as "real-life" people, visibility and identification contribute to and follow a shift to a character-centered consumption of narrative that, in turn, fuels and supports the politics of visibility. But this even tighter causal circle of visibility and identification not only further conceals its underlying narrative rationale but also obscures real problems with a process of identification that is itself narrative. And an emphasis on character and visibility is not in the least radical or subversive; seeing the effects of narrative's power on characters whose lives are transformed both produces and reinforces faith in a naturalized heteroideology in whose form and by whose agency such transformations are accomplished.

Just as visibility eclipses the narrative that situates it as a triumphant resolution, characters absorb and represent the ideological weight of narrative transformations, acting as synecdoches of ideological positionings. Because characters both screen and imply a triumphant heteronarrative, narrative appears to be flexible about the kinds of characters who can conceivably occupy the position of protagonist. As I have already discussed, lesbians can be protagonists, but only as long as they operate within the heteronarrative dynamic. And because of the sexual ideology by which the exposure of lesbian sexual identity is significant, lesbians can be protagonists only *as lesbians*. The lesbian character's personal sexual trait acts as the screen that hides the heterologic by which the lesbian is significant in the first place and the narrative ideology by which her occupation of the protagonist position is a recuperation. Even when a lesbian is a protagonist, whether in a fictional narrative or a "real-life" admission, the sexual ideology implicit in twentieth-century understandings of narrative does not work to counter the dramatic maintenance of sexual categories located in the characters' personae (female and male heterosexual, homosexual, lesbian) but, rather, resists the disestablishment of those categories or any shift, slippage, or disruption in their ideological inter-relation that would enable a subversion of the sex/capital/reproductive system as narratively replayed and sustained. Thus, confessing lesbian identity may gain a certain audience share (and lose another) within an identity/consumer logic, but it also forever marks any celebrity who so confesses. She becomes a special case whose artistry or prowess is subordinated to the spectacle of her sexual identity.[3]

This emphasis on visibility, character, and image actually prevents other kinds of political action by seeming to fill the space of praxis and of possible response. Making the lesbian fit the heteronarrative provides the illusion of mastery that prevents analysis of the story itself, resulting not only in a belief in visibility as a political panacea ("we're here, we're queer, get used to it") but also in an endorsement of the narrative ideology by which lesbians and gay men are contained. Once a lesbian character is positively portrayed, once narrative seems to work for us, somehow we think we no longer need to tinker with—or even recognize—the mechanism. The ideological insistence of narrative with its offer of closure, pleasure, and mastery underwrites our credence in the efficacy of the highly visible protagonist, who, when lesbian, shares in the mainstream booty of narrative largess.

The victoriously visible lesbian protagonist represents finally neither a relaxation of heteronormative thought nor the political or social liberation of lesbians in general, although we might be justified in believing that the portrayal of lesbians as "real people" protagonists represents an affirmative shift in real-life attitudes. To some degree visibility does represent change in the sense that any representation that can survive the censoring powers of commercial sponsors must be acceptable to those sponsors' perception of a substantial buying public. Heteronarrative recontains the supposed social transformation represented by the appearance of lesbian-positive narratives, while staging the appearance of a more liberal and less-heterosexist universe. And in so far as visibility might represent change, it becomes a restrictive barrier to any further change.

The heteronarrative politics of visibility is also reiterated in the narrative attached to the role model. A mainstay of visibility politics, the role model works on a set of unexamined assumptions about the identificatory mechanisms stimulated by the mere fact of visibility. Cited as a rationale by outing enthusiasts, and as something we all would like to see on television and in the media, a role model is someone who, exhibiting an aspect of an oppressed identity, a) succeeds in being visible; b) succeeds in making his/her oppressed identity visible; and c) succeeds in some aspect of Western capitalist production. In Horatio Alger fashion the role model is testimony to the ability of an oppressed minority character to occupy the position of protagonist in the victory narrative; his or her very presence is proof that the story can belong to anyone. Establishing this ascendancy in the heteroideological narrative of Western capitalist production provides hope that those seeing such exemplary instances will link themselves to the character by virtue of shared identity and thereby understand themselves as potential protagonists able to live out the same success story.

Apart from role modeling's obvious ideological problems such as its capitalist inscription of the heteronarrative, role modeling also depends upon some account of identification to work. In role model logic identification is conditioned both by an understanding of positive cultural values and an assumption of similarity. One does not identify with bad, but visible models (one does, but they are not called role models) and that kind of identification serves no "positive" political purpose. One presumably does not identify with those who are unlike one, especially when the other terms of the success narrative depend upon aspects of culture or identity one does not share. But seeing oneself as a potential protagonist and being that protagonist are two different things. Perhaps the vision of success might enable hope of its reality, but the mechanism upon which all of this depends is identification, which, as a narrative process itself, may be more a heteroideological fiction than a useful assumption of praxis.

2

Coming Around

Why would the problem of identification not be, in general, the essential problem of the political?
—Philippe Lacoue-Labarthe, *Typography*, p. 300

Identification is the mode of joinder that brings narrative and life together. While narrative's transformations may appear to be internal to any specific story, social benefits come from the assumption that narrative's content will effect, reinforce, and shift social behavior. The mechanism for such affect is not simply narrative's irresistible offer of mastery but also some form of imitation that initiates the story's reproduction elsewhere. Imitation is understood in terms of identification, a more psychically specific mechanism whose assumed site in the person (instead of in culture or in the story) presumably accounts for how narratives get from culture to the individual, from example to praxis. Whether one identifies with a character (via the notion of "role model") or with agency in relation to the power protagonists seem to wield, identification is assumed as the mechanism by which narratives afford pleasure as narratives and provide the possibility of social transformation.

Identifications are not made in the absence of narrative, either express or implied, which suggests that in some way narrative and identification are different modalities of the same ideology. In other words, we understand identification in the way we do because identification is both narratively informed and premised upon the same reproductive heteroideology as narrative. Even understandings of the process of identification follow the larger pattern of narrative; identification proceeds from difference (or unperceived sameness) to recognition to a form of joinder that reproduces elements of the protagonist in the reader or viewer as wishes for attributes and power, as imitated actions, or as empathy with narrative position. Understanding the relations between narrative and identification means taking into account the ways both enact a specific dynamic by which differences are produced then conjoined to spawn a product that, in the case of identification is either part of an identity or pleasure or even some life change.

Identification is also preeminently narrative in the sense that identifications with characters or positions in narrative are produced not so much by image gestalt but more by a self-placement in a narrative economy that is partially determined by the dynamics of that narrative. For example, because narratives focus on protagonists, whether or not we are like specific protagonists, we can and do identify with them because of their position in the narrative dynamic that invests power and effect in the protagonist. Hence, I, as a white, feminist lesbian can identify with James Bond; the dynamics of narrative that underwrite identification enable multiple contradictory identifications with completely or largely dissimilar characters.

But just as narrative is often defined by its end and its action displaced into actors, identification is also sometimes conflated with identity. Identity and identification form a tautology where identities catalyze identifications and identifications produce identities. If identity is a larger version of sexual identity, then it functions as the self-delimiting measure of the self-sameness that both inhibits and catalyzes narrative. Identity as an end is an end in itself and really the self-absorbed middle of a larger story. The relation of identity and identification replicates the self-limiting dynamic of the coming out narrative in its tautology, retroactivity, and illusion of mastery.

In 1970 at the heroic stage of burgeoning feminist activism, Radicalesbians published a short essay, "The Woman-Identified

Woman," which offered what turned out to be an influential analysis of the relation between the category *lesbian* and patriarchal oppression of women—between identity and identification. Working in relation to a feminist environment that marginalized lesbians (when it considered them at all), Radicalesbians argue that marking as lesbian those women who refuse a male-identified role would challenge male oppression of women. The male-identified role accepted by many women is one way women cooperate in misogyny:

> Women hate both themselves and other women. They try to escape by identifying with the oppressor, living through him, gaining status and identity from his ego, his power, his accomplishments And by not identifying with other "empty vessels" like themselves, women resist relating on all levels to other women who will reflect their own oppression, their own secondary status, their own self-hate. *(176)*

Homophobia, Radicalesbians contend, is complicit with this male identification; their conclusion is that to liberate themselves from a sexist hegemony women need to identify with women: "Only women can give each other a new sense of self. That identity we have to develop with reference to ourselves, and not in relation to men. This consciousness is a revolutionary force from which all else will follow, for ours is an organic revolution" (176).

This victory narrative poses identification as the means to an end from "which all else will follow." Identifying with women instead of with the oppressor will raise a new consciousness of female identity and disarm part of the oppressor's means of preserving his dominance. Radicalesbians' appeal to identification as a mode of political action overtly acknowledges what has often been assumed by a politics premised upon identities. Presuming that identification is the mechanism by which individuals relate to and form ties to groups is linked to the assumption that one will identify with groups that exhibit something in common with one's identity and/or interests and that one's identity will be in part constructed from one's affiliation with groups.

The centrality of identification as a means to a political end underwrites many attempts to understand the interrelations among lesbians and their potential for political action. In 1990 Bonnie Zimmerman understands lesbian fiction as a similar means to a political end:

> The significance of lesbian fiction lies not so much in the indi-
> vidual text abstracted from its political and social context, but in
> the genre taken *as a whole*, in its interplay of ideas, symbols, images,
> and myths. The purpose of this writing—self-aware or not—is to
> create lesbian identity and culture, to say *this* is what it mans to be
> lesbian, *this* is how lesbians are, *this* is what lesbians believe."[4]

Assuming, but not specifically positing identification as the agency by
which this fiction works to define lesbian community, Zimmerman
locates literary representation as an important locus for identification;
"Lesbian resistance to this oppression," she says later, "necessarily lies in
telling our stories and naming ourselves" (74).

This politicized mode of identification presumes an attraction of like
to like; lesbians will discover and reinforce their lesbian identity in a literature addressed to them. The search for this likeness does not stop with
recognitions that identity might be contingent, fragmented, or illusory.
Many of the authors in the recent *The Lesbian Postmodern*, for example,
evince a nostalgia for identification; recognizing that identity is constructed and contingent seems to produce a desperate need to identify,
if only with the very fact of contingency (i.e. *as* the postmodern) or with
figures who question the primacy of identity.[5] Identification represents
a conservative trend, a reluctant and perhaps understandable difficulty
with leaving behind the comforts of the story, the reassurance of assimilation, and a belief of the liberatory value of the mere fact of being a
lesbian, since in a very real sense, being a lesbian does represent some
kind of victory.

What is at stake in privileging identity as a politically useful category? How can we understand identification and identity differently or
displace the concept in such a way that we are not trapped by the narcissistic illusion of perpetual self-production?

3

Becoming

When she fell in love it was with a perfect fury of accumulated dishonesty; she
became instantly a dealer in second-hand and therefore incalculable emotions. As,
from the solid archives of usage, she had stolen or appropriated the dignity of speech,

so she appropriated the most passionate love that she knew, Nora's for Robin. She
was a "squatter" by instinct.
—Djuna Barnes, *Nightwood*, p. 68

Jenny Petherbridge, the "squatter" in *Nightwood*, invades and inhabits
the narratives of others. Identifying with Nora's role as lover, Jenny literally takes her place with Robin, becoming not Nora but she who
occupies Nora's place, consuming both role and object. Shamelessly
stealing an identity, Jenny is attracted to the lover's position by the narrative disposition of that part in other women's lives rather than
through any recognition of a similarity to Nora or an attraction to
Robin. Made through narrative, Jenny's identifications also represent a
narrative of their own, a story that ends with a happy merger, not with
either a character (Nora) or with another person in "real" life (Robin)
but rather with being one with Nora's role. The embarrassing revelation of emptiness exemplified by Jenny's overzealous, overly embodied
identifications points to her misapprehension (or canny understanding)
of the nature of identification. Making grotesquely literal identification's typically figurative, fantasmatic processes, Jenny's identificatory
incarnations betray identification's consumptive narrative.

The relation between Jenny's embodied identifications and her anxious, disjointed sense of self—what we might call an identity—also
clarifies the connection between identification and identity. The way
her identifications actually fabricate an identity presents what seems to
be a travesty of both identification and identity, the reduction of an
unconscious cumulative process into the tawdry willed absurdity of
Jenny's desperation. There is nothing really Jenny nor is there a quintessentially "Jenny" identity; Jenny is a composite of effects from elsewhere, a pastiche of borrowings, a collection of stolen photographs and
proliferated miniature elephants, a visible nervous anatomy of the dangerous conflation of identification and identity that haunts assumptions
about narrative pleasure and the value of identity as the synthetic victor of narrative conflict.

If the empty Jenny is, however, only the product of her appropria-
tive identifications, what determines her choice of positions—lover, for
example, as opposed to beloved—with which to identify? Is it the
attractions of specific positions within a narrative dynamic? Is it the
function of some predisposition, perhaps some identity, that determines
which roles are more attractive to her? If Jenny only lives vicariously, if

she is only the sum of stolen parts, what predisposition might she have except one whose premier function is occupation, substitution, and consumption instead of creation or production?

Coming to Be

The ego is the sum of the identifications of the subject, with all that that implies as to its radical contingency. If you allow me to give an image of it, the ego is like the superimposition of various coats borrowed from what I would call the bric-à-brac of its props department.

—Jacques Lacan, *Seminar II*, p. 155

Nightwood's portrait of Jenny as the squatter whose identificatory difficulties sunder Nora and Robin enacts a meditation on the relations among narrative, identification, and identity. If *Nightwood* is perverse in its narrative, it is forthright in its exposure of identification's imbrication in narrative. *Nightwood's* proliferation of awkwardly narrativized identifications—Jenny, Felix, Dr. O'Connor—demonstrates the connections among narrative, sexuality, and identification in the register of the literal and the perverse, illustrating the complex ideological stakes of reproduction, consumption, and loss through the characters' labored hyperbolic assumption of others' roles, clothing, and histories. If Jenny's identificatory predilections are cannily correct, identification is a term of conjunction between the individual and culture, an effect of discourse, a motive for consumption, the copula by which cultural significance is transmitted from the general to the specific.

Like *Nightwood* (or *Nightwood* like them), narrative theories and psychoanalysis understand identification as one way to bring together elements of different orders—the social and the individual, narrative and psyche—to produce both cultural engagement and ego. Making a nineteenth-century appearance roughly coterminous with the appearance of the term *sexuality*, "identification" in the sense "of becoming or making oneself one with another in feeling, interest, or action" shares in the same sexualized bourgeois ideology of capitalist (re)production. If the *OED* definition is any indication, identification's conceptualization echoes the caginess of structuralist narrative theories that avoid any specification of just how that coming together is motivated or accomplished. To borrow the terms of one of those structuralist accounts, identification works like the Todorovian "verb" to narrative's "adjective," acting, on a cultural level, as the force that brings together narrative and reader, image and viewer, and role model and potential success story. In the realm of the intrapsychical, identification is the catalytic activity by which the subject joins with image, object, or desiring position. *Nightwood*'s identifications bring culture and psyche too close together in a travesty melodrama of false identities.

Unlike *Nightwood*'s rendering of identification's disjunctive impropriety, most representations of identification seem to be missing difference. Identification's etymology appears to trade the vital differences that scuttle through narrative's theories for a shameless sameness that should, in narrative's heteroideology, locate identification in the place of Brooks's potential short circuit, the self-delimiting stasis of a mirror-like fixation on self-same, the homosexual. As the "woman-identified woman" illustrates, the mechanism of identification appears to be an attraction of same to same in a narrative of joinder. "Becoming . . . one with another" recalls the nostalgic attraction for a previous wholeness that pulls Aristophanes' celestomorphic beings back together.

Since the product of this coming together seems to be an identification, a metaphorically enlarged or doubled self or a consciousness of likeness, the typical narrative of identification might present an example of how the joinder of sames is productive instead of arresting, and productive precisely as the result of bringing sames together. But identification produces itself, replaying the self-cycling narrative of identity we first saw in the coming out story (which is, after all, mainly a narrative of identification). Neither identification nor identity survive long as ends in themselves because they are neither produced by nor productive of differences in an ideology that values heterology. Representing a sameness economy, they become temporary stops—the locus of the difference to difference—on the way to another story and a different end.

Identification as sameness, however, is produced by heteronarrative rather than being an effect of some intrinsic identificatory sameness. Situated in the place of same, identification is thus depicted as same; depicted as same, it is situated as same. While this circular analysis seems tautological or at best an adherence to the very ideology I am trying to identify, even the perception that identification is a logic of sameness is an aspect of the heteroideology by which sameness is the necessary difference to difference and by which identification is different from desire or mastery or even knowledge of anything other than self.

In the context of this identificatory narrative, Jenny Petherbridge's identifications seem perverse because they try to weld obvious disparities in an economy driven by similarities. If identity, like the ego, is dressed in layers of bric-à-brac, Jenny's clothes are more than unusually ill-fitting. The unseemliness of her squatting comes from the dissimilarity between her manifest persona and the identifications she tries to make; she twists the story in the ill-managed gestures she employs to wrench identifications into identities. Making visible our assumptions about identification's presumptive sameness, Jenny's perversely awkward actions demonstrate the extent to which we normally suppose identification to be an economy of similitude even as it sometimes might represent the dreams, hopes, or delusions of similarity nursed by the obviously dissimilar.

But Jenny's example also illustrates how identification, despite its gloss of sameness, is also a negotiation of differences. If Jenny's identifications exhibit the discomfiture of the unsuitable, they also show the extent to which identification renders differences as same. Identification's differences are discounted in favor of some imagined similarity in narrative position, trait, or identity. Understanding identification as an economy of sameness thus requires the repression of differences. Clearly portraying an unwieldy measure of difference, *Nightwood* best illustrates how absurd identifications are or how courageous.

The question, then, is why heteronarrative requires that identification be situated as sameness, if identification actually manages sameness and difference or sameness in relation to difference. Neither identification's self-productive quality nor its facade of excessive sameness seem to account for the almost careless attributions of presumed similarity that sustain discussions of lesbian identifications. Radicalesbians' appeal to identification, for example, assumes there is no difficulty with women identifying with women except that posed by the countervalent force of patriarchy. The problem for them, in fact, is the political dissonance of identifying against one's own interests manifested by male-identified women. Zimmerman's account of the function of lesbian literature presumes that lesbian readers will necessarily identify with lesbian texts and find their place in the community the texts share in constructing. Both assume a sameness linked to identity necessary to sustain a notion of lesbian community that becomes the bulwark against heterosexual hegemony and the political dominance of the gender system.

But what if identification is glossed as sameness to hide its negotiation of differences in a sort of political teleology? Repressing differences would serve a political purpose if it is important to make and sustain a community understood as a collection of those with similar purpose and identifications. The political narrative produced through an understanding of identification as same is, as I have previously pointed out, self-cycling and self-containing. The consciousness it produces is temporary, fantasmatic, and utopian, fraught with guilt, tension, and zealous policing spurred by the differences identification represses. But if the narrative of identification as sameness were discarded in favor of a narrative of identification *as the management of differences*, how might we understand the value of identification?

Beneath the tidy, but mythical self-same circle of its veneer, identification is the alibi for a range of contradictory, sometimes incoherent positionings. In its guise as the surface narrative of the attraction of sames, identification is a cover story for a more complex negotiation of differences whose crafting into ego results not in any unified whole entity or identity, but rather in the split subject and multiple fragmented identities. Its organizing logic is neither similarity nor opposition, but narrative itself as an ideologically-informed cultural dynamic that distributes various personae in ideologically inflected parts. Identification *is* narrative. As a catalyst, as one of Barthes's "cardinal functions," or Todorov's "verbs," identification actually converts difference into sameness, managing the two in a neat replication of productive heteronarrative dynamics. In this sense identification as sameness covers and disavows narrative's failure to produce a whole represented in the differences and dissolution that adhere to endings. At the same time identification provides a narrative by which narrative itself is consumed.

This heteronarrative version of identification is not the real "truth" of identification that betrays the lie of its ideological sameness; rather, the surface/depth, sameness/difference interplay of these two different narratives of identification constitutes its ideological rendering and enables its function. That its politics of difference is masked by a gloss of sameness replicates the way identification works as the arbiter of difference and sameness, the mode by which an illusion of sameness transmutes unnecessary conflict in the service of a greater wholeness to come.

Heteronarrative's displacement of identification into the locus of sameness functions as a way of occupying even sameness with a narrative whose function is to process difference productively. Although it appears to be a way of disavowing differences, identification is also a way of disavowing sameness at the point in narrative where sameness seems to reign. And this is why *Nightwood* is really so perverse: it exposes identification's operations of disavowal by showing just how forced identifications really are. If sameness is the alibi of identification and if identification is the way differences are rendered same, then by parading as sameness, identification stands in the place of a scary lack of difference. In a fetish logic, identification becomes the sameness that is missing, disavowing the possible lack of difference that is so frighteningly deadly to heteroideology. While this might seem overly complex or far-fetched, identification has become a kind of political fetish, not because it consolidates sameness in politically effective ways or disavows disruptive differences, but because it stands in as an arbiter of difference and sameness that makes sure difference won't disappear.

Identification is part of heteronarrative's middle at the same time that it seems not a part of narrative at all but an appendage. It poses as a condition of reception, acquisition, and growth instead of a narrative unto itself or a part of narrative's intrinsic dynamic. Identification's relegation to narrative's murky middle and marginal edges makes its pervasive operation ubiquitously insistent; it seemingly operates in multiple cultural sites as the unspecified go-between in processes of consumption. By casting identification both as a narrative part and as sometimes apart, the workings of heteronarrative displace into identification's ubiquity and disguise the very different play of differences identification actually negotiates.

Identification's "cover" of sameness also enables its subordination to narrative, a hierarchization necessary to the exigencies of reproduction that demand not identity but the joinder of identities. But in its negotiation of differences, identification's narrative of sameness also masks heteronarrative processes. Thus the power of identification comes not from its metaphorically median location but rather from its performative masquerade that perversely hides its heteronarrative of difference under a studied gloss of sameness. Identification is heteronarrative in drag.

Freud's Comeback

As the productive manager of differences that might otherwise threaten mastery, identification's story parallels the narrative of sexuality—

though in Freud's work identification is a late bloomer. Freud initially mentions identification in a letter to Fliess (February 8, 1897, and Manuscript L of May 2, 1897) and first develops an incipient theory of hysterical identification in his analysis of the Witty Butcher's Wife's dream in *The Interpretation of Dreams*. His patient, the wife of a butcher, believed she had had a dream that contradicted Freud's theory that all dreams represent the fulfillment of a wish. Dreaming that she wanted to have a supper party but couldn't because all of the stores were closed and she couldn't buy smoked salmon, the patient, according to Freud, presents the dream as a challenge to him.

Insisting on analysis as the only way to determine the wish content of the dream, Freud proves his patient wrong by showing how her dream of the unfulfilled wish to have a supper party was the fulfillment of a wish that her slim friend (in whom she imagined her husband was interested) not have the smoked salmon that would make her fatter and thus more attractive to the patient's husband. Since the patient had also disclosed that she wanted her husband not to grant her wish for a daily caviar sandwich, Freud discerns what he calls an "hysterical identification" between the patient and her friend. Tracing the meaning of the absence of smoked salmon that would have enabled the supper party to the friend's fondness for smoked salmon, and linking the wished-for salmon to the wished-for caviar, Freud ties his patient's wish for an unfulfilled wish to her wish that her friend's wish be unfulfilled. He concludes that by dreaming that she had an unfulfilled wish, his patient had put herself in the place of her friend in the scenario of the unfulfilled wish, not by becoming her but by standing in for her in a representative capacity:

> Identification is a highly important factor in the mechanism of hysterical symptoms. It enables patients to express in their symptoms not only their own experiences but those of a large number of other people; it enables them, as it were, to suffer on behalf of a whole crowd of people and to act all the parts of the play single-handed. *(182–183)*

The representative quality of this identification is acutely narrative; it is the substitution of one person for another in a story. According to Freud, his patient, working through displacement and substitution, replaces her friend as the suffering protagonist, then plays out the entire

narrative of the unfulfilled wish. At the same time that Freud can displace his connection between his patient and her friend onto the
patient, he sees a similarity between the patient and her friend's positions in the narrative of wish fulfillment. Whether Freud makes this
connection or it is made in the patient's unconscious or both, the
recognition of their similarity comes from perceiving an analogical
position in a narrative dynamic rather than from recognizing a preexistent similarity between the women. The narrative of the women's
identification, then, would seem to be both the patient's way of making her different, slim friend the same as her and Freud's way of making the dissimilar women the same in some larger drama of desire.

Freud premises his conclusion of identification upon the assumption
of a similarity that he attributes to the processes of the patient's unconscious, but this similarity is in fact only a similarity in the layered narratives Freud devises. In other words, the wish fulfillment narrative is
Freud's story, *his* understanding of dream work. By narrating a dream
she believes is about an unfulfilled wish, the patient tries to counter his
theory. To show how his theory is in fact correct, Freud surmises an
identification between the women based on their assuming the same
place in the narrative of the wish for an unfulfilled wish, a wish that is
paradoxically fulfilled by their other wish's failure. The dream narrative
thus becomes a part of a larger story of conflict between patient and
analyst where the stakes are the truth of theory. By showing how her
dream was really the fulfilled wish for an unfulfilled wish, not only on
her own part but on the part of her friend, Freud situates the dream
narrative and its identifications in the context of the larger difference
between him and his patient. Interpreting the patient as representative
of all hysterical women who exhibit the symptom of a wish for an
ungratified wish, Freud pits himself against all women who would
doubt his theory through his identification of them as all the same,
occupying the same place in the conflict.[6]

That Freud's notion of identification depends upon narrative instead
of simple similarity is also evident in his ensuing description of identificatory hysterical symptoms. Noting that ward patients will often display the same symptom through time, Freud attributes this contagion
not to simple imitation but rather to the patients' narrative reasoning:
"If a cause like this can produce an attack like this, I may have the same
kind of attack since I have the same grounds for having it" (183).
Because this cause/effect reasoning is not conscious, it emerges as a

symptom; thus, symptoms might be seen as evidence of unconscious or repressed narratives. But despite the overtly narrative process by which these patients display their symptoms, Freud reduces this instance of identification to commonality. "Thus identification is not simple imitation but *assimilation* on the basis of a similar aetiological pretension; it expresses a resemblance and is derived from a common element which remains in the unconscious" (183).

The difference between "imitation" and "assimilation on the basis of a similar aetiological pretension" is the difference between a simple logic of same to same and a logic by which differences are rendered same by one's insertion into an analogous narrative (aetiological pretension) as the symptomatic site of a cause/effect relation. As assimilation, identification reduces differences into an appearance of same which that is not sameness but analogy. The recognition of sameness is not the perception of a symptomatic similarity akin to mimesis; rather, it is a narrative interpretative process by which story elements are taken apart and remade into a new narrative featuring a different protagonist. In a very real sense identification's narrative is reproductive, causing the generation of myriad versions of the narrative that initially informed the identification.

Twenty years later, Freud elaborated his notion of identification through a more complex narrative of developmental stages. In *Mourning and Melancholia* (1917), Freud understands melancholia as an "*identification* of the ego with the abandoned object" (249). This identification results from the loss of the person who served as a point of object cathexis through "slight or disappointment." The loss of the object frees the libido, which, instead of substituting another object for the original, is "withdrawn into the ego," establishing there an identification with the lost object, whose loss becomes an ego loss.

According to this narrative, identification combines and rearranges heteronarrative joinder by transforming or hiding an originary object cathexis (a kind of joinder with other representing an end) in an interior dynamic of making same. Tracing back the conditions that enable this substitution, Freud sees the process of melancholia as itself regressive, reverting from object cathexis (the "better" joinder, which, we find retrospectively must have been narcissistic) to a narcissistic identification or coming together of sames in the self. Narcissism, or sameness, provides a preinscribed path for the libido's progression and regression, just as in Freud's account it provides a preinscribed rationale for regression to an identification that becomes retrospectively "a preliminary stage of object-choice" (249). Freud's narrative of melancholia, which seems at first to go forward to an identification, actually characterizes this identification as a reversion to what retrospectively was always an originary condition and process. This originary identification, Freud goes on to say, is a product of "the oral or cannibalistic phase of libidinal development" where the different object is quite literally assimilated or made a part of same by the ego's wish to devour it.

This oral assimilation literally makes same from different, but in his next paragraph Freud returns this assimilative process to an even more elementary expression of sameness when he discusses the distinctions among narcissistic and hysterical identifications, and transference neuroses. Distinguishing the two identifications on the basis of whether the cathected object is lost or retained, Freud ends by commenting that in the transference neuroses, "identification is the expression of there being something in common, which may signify love" (250). Ordering these various identifications in a developmental chronology, Freud sees narcissistic identification as being the "older," a primitive self-same that gives way to a more mature, more or less heterological object cathexis that then might become transferential love in an apparent return to commonalities. The trajectory from the oral to the narcissistic to the hysterical to the transferential follows the heteronarrative trajectory from self-same single to the different same of narcissism to hysteria's threat of renewed sameness to transference's conjoined and productive difference. Becoming an object-cathected love by the story's transferential conclusion, identification is again rendered simply as having "something in common."

Freud's account of identification in melancholia situates identification as a problematic regression, an almost-literal short circuit in the ego that tragically supplants object cathexis. Identification is a regression because it is narcissistic, a politics of same in retreat from the more productive politics of difference represented by object cathexis's conjoinder of self and other.[7] And identification becomes narcissistic *because* it is a retreat. The relative valuations of identification and object cathexis and their location in a developmental chronology reflect and enact a sexual heteroideology (the same one that locates homosexuality as same on a path to the heterologous joinder of differences). The apparent conjoinder of difference (albeit in the limited form of cathexis) is narratively positioned as more developed than the narcissistically associated identification that becomes retrospectively even more of a dynamic of sameness than Freud depicts it at the narrative's beginning. What is revealed in Freud's narrative of melancholia is not the essence of identification's mechanism but its placement in relation to other forms of relating, a placement that follows and reinscribes heteronarrative. Identification is regressive not because it is intrinsically more primitive but because the narrative, ideological disposition of sameness and difference requires it to be. In Western culture, could identification ever possibly be perceived as an advance from a barbaric and misled heterological object cathexis?

Freud elaborates his understanding of identification as assimilation in his venture into group psychology, *Group Psychology and the Analysis of the Ego* (1921). As in *Mourning and Melancholia*, Freud defines identification via the narrative of its development, a narrative fraught with retrospective revisions. Devoting an entire chapter to identification, Freud locates a difference within identification itself, splitting it into two types whose confluence produces the Oedipus complex. The first type, which Freud regards as, "the earliest expression of an emotional tie with another person" (46), grows from a same-sex "special interest" where (in this case) the boy takes his father as an "ideal." Although Freud does not further specify the actual mechanism of this identification, his appeal to a same-sex ideal suggests that it is a dynamic of same to same based on gender. Simultaneously, Freud recounts, the boy develops another kind of identification with his mother, "according to the attachment [anaclitic] type" (46). Implying a kind of protodesire, this second identification works like heterosexual attraction. These "two psychologically distinct ties: a straightforward sexual object-cathexis toward his mother and an identification with his father which takes him as his model . . . subsist side by side for a time" (46). Propelled, however, by what Freud calls "the irresistible advance toward a unification of mental life" (not the heteronarrative again!), "they come together at last; and the normal Oedipus complex originates from their confluence" (46).

Driven by an "irresistible" heteroideology, the little boy's development occurs through yet another heteronarrative of conjoinder where two kinds of identification, the one informed by sameness and the other by sexual difference, come together to produce the Oedipus complex, a step in the "unification of mental life." Freud's splitting of identification into economies of same and different signals both identification's management of sameness and difference under a guise of sameness and its reiteration of the heteronarrative. Identification, which when unspecified connotes similitude, becomes the complex interplay of difference and sameness when it is defined. At the same time, it is the same old story all over again.

This simple, almost happy narrative of oedipal unification is beset, however, by inevitable problems. When the two identifications converge, they not only produce unification, they also produce conflict located not in the heterological object cathexis with the mother but in the boy's idealization of the father. An unstable connection (as all relations between sames are in heteroideology), the boy's identification with his father turns out to have been "ambivalent from the very first." What we had thought was same—even an idyllic same—turns out also to have been replete with differences from the start. Necessarily same for the purposes of the oedipal narrative, once the oedipal is achieved and once sameness becomes its own story, sameness turns out to have always been a negotiation of differences.[8]

The narrative of Freud's first of the two types of identification is the narrative of assimilation by which Freud first defined identification in *The Interpretation of Dreams*. Slightly recasting this first version, Freud links identification to "the first, *oral* phase of the organization of the libido, in which the object we long for and prize is assimilated by eating and is in that way annihilated as such" (47). In this reference back to the first oral phase, Freud refers back to his own "Three Essays on the Theory of Sexuality" (1915), evoking a sexual parallel to the identification narrative. Pointing in a footnote to a section of "Infantile Sexuality," he links this first kind of identification to the first pregenital sexual organization where "sexual activity has not yet been separated from the ingestion of food" ("Three Essays" 64). The sexual "*aim*" of the organization is "the incorporation of the object" ("Three Essays" 64). As in his 1921 account of the development of identification, the story has taken a regressive turn, one that leads back to a 1915 revision of "Three Essays." But, curiously, the 1915 "Three Essays" already expressly contains part of his 1921 explanation of identification: "the sexual *aim* consists in the incorporation of the object—the prototype of a process which, in the form of identification, is later to play such an important psychological part" ("Three Essays" 64).[9]

Producing a self-reflexive circle in his own work where 1921 refers to 1905 and 1905 to what turns out to be 1921, Freud performs identification's self-cycling propensity. In a sense this incorporative notion of identification consumes itself; incorporation or consumption defined as both sexual and identificatory represent a narrative of joinder, where "the object that we long for and prize" is taken in, becoming part of the (nascent) self. But Freud never illuminates what determines this longing and prizing in the first place; in *Group Psychology* that longing refers back to the boy's "special interest" in his father, or a species of like to like. In "Three Essays," though unspecified, the draw seems be food or the source of food, which Freud notes, is later replaced by the thumb which literally represents the self-cycling of aim and object as the infant incorporates itself.

This turn back to an instance of incorporation simply repeats the narrative of identification where the principle that motivates an identification is omitted in favor of a narrative of self-cycling that actually hides the differences identification manages. In the case of Freud's assimilative model of identification, this first model turns out to have been already "ambivalent," embodying love and hate, not in its motivation but in its paradigm for consummating that attraction as it destroys what it loves. This originary, still enigmatic (i.e., sourceless) ambivalent identification, however, affords the pretext for oedipal stories in which identification goes wrong. Supplying the binary model for a list of identificatory permutations, including the appearance of the "wrong" type of identification (anaclitic instead of assimilative), the originary difference contained by and glossed over by identification accounts for all of the narrative developmental difficulties that, in the oedipal narrative, determine the sexuality of the story. In other words, this first type of identification already contains all the possible ends to the story of sexuality and, in the "reversal of affect" so typical of Freud's analyses, the story of sexuality becomes the story of identificatory mishap.

Freud's first example of such infelicity is the inversion of the Oedipus complex where, in identifications linked to a gendered paradigm, "the father is taken as the object of a feminine attitude, an object from which the directly sexual instincts look for satisfaction" (47). Enabled by the ambivalent identificatory track already in place, this inversion, Freud notes, is the effect of the deployment of the wrong version of identification. "The identification with the father has become the precursor of an object-tie with the father. The same holds good, with the necessary substitutions, of the baby daughter as well" (47). Assimilative identification becomes anaclitic; gendered sameness becomes same-sex desire.

In light of these larger oedipal narrative and developmental consequences, Freud reexplores the nature of identification, this time elabo-
rating more fully its very binary attributes. Assimilative identification
becomes simply "an identification with the father," where "one's father
is what one would like to *be*" (47). This contrasts with "the choice of
the father as an object" where the father becomes "what one would like
to *have*" (47). Locating the mechanisms of identification in verbs, Freud
exposes the larger ideological stakes of the two modes of identification
which reiterate the ideologies underwriting narrative. That assimilative
identification is *being* recalls the self-same essentialism of identification's
first narrative, itself enigmatically premised on a wanting to be like that
simultaneously betrays a preexistent likeness or commonality and provides one as its result. *Having* belongs to a logic of difference, property,
and production, where one has what is different from what one is and
where the inevitably sexualized "having" portends future desire.

Freud also orders these two types of identification chronologically
by linking *being* to the ego's subject and *having* to its object. Since in
Freud's narrative of development, subjecthood precedes the ability to
have objects, *being* necessarily precedes *having*; the first type of identification "is therefore already possible before any sexual object-choice has
been made" (47). That *being* precedes *having* seems a necessity, but it also
conforms to and reinscribes narrative heteroideology where a politics
of sameness precedes, enables, and is superseded by a politics of difference. This heteronarrative chronology accounts for Freud's understanding of assimilative identification as a regression, as a going back in the
story. Having located it in the beginning as that which enables the narrative's end in object choice, assimilative identification becomes a
regressive substitution for object choice, a retreat from the difference
and sexuality object cathexis represents. Such regressions write the narrative of a cure in the reinstallation of the proper heteronarrative and
also evidence the way heteronarrative defines proper chronology. The
problem with these patients is that they occupy the wrong place in the
story at the wrong time, a disfunction that recalls Freud's narratives of
homosexual development.

This narrative ordering finally opposes identification, which has
become primarily the assimilative type, to object cathexis, which represents the development of anaclitic identification. Identification as
assimilation is relegated back to the pregenital, oral, narcissistic, self-
same that stops the story if it occurs in the wrong place. Functioning

as a switch, assimilative identification works as a kind of Todorovian "verb" or catalyst, providing the alternate narrative paths of human sexual development. That assimilative identification is basically self-cycling, tautologically hiding its management of differences in the first mythical instance of attraction or need, is symptomatically repeated in the limited nature of the binaries (assimilative/anaclitic, male/female, same/different) that structure the developmental narrative. Identification, then, seems the self-contained kernel of Freud's narratives of development and sexuality and is also posed as the self-contained core of its own narrative.

Having ordered and transformed identification into a narrative of sexual development, Freud illustrates the various permutations that might produce or explain neurotic symptoms. The oedipal symptom where one identifies with the same-sexed parent is the display of object love toward the parent of the opposite sex. In an identification with the parent of the opposite sex (Dora's cough like her father's, for example), object choice regresses to identification. In hysterical symptoms "based upon the possibility or desire of putting oneself in the same situation" as another, "the identification by means of the symptom has thus become the mark of a point of coincidence between the two egos which has to be kept repressed" (49). This final permutation offers another clue to the ideological stake in placing identification in the locus of same. Producing a symptom that represents the repression of the "coincidence of two egos," identification enables the perverse as well as the "healthy" merger of same with same and different with different. While the politics of difference goes on to produce "normal" individuals, the politics of same produces the non-productive, homological, homosexual who becomes identified with neuroses and hysteria, forms of identification gone awry, not because homosexualities are about identification, since Freud clearly locates homosexual perversity in aim and object choice, but because the parallels between the story of identification and the story of sexual development reflect their genesis in the same reproductive heteroideology that requires their alignment with one another stage by stage.

Freud does add a third kind of identification to his list, a kind of postdevelopmental affiliation necessary to understand group processes, the addition of which precedes his discussion of groups. Identification "may arise with any new perception of a common quality shared with some other person who is not an object of the sexual instinct" (49–50).

After its affiliation with sexuality, identification itself is freed from the obligations of object cathexis and desire. Emerging from the intrapsychic, identification becomes interpersonal, the basis for a tie among members of a group or with a leader. While the evocation of commonality refers back to the assimilative type of identification, this third, postdevelopmental type of identification is a productive progression instead of a neurotic regression, openly enabling the negotiation of differences rather than hiding the differences it negotiates. In this sense identification has been sanitized; displaced from its ideological function and glossed with heteroideology, it becomes an incipient mode of positive inter-personal connection that is, importantly, not sexual.

Freud's narrative of identification exemplifies the ambivalent place of ambivalence identification occupies, an ambivalence recuperated as sameness (regression) or difference (progression). What is important in this is not the politics of same or the dynamic of returning to same, but the fact that identification is both definitionally and ideologically narrative in both its inception and function, even though it appears to escape the story. Freud's understanding of identification is overwhelmingly narrative; he is ultimately unable to explain the closed circle of attraction that initiates identificatory processes. The very absence of definition means that the narrative deployment of identification makes it what it is. The moment when attraction or likeness is perceived evades narrativization except through the narrative of self-sameness by which attraction is later glossed and from which sameness is retrieved by the attribution of originary ambivalence. Because what is located as the incipient moment of identification is never defined, identification resists all but a functional definition. It becomes the emblem of the narrative of reversion itself—a narrative of reversion to self that both characterizes and hides a narrative of consumption and assimilation. Thus, identification is the undefined process that stands for the process of consumption in a narrative ideology about production. It is both complement to and a complementary part of heteronarrative (re)production.

As the metanarrative of consumption, identification seems to occupy the site of connection, but it is located there as an effect of a narrative ideology that, in its fix on joinder, must relegate the other half of that story—the portion whereby it and its products are received, understood, consumed—to its narrative double. The narrative of identification performs an inverted parallel (difference hidden by sameness) to the heteronarrative dynamic. While identification is the complement of narrative, identification also reproduces a version of the heteronarrative as the operation by which narrative itself is consumed. This is evident not only in critical understandings of the process of reading but also in narratives of cultural production that which require, imply, and import an accompanying narrative of consumption.

Narrative is still a part of consumer culture's simulacra, motivating consumption. Production is to consumption as narrative is to identification; the first terms seem progressive, fertile, and inventive, the second, regressive, sterile, and repetitious. By displacing (re)production's necessarily correlative consumption into the seemingly extranarrative but parallel process of identification, the two together actually render ideology consumable. Identification becomes a process by which the difference between self and narrative, between self and others, between experience and fiction is disavowed. This disavowal allows ideology to work in the face of experience otherwise. Simultaneously, identification is the way sameness is managed and controlled, prevented from engaging in some wild Aristophanic merger that would set hetero-ideology awry.

4

I Am What I Am

> Identity at the level of the social may be oppressive, and identity at the level
> of the psychical may be fictional, but what about identity at the level of
> the political?
> —Mary Ann Doane, "Commentary: Post-Utopian Difference," pp. 76–77

Envisioned as a way to promote and consolidate strong minority identity, identification as a narrative of consumption already locates consolidation within a heteronarrative status quo. While the ideological workings of this highly structural narrative seem perhaps all too closed and determinate, what they determine are not the possibilities for change but rather the choice of the means by which to effect change and the ways that change might be defined. When the means are provided by the narrative that incorporates them, it is difficult to do anything but to play in the same arena. And what we think seems radical, subversive, and challenging seems logically and psychically so because it is already a part of the story just as villains and antagonists, minor characters and homosexuals are already a part.

The choice of identification as a consciously wielded political tool is not only informed by the assumptions of visibility politics, it is also affected by the consumption narrative as that is writ large in culture. In an analogy to identification's narrative of consumption, the literal, pervasive narrative of commodity consumption in contemporary culture offers the seductive promise of fulfillment, affiliation, and meaning via the exchange of money for objects. Appearing to bypass most elements of heteronarrative struggle, consumption seems not to short-circuit but to shortcut the route from beginning to end. Its emphasis on commodity over the toils of acquisition foregrounds the narrative's conclusion of product over the process, downplaying even narrative's character as exchange. Appearing to be the effortless, magical route from unhappiness to consummation and from lack to plenitude, consumption, like identification, is the narrative of easy trade and high return whose very facility masks the difficulties and differences it manages and whose narrative in contemporary culture always makes it seem that one gets more than one pays for. Structurally and ideologically but not really consciously linked to identification, the narrative of consumption that underwrites identification offers an attractive alternate route for liberationist politics. As a strategy already available in a media-dominated culture, consumption is an approach that inveigles instead of convincing, allures instead of confronting, and gives a lot for relatively little effort. This is not to suggest that lesbian and gay activists want to take the easy way out; it is to suggest that the means that present themselves present themselves as an effect of the apparent, very ideologically inflected interplay of conjoinder and consumption.

Identification also becomes an appealing political tactic because it seems to provide a connection between narrative, culture, and the individual with which we can interfere and in which we can intervene by using narrative propensities in our favor and by inhibiting their effective perpetuation of heteroideology. Narrative, though structurally redundant, seems to offer the opportunity for alteration and endless permutation; its mediate moments seem to furnish an opportune site for intervention. In another confusion between process and product, however, what identification's narrative alters is not the scene of consumption but the objects to be consumed. This results in attempts to manipulate the identities of characters featured in narratives and their roles in narrative dynamics. Offering the possibility of new identities to identify with adds up, however, to the production and reinforcement of new identities. The imagined result of shifting the roles to be identified with is individual liberation and the emergence of large numbers of counterideological players in the same old story.

Created in part by the conflation of identification and identity, this circular process replays the same old narrative of a self-cycling and self-referential identity, since if identities spark identifications and identifications produce identities, the illusion of a change depends upon finding a place in the story to change the terms as they cycle. The illusory problem, as it always is, seems to be where to start (and illusory because there is never a start). Despite or because of its position as "verb" connecting identities in the cycle, identification seems the logical, almost the weak point, since it seems more easily altered than the stalwart, but imaginary fortress of identity or the insistence of heteronarrative itself. And because identification offers the gloss of an alternate narrative of consumption instead of a narrative production that must be consumed, identification seems able to provide an "in," the rationale for altering the nature and character of who plays the parts in narrative. The narrative of identification, however, does not supply an answer to how one plants a positive (i.e., anti- or nonideological) role model in the story in the first place.

But while this fantasy narrative of identificatory liberation appeals to our already ideologically inflected understanding of the problem of social oppression as one of invisibility and nonrepresentation, what can we really expect if we follow the story? What if Martina Navratilova, for example, is a role model? How can her visibility as a successful lesbian tennis player effect political and social change? Would change come as a result of her success, inspiring us individually in some kind of narcissistic assimilation of her achievement as our own in the same logic by which major league sports franchises inspire loyalty among their fans? Is her life a narrative pattern for all to follow? Do we simply revel in the fact of her lesbianism? (Is this just self-reifying pleasure?) Does her success suggest some useful way out of the conditions by which gay men and lesbians are oppressed? If so, is the point that we all become champion tennis players (and simultaneously engage in the narrative of capitalist success) or that we all persevere to become champions at whatever (in the same narrative)? Is the point that a lesbian can succeed (lesbians can have the capitalist narrative of success)? My argument is not that Martina's success is bad nor that her public acknowledgement of her sexuality is not admirable, but that without challenging the underlying ideologies that inform these cultural narratives in the first place, including that which situates identification and identity as answers, we simply live the fantasy of liberation already inscribed in the heteroideological story.

We might argue that because identification is an unconscious process, we cannot avoid the story; therefore, we might as well employ what is there and what is going to happen anyway to our advantage. Such a strategy is a matter of wielding the unconscious, an old trope of cultural manipulation suspected in advertising's sublimations, campaign tactics, and the work of ideology itself. The problem with this is precisely that identifications are *unconscious*; we cannot control or even always predict them. While the heteronarrative situates identification as a politic of sameness, and while we accept that premise as a basis for identification-based praxis (outing, for example), and while we envision political mileage in a homosexual character's "positive" position in the narrative, we can't control the idiosyncratic course individual identifications will take (though we think we can). How does the liberation narrative work, for example, if (hypothetically) I find Sandra Bernhard repulsive? How does it work if I form anaclitic instead of assimilative identifications, wanting to "have" instead of wanting to "be" Deanna Troi in *Star Trek: The Next Generation*? Since the character's dress, posturing, and cleavage-centered decorativeness are there to be consumed anaclitically, does it matter that such reading is accomplished by a female instead of a male? While lesbian desire might produce a radical consumption against the heterosexual grain of *Star Trek*, does it change the way the story finally goes or does it provide me with a place in it? Does k. d. lang's coming out do anything more than reinforce our "radar," our sense of being able to identify the already-identifiable correctly? Doesn't her open stardom reproduce in lesbian form the same commodity cultural illusion of pleasure in consumption? Does having that political and social visibility constitute liberation or does it finally forestall efforts to gain enfranchisement by appearing to include lesbians within the commodity market—by making it appear as if we have already won?

Some might answer yes to the penultimate question, for at least having pleasure is better than having none. That there are open, visible lesbian "personalities" seems an acknowledgment of our presence and a recognition of our identity as a cultural part instead of something that "dare not speak its name." And reading Sandra Bernhard as subversive cleanses the lesbian pleasure Bernhard might provide of whatever sense of heterosexual or ideological complicity might adhere to its provision. Proof of the strength of this imaginary and its disarming function in lesbian practices of identification and cultural consumption comes in reading her *Playboy* spread as subversive high camp. Similar to readings of pop star Madonna as subversive, interpreting Bernhard as a complex countercultural figure has to do with the way she is perceived as playing on the narrative of consumption; she is visible and successful despite her open contravention and complex parody of forms and ideologies of gender and sexuality.[10] While various analyses can be more or less convincing about this, such analysis also seems motivated by a desire to see what we like as somehow subversive because doing so provides the illusion that we have challenged the story, that Davida has vanquished Goliath. So when k. d. lang is adamantly vegetarian in cattle country, the link between that radical stance and her lesbianism seems to make the lesbian even more of an influential cultural outlaw, one whose bandit status is simultaneously rewarded. Her implicit narrative seems to challenge capitalist ideology by providing the story of someone who, working against capitalist interests on one level, can be a star because hordes of lesbians are buying her albums. But what narrative is this? As we have well learned from the experience of feminism, reproducing the same narrative with different players is no change at all.

Identification's narrative product, identity, inherits the same problematic narrative logic. For Lacan multiple, layered identifications produce an ego; in more popular cultural terms, identifications produce identity and vice versa. While the relation between ego and identity is unclear (Is ego identity? Is identity only the socially-relevant part of ego? Is identity different from ego and wielded by it? Is identity larger than ego?), the relation between identity and culture is more clearly complex, so complex that we all experience multiple appeals to the multiple identities with which we identify. And while we may each have an identity, the singular standing for the complex intersection of ideologies, narratives, and culture, identity also seems to stand apart from us, as something to identify with in the assimilative sense. As Judith Butler so eloquently describes it, "the source of personal and political agency comes not from within the individual, but in and

through the complex cultural exchanges among bodies in which identity itself is ever-shifting, indeed, where identity itself is constructed,
disintegrated, and recirculated only within the context of a dynamic
field of cultural relations."[11]

Part of that mode of "complex cultural exchange" is narrative as it
both organizes our perceptions and locates and underwrites identification itself. Like identification, identity hides its own process, standing as
the deceptively complete and whole product of individual development. While identification manages differences in the guise of an appeal
to sameness, identity hides the contingent, multiple, conflicting possibilities produced in and through narrative ideology (among other
things) under a guise of self-same unity linked umbilically to a discernible, distinct, culturally defined position. In the adoption or forma-
tion of identity, which is always in relation to social forms of identity
available, the narrative that inscribes identities as if they were static positions or gestalts is elided in and by the product it generates. The notion
of identity, thus, depends not only on the repression of fragmentation
but also on the repression of the story by which any identity gains significance and cultural valence in the first place.

If this is the case, then, how do we interfere in that narrative circle
whose seamlessness produces such a creature as identity politics in the
first place? In her analysis of the identity politics' liberalism, Shane
Phelan argues that "the experience of oppression" is not so much the
"*what* we are told we are like" as "the rigidity with which we are
told."[12] Locating the force of narrative ideology in force itself—"state
terrorism, disappearances, forced psychiatric commitment or treatment, sterilization, and so on"—Phelan suggests countering that force
through several possible strategies: "light-heartedness—the humor that
comes from seeing all categories, all explanations, all identities as provisional" (156), rejecting identities, consciously recognizing ideology for
what it is ("we do not live the lives that our theoretic representations
would suggest"), or returning to Foucault's notion of "genealogy" or
"counter-memory."[13] Genealogy or countermemory is a narrative
counternarrative practice where myths of origin and causality are
replaced by the elaboration of detail, the analysis of descent exposing
the body "imprinted by history," producing a more knowing history
that, parodical, is able to dissociate identity and finally sacrifice the subject of knowledge itself. Reiterating precisely the dilemma of heteroideology, Phelan replaces narrative with a better, more detailed

genealogy, one whose attention to fact and changing modalities provides no unified view.

The counternarrative of genealogy is one in which narrative ideologies are exploded from within, overfull of the detail that prevents easy ideological reassimilation. If we could do this on a broad cultural scale (or do it at all) and if we could thereby disturb the circular narrative that weds identification, identity, and heteronarrative, we might succeed in disimbricating narrative, sexual ideologies, and the location of individuals in that schema. The problem is, of course, a) how well genealogy can be accomplished, by whom, and on what scale; and b) how well a genealogy would actually resist or counter the heteronarrative without being recuperated by it. In the context of the problem posed by the imbrication of narrative and heteroideology (or that our notion of narrative *is* heteroideology), genealogy finally appears to be an advanced form of consciousness that would need to be applied not to identity or to its production but to the very ideologies by which identity is produced.

That we all have multiple identities and are aware of that multiplicity does not inhibit the constant appeal to identity as a finished acquisition whose loss (an identity crisis) signals the dubious confusion of the culturally dislocated. While sufferers of identity crises might not see their suffering as a positive condition (in the narrative heterologic by which identity is supposed to be whole and singular), perceiving splits, contradictions, and fragmentation in identity might be a temporary breakdown in heteronarrative hegemony as long as that perception is not part of the larger mastery narrative whose comprehension of fragmented identities bespeaks a delusively knowing persona elsewhere (as in this argument).

This is not to claim a subversive power for psychotics nor to install a consciousness of split subjectivity as itself liberatory (since some ego somewhere makes that recognition); rather, it is to suggest that the recognition of a loss of identity represents the simultaneous failure and momentary visibility of the heteronarrative as both ideology and identificatory process. If narrative works to seal over the splits and contradictions inherent to the always ever-partial identity, then having a crisis indicates the failure of that narrative, unless, of course, the crisis is the fragmentary middle of another narrative by which identity will be reconstituted as whole again. (In which case such fragmentation actually serves as a necessary part of the story. Am I not recuperating fragmentary identity even now in a larger narrative in which it becomes the answer to another question?) But even if that fragmented identity will be eventually recuperated or healed, the moment of its fracture signals a breach that, like the middling moments of lesbian exposure, shows up the terms and investments of the system itself. The practical limitation of seeing identity crises as any real site of contestation is, of course, where this recognition takes place. The individualized locus of such crises restricts their generalized applicability.

The problem of identity and social action in relation to an understanding of the pervasive power of narrative heteroideology is twofold and self-contradictory: 1) If heteronarrative locates identity as the space for political action around that identity and at the same time produces that identity in certain forms in the narrative that effects that oppression, how can identity ever counter oppression? 2) How do we disimbricate narrative from heteroideology and still recognize narrative? 3) If disimbricating narrative from heteroideology would displace or radically redefine identity, how do we retain the ground for political action? Or is the second question really already the answer to the first and third, disposing of the oppression and hence the need for certain kinds of identity? While this same heteronarrative seems to compel me to provide an answer to these questions, the best I can do is resist that compulsion and enact my own failure in that narrative (which gets us nowhere) or try to provide a theory, in which case I reinforce the narrative and more than likely suggest strategies that come from and are easily recuperated by heteronarrative. I know, but all the same . . .

That the heteronarrative can fail or appear to fail, even temporarily, suggests the possibility of intervention at its points of failure, of making more permanently visible just how we got to that point and defining the terms, stakes, and ideologies that always return that failure point to a "happier" wholeness. Though in recognizing failure, we risk making failure itself another answer to the question of how to overcome narrative hegemony, widening the narrative middle, even as an end in itself, may make it difficult or impossible for that particular narrative to continue. And in spelling out narrative's terms, in forging its genealogy, we also discover the logics of repetition, alternation, and accrual that have always sustained, accompanied, and provided sense both within and outside of narrative, which, camouflaged (like a trick 3-D picture) within the ideological imperative to combine, nonetheless function to pattern, sustain, and carry narrative from one end to the other over and over again and function on their own to make sense out of such arguably nonnarrative patterns as music.[14]

This may finally be why identification might really be a valuable site of intervention in narrative, not as a process with identity as its positive result but as a location where narrative's differences are variously managed and visible. While identity may seem to be a baseline presumption for narrative consumption in the narrative logic of identification (providing the same with which to compare same), it is also the illusory product of another narrative whose logic, like Lacan's logic for the construction of the ego, is as much repetition and accrual as it is the product of heteronarrative's shifting play of sameness/difference. Identities are always multiple in the social sphere; the ego maintains its illusion of unity in an intrapsychic sphere. They both coexist as the disavowed shadow of the other. Identity's crisis (in the pop psychological sense) occurs when ego and identity come together as the same thing and manifest a split and lack of center. This crisis reveals not only the overidentification of ego with social identity but the intersection of heteronarrative with the logic of accrual also associated with identification and identity, simultaneously exposing both logics and their interdependence. The logic of accrual, already in operation, provides a possible alternative to the heteronarrative even as it is a necessary part of it, since despite the fact that accrual masks the negotiation of differences, it works counter to the heteroideological presumptions of complementary or oppositional joinder, terminal (re)production, and consumption. But to what extent can this intersection of logics be deployed as a way to disrupt their cooperation? And would this disruption explode heteronarrative's relation to sexual ideologies?

The simplest example of the potentially opportune intersection of narrative logics is the narrative of American national identity. Sustaining the ideology of statehood with all its dispositions of power, underwriting such concepts as loyalty, patriotism, and political survival, and grounding exclusionary practices, imperialist maneuvers, and self-protective economies, the notion of American identity is a fragile, highly defended, constantly and anxiously tended precept. For historical reasons having to do with successive waves of markedly different immigrants and the needs of a capitalist ideology that produces and maintains a ready market for a particular species of aggressive consumption, American identity is much alluded to, proudly displayed, and belligerently and aggressively expounded ("America, love it or leave it;" "Buy American").

But its overt promotion bespeaks its constant need for preservation, because American national identity always threatens to reveal its fragmentary, fractured, and layered quality. If you ask white Americans, for example, some version of a question about where they "originally" came from—meaning both nationality and ethnic origin—many will respond with a list of European nationalities. For other (except native) Americans, racial background in addition to origins elsewhere signals that fragmentation. We are American but we are also and originally from someplace else, each representing a set of fragments which the 1980s' genealogy craze would track down and quantify as a source of individual identity that coexists with the more encompassing identity of "American."

Listing of multiple other nationalities demonstrates the contingency of American identity, revealing a fractured quality that, though normally taken as innocent pride in descent (which also forms part of individual identity), can produce dangerous breaches if taken too far. For example, white supremacists, identifying with an Aryan heritage or the narratives associated therewith (fictional as they might be), intervene in American identity's fragmentation to rescue and elevate one term as the basis for a corrected narrative of national production (and the production of a nationality), one that is predictably counter to notions of liberal democracy. Equating a very limited notion of whiteness with American identity, supremacists essentially take advantage of American identity's fragmentation to cut out and exclude all fragments but one, recuperating the wholeness of identity by wrenching it into an extreme (pathological) unity. While this is almost a parody of the heteronarrative's drive to unity (especially in its appeal to "purity" and sameness), it also demonstrates the identificatory point at which the narrative has been wrested from its course to serve another, fairly perverse, but very monolithic end.

Following the tactic of white supremacy, it might be equally possible to open up identificatory stories instead of closing them down by intervening in the narrative of the production of identity, especially if we understand identity as contingent, multiple, but necessary. Where white supremacists select and privilege a racialized nationality associated with the most single-minded notion of identity possible in the post–World War II world, it would be equally possible to break the story up at the same point, not just to pluralize identity (a makeshift substitute for the illusion of unity and its complement) but to displace identity as the end of the story. In other words, by intervening at the same point as white supremacists who then write the story in its most egregiously monolithic terms, we can break the story down so that it cannot end at all, working not only against identity (in the narrative sense) but against the ideological and sexual dynamic of an end product enacted by narrative itself. We might argue that as the product of identification, identity, too, is unconscious and therefore cannot be wielded this freely. This is true to the extent that identity refers to ego. But it is also true that we consciously adopt identities; those we might mess with, see as constantly accruing, never finished.

The problem of course is how one does this, since even suggesting such a possibility may stimulate reactions that range from instinctive skepticism to self-protective denial to reasoned evocations of the importance of identity to political action. How, in other words, can we mess with the identity narrative if the narrative is a) already strongly ideologically implanted; b) necessary for political action; c) essential in the intersection of self and world? While a consciousness of the multiplicity of identity seems helpful—and in fact optimistic in light of the kinds of monolithic identity narrative fabricated by the Ku Klux Klan—consciousness of identity's multiplicity itself is probably not enough to alter or break apart the narrative. Instead as an answer, multiplicity becomes its own species of monolithism, losing its fragmentary and indeterminate quality in the illusion of comprehensive listing and acknowledgement. Nor is the answer an insistent display or performance of multiplicity, which, like the plethora of men's club symbols that huddle around the sign adorning the ingress to small midwestern towns, signals identity as the sum of components. Nor is the answer humor or performativity as practices that refer back to and illustrate identity's contingency. Both depend upon another, more secure (if not unified) identity or ego elsewhere that perceives and critiques the fiction of unity in the first place. Playing in or with the narrative does not disturb the narrative no matter how much the middle is widened, the terms made conscious, or the details listed.

Rather, breaking up the heteronarrative by which differences come together to produce a unified product would mean not just never ending, but never perceiving an end as a possibility, as something missing, sacrificed, or displaced. In concrete terms this means emphasizing, privileging, locating the repetitions that constitute the terminally unfinished presence of existence, putting repetition, alternation, and accrual in place of progress and closure. There is pleasure in repetition, a pleasure associated with the infantile and mentally infirm. Permitting that pleasure as a positive pleasure might begin to counteract the particular species of drive toward an ending that characterizes the heteronarrative and cooperates with its (re)productive ideology. Because, however, repetition always risks ideological recuperation (witness the repetitive quality of television reruns, exercise programs, and even American cityscapes), repetition is not an answer in itself but only a suggestion about what might counteract the hegemony of end-orientation.

If repetition, too, is already a component of the heteronarrative, if its sameness provides the necessary difference to overcome, then emphasizing repetition risks recalling the heteronarrative anyway and maybe that is unavoidable. Perhaps, then, the point is one of emphasis instead of totality, of finesse instead of confrontation and opposition (which would inevitably reproduce the heteronarrative) so that all of the possible ways repetition might be addressed or evoked—consciousness, performance, evocations of multiplicity—accomplish some small measure of challenge, which is why they generally have to be shut down or recuperated. Repetition seems pointless, but of course, that is the point. And suggesting the value of something that has an end in itself is tantamount to valorizing that place of sameness metaphorically linked with the lesbian and gay male, a space infantilized, made primitive and meaningless in the same logic by which the end is valorized and enjoyed. In suggesting repetition as a counter, am I only playing out the role of the homo again?

And what form might repetition take? Where would it manifest as a counternarrative possibility? In music, which already sells itself in large degree on repetition? In popular narrative and television, where repetition reigns not only within each story but among them? In a kind of protracted honesty about the impossibility of answers and endings and knowledge? And how might that relate to the very ideology that underwrites and demands economic, scientific, humanistic, evolutionary, social "progress"?

Another other possibility for counteracting the heteroideological power of narrative is constantly to ignore or devalue the end as a way of challenging and altering the reproductive ideology that shapes this particular notion of progress. Or vice versa, in an overpopulated world, challenging the value of reproduction as a way of at least disimbricated sexuality from narrative. The demise of the repro ending (and its analogies) would relieve the mastery narrative of its heterosexual impetus, possibly providing an opening for multiple, nonreproductive sexualities and non-ending patterns. The best way, finally, to really get rid of the end's valence, however, would be to defeat death. And if we did that we would need narrative to pass the time, perhaps endless narratives of endless repetitions, but without reproduction because that would have become unnecessary.

While this final solution seems absurd, it seems to me that really it is the only way to escape the heteronarrative. The point is finally, that no matter what tactic one takes in relation to narrative and heteroideology, it is bound to be temporary, provisional, makeshift, and responsive. If there is ever to be a culture in which sexualities lose their ideological valence and actually cease being "sexualities," such a culture would need a very different relation between narrative and ideology as well as a very different ideology whose layered referents no longer coalesce in the pattern that conveniently welds the social, the psychical, the economic, and the "biological." But in challenging this twentieth-century structuralist monolith as it so easily adjusts to (and underwrites) commodity culture, many approaches are better than one, several simultaneous strategies are better than a single approach, an identity crisis may be better than certainty, no conclusion is better than mastery's illusion.

CHAPTER SIX

Come Again

Surely some revelation is at hand.
—W. B. Yeats, "The Second Coming"

I KISSED A GIRL

1995 witnesses the mainstream, MTV imaging of lesbian desire in Jill Sobule's music video, "I Kissed a Girl." Narrating a suburban housewife affair, the video images blond and brunette next-door neighbors flirting, hugging, and rubbing feet under the table while participating in the exaggerated daily humdrum of suburban family life. All signs are that this could represent a positive change in narrative, in visibility, in public acceptance of alternative lifestyles.

But look carefully. The video ends with both women pregnant. They never leave their husband or boyfriend. One dreams of standing beside her boyfriend in courtly costume. The other dreams of standing beside her girlfriend dressed as the courtly knight. And although they share that dream for a moment near the end of the video, that sharing inau-

gurates the family barbecue that precedes the image of the two pregnant women getting the morning paper. Sound familiar?

There seems to be something subversive about this video. Its pastiche style, the cartoon-balloon dream scenes, the exaggerated secrecy
of the women's trysts, the overly stereotypical romance signifiers of its
imagined courtship, the delight in the fact of the kiss, the continuation
of the relation in the husband/boyfriend's absence seem to undermine
the American dream quality of the suburban scene. Is the video's
apparent parodical consciousness of the heterosexual nuclear family a
way of undermining the story? Is this an example where presenting
the narrative "with a vengeance" shows heteronarrative up or is it
another instance of lesbian recontainment by the reproductive narrative? Or do these women illustrate a borderless sexuality, a polymorphous perversity that breaks down the binary distinctions between
hetero and homo?

I would like to answer yes to all of these suggestions. But alas, I think
this video is really another recontainment that merely poses as parody.
The video's osculatory glee seems refreshingly triumphant; its mood
overtakes the video's shaping narrative. But even so, the song's lyrics
openly admit that kissing a girl won't transform the world and the
video's narrative illustrates a tupperware-party-filled, nostalgic suburban landscape whose subversive hidden homosexuality doesn't disturb
the status quo and in fact seems enjoyable only because it is secret. Even
if the nuclear family story is not what it seems, we already know that it
never is; it is always supported by a measure of the homosexual. The
video is a paradoxically visible closet redux.

So in 1995 things have not changed much unless we count the fact
of visibility itself. What is scary is the way the heteronarrative insistently
reappears, here as a product consumed under the aegis of the most idyllic, innocent moment of the incipient lesbian. But the lesbian has always
represented a kiss on the way to narrative reproduction. The possible
insurrections of repetition, accrual, or alternation, typical of MTV fare
are absent in this very narrative music video.

The second coming is never as good as the first, but we live lives of
second comings. As I reread this manuscript, I realize how hegemonic
and pessimistic this analysis seems, with little room for challenge, subversion, or transgression. To combat heteroideology would mean thinking outside the system altogether, changing conceptions of time, cause
and effect, and knowledge. To effect such a change will take more than

narrative or a consciousness thereof. I do not believe all is as hopeless as I draw it, but drawing it was necessary to begin to see where hope could lie and to dispel the illusory answers offered by narrative itself. So I would like to end this book with hope, a hope that was there from the beginning: that by defining what we seem to take for granted, we might find a way to begin to think in a radically different way, at least I hope. This radicality has to do with seeing what has always been there: the patterns in narrative that have never counted because they did not lead to closure or production. It has to do with never assuming that effect necessarily precedes cause, with understanding that time can move two ways, and that meaning lies not in the lure of knowledge but in the repetitions, accruals, alternations, and nonsense of maybe never getting there. Or in knowing there is no there to get.

NOTES

Introduction

1. Hayden White, "The Value of Narrativity," 1.

2. Roland Barthes, "Introduction to the Structural Analysis of Narratives," 79.

3. See Dana Polan, "Brief Encounters," for his statement of the meaninglessness of culturally pervasive narrative.

4. Louis Althusser, "Ideology and Ideological State Apparatuses."

5. Roland Barthes, "Myth Today."

6. Terry Eagleton, *Literary Theory*, 135. See also Terry Eagleton, ed., *Ideology*.

7. Teresa de Lauretis, *Alice Doesn't*, 157.

8. Michael Warner outlines the function of the homosexual as the displaced locus of heterosexuality's shaping narcissism in a series of complex mirrorings that are shaped by this same narrative of blockage in "Homo-Narcissism." Teresa de Lauretis examines the interrelation of the lesbian and the perverse in depth in *The Practice of Love*. For other insights on the possibilities of the perverse, see Jonathan Dollimore, *Sexual Dissidence*.

9. D. A. Miller, *Bringing Out Roland Barthes*, 44. See also Paul Morrison, "End Pleasure."

10. Roland Barthes, *The Pleasure of the Text*, 14, 10–11.

11. Teresa de Lauretis, *Technologies of Gender*, 25.

12. Monique Wittig, "The Straight Mind," 105.

13. Judith Butler, *Gender Trouble*.

14. Here I cite Butler's entire book as raising a problematic about the systems of gender and ideology and the possibility for a praxis.

15. Michel Foucault traces the rise and discursive functions of the category sexuality in *The History of Sexuality*, vol. 1. See also David Halperin, *One Hundred Years of Homosexuality* and Eve Kosofsky Sedgwick, *Epistemology of the Closet*.

16. For an exposition of this hypothesis see my *A Lure of Knowledge*.

17. Wallace Martin's *Recent Theories of Narrative* is still staunchly structuralist, perhaps because what is defined as narrative theory is only defined as such because it is structuralist, that is, appended to the narrative understood structurally. The furthest from the textual narrative theories get is communication theories that simply displace the structure from one locus to another.

18. In *The Postmodern Condition*. Lyotard hypothesizes that the absence of a belief in the possibility of regulating "the totality of statements circulating in the social collectivity" is the absence "for which the ideology of the 'system,' with its pretensions to totality, tries to compensate and which it expresses in the cynicism of its criterion of performance" (65). This book is such a system. See also Jean Baudrillard, "Symbolic Exchange and Death."

1. The End Is Coming

1. Roland Barthes suggests this narrative disavowal as perverse, particularly in tragedy "*whose end I know*: I know and I don't know, I act toward myself as though I did not know." *The Pleasure of the Text*, 47.

2. *The Pleasure of the Text*, 47.

3. Robert Scholes, *Fabulation and Metafiction*, 26.

4. Walter Benjamin, "The Storyteller." He says, "Death is the sanction of everything that the storyteller can tell. He has borrowed his authority from death. In other words, it is natural history to which his stories refer back" (94).

5. This is from Teresa de Lauretis's translation of Propp's "*Edipo alla luce del folclore*," ed. Clara Strada (Turin: Einaudi, 1975), 85–87, quoted in *Alice Doesn't*, 113–114.

6. The importance of narrative in Freudian psychoanalysis is explored by a number of critics, including Steven Marcus, "Freud and Dora"; Shoshana Felman in "Beyond Oedipus"; and Roy Schafer, "Narration in the Psychoanalytic Dialogue."

7. In "Fragment of an Analysis of a Case of Hysteria," for example, Freud not only says that he begins with narrative but begins his narrative with a long discursus on why his narrative isn't complete.

8. Aristotle, *Rhetoric and Poetics*, 232. All subsequent citations are from this edition. See also Sophocles, *Oedipus Tyrannus*.

9. Freud confesses to Wilhelm Fliess that he has found this is his own case (October 15, 1897) in *The Complete Letters* ; and see *The Interpretation of Dreams*. Freud sees the Oedipus pattern as fairly universal (except in the difficulty of fitting

it to females); however, the plot of familial jealousies within which children are introduced to gender and law is always retold from the point of view of he who has mastered the plot—from the end, retrospectively.

10. René Wellek and Austin Warren, for example, exhaustively explore the status of literary criticism in *Theory of Literature*, where the basic underlying premise is that one can define a whole work of literature and enact upon it an "intrinsic study" of its parts to itself.

11. Most narrative theorists distinguish plot from other narrative elements such as sequence. Tsvetan Todorov, for example, defines the "minimal complete plot" as "the passage from one equilibrium to another." *The Poetics of Prose*, 111. See also Gerald Prince, *Narratology*.

12. Fredric Jameson, "Pleasure," 71.

13. Barnes takes this one step further in *Nightwood* by ironizing the irony through a consciousness of the pathetic all-too-typical storiness of the story of heredity and generation.

14. Though contemporary theorists would make a distinction between the terms *sexual instinct* and *sexuality*, Freud does not seem to, using them as synonyms, his choice of term based primarily on whether he wants to evoke the idea of instinct or emphasize its sexual nature. He says, for example, "even though it is certain that sexuality and the distinction between the sexes did not exist when life began, the possibility remains that the instincts which were later to be described as sexual may have been in operation from the very first" (34). The terms do not have quite the same meaning, *sexuality* appearing to be a larger category than *sexual instinct*. It is possible that the difference in Freud's usage is related to the relation he describes above: sexuality is more general and less primitive; it is a retrospective mode of organizing and understanding certain behavior, while sexual instincts are germinal and linked to reproduction.

15. Plato, *Euthyphro, Apology, Crito, and Symposium*, trans. Benjamin Jowett (Chicago: Henry Regnery, 1967), 98–102. This is the same translation employed by Freud's translator.

16. Freud's footnote devotes an entire paragraph to discussing the probable precedence and influence of the *Brihadaranyaka-upanishad* on Plato's anecdote.

17. Jean-François Lyotard, *Libidinal Economy*, 27.

18. See for example, Slavoj Zizek, *For They Know Not What They Do*, and Jacques Derrida, "The Purveyor of Truth."

19. The *OED* lists three different meanings for narrative, the first being a formal legal term referring to the "recital of facts" part of legal documents or pleadings. This particular use, though formulaic, is linked to our notion of narrative itself as a formula requiring certain parts. All discussion of the meanings of the term *narrative* and their dates of appearance are from the *OED*.

20. See also Stephen Heath's discussion of the entire phenomenon of the rise of sexuality as a category in *The Sexual Fix*.

21. See Melissa Mowry, "(Re)Productive Histories," and Susan Stewart, *Crimes of Writing* for excellent accounts of how issues of reproduction were instrumental in shaping late seventeenth- and early eighteenth-century print culture.

22. See Sander L. Gilman, *Difference and Pathology*, for an extended discussion of representations of prostitution in the nineteenth century.

23. *The History of Sexuality*, vol. 1, 127, 123.

24. It could be said that conservative, right-wing politicians find good use for lesbians and gays, using them as the pretext for more restrictive educational and funding policies and as the evil whose very presence should vault them right back into office. Without the best evidence of homosexuality, what pretext could the Right manufacture to illustrate the patriarchal panic that underwrites conservatism?

2. Come Together

1. In *Bringing Out Roland Barthes* D. A. Miller locates narrative's heterosexuality in the accumulated weight of plotting habits. Insofar as such habits reflect ideology, or at least the degree of cultural interest or obsession in particular contents in relation to particular patterns, this might be an astute observation. To the degree that the habitual choice of certain contents is already determined by the ideological weight of the organization of meaning, Miller confuses surface accumulations (which are an effect) with cause, which drives the particular understanding of shape in the first place. In so far as that shape is ideologically appended to contents, narrative is heterosexual.

2. Thomas Leitch, *What Stories Are*, 4.

3. Gérard Genette, *Narrative Discourse*, 25.

4. David Bordwell and Kristin Thompson, *Film Art*, 55.

5. Robert Scholes and Robert Kellogg, *The Nature of Narrative*, 4.

6. Wayne Booth, *The Rhetoric of Fiction*, and even Northrup Frye, *Anatomy of Criticism*, assume and treat a more traditional literary notion of narrative. Later structuralist narrative investigations treat narrative as a larger cultural phenomenon that may be literary, mythical, or cultural.

7. Claude Lévi-Strauss, "The Structural Study of Myth," 210.

8. See Todorov's essay, "The Secret of Narrative," in *The Poetics of Prose*.

9. Algirdas J. Greimas, *On Meaning*, 64–65.

10. J.-A. Berthoud, "Narrative and Ideology," 102.

11. Barthes cites Claude Bremond's "Le message narratif," in *Communications* 4 (1964): 98, n. 2.

12. See generally *Alice Doesn't*, 125–134.

13. Freud's letter to Fliess of October 15, 1897 in *The Complete Letters*.

14. Anthony Kerby, *Narrative and the Self*, 12.

3. Coming Apart

1. *Victor/Victoria* is complicated again by the politics of identification and working of the cinematic apparatus that itself organizes image and narrative in ways that

reiterate Western ideologies of the masculine subject and emphasize mastery. See Laura Mulvey, "Visual Pleasure."

2. This is Octave Mannoni's formula for the disavowal associated with the fetish in *Clefs pour l'imaginaire*.

3. One of Q's worst nightmares was to be condemned to a single gender and body that shifted him from the position of manipulator of narrative to its gendered and very trapped victim.

4. The J'nnai look female and all look very much alike, presenting the visual spectacle of no difference. Matching this no difference, they police their species' desire through psychotechnology.

5. This is like Joan Riviere's notion of masquerade as an over-compensatory femininity in relation to an underlying masculinitity and possible homosexuality in "Womanliness as a Masquerade."

6. This assumes a Lacanian understanding of the term *phallus* as a signifier of desire, as that which cannot be realized, as the signifier of separation and law. See Jacques Lacan, "The Signification of the Phallus." All citations are from this version. Or see "The Meaning of the Phallus," in *Feminine Sexuality*, which is a different translation of the same essay. For a discussion of the difference between the phallus and the penis, see Jane Gallop, *Reading Lacan*.

7. Jacques Lacan, "Guiding Remarks," 96.

8. In *Bodies That Matter*, Judith Butler plays through Freud's and Lacan's "plastic" idealization of the phallus that functions in itself like the dynamic of desire; she says, "The phallus will thus always operate as both veil and confession, a deflection from an erotogenicity that includes and exceeds the phallus, an exposure of a desire which attests to a morphological transgression and, hence, to the instability of the imaginary boundaries of sex" (88). Butler's reading of the "lesbian phallus" returns to and questions the relation between anatomy and sexual difference as a possible way to open "up anatomy—and sexual difference itself—as a site of proliferative resignifications" (89). She sees the lesbian phallus as an alternative imaginary, one that would presumably mitigate against the heteroideological weight of narrative for example. The lesbian phallus is also different from the lesbian *as* phallus suggested here, since the lesbian as phallus is the logical conclusion of the inmixture of sexual difference and heterologic.

9. Ellie Ragland-Sullivan, *Jacques Lacan*, 287.

10. See Ragland-Sullivan's explanation of this in *Jacques Lacan*, 88. In *S/Z* Roland Barthes suggests that castration (having or not having the phallus) governs the structure of the sexes in Balzac's *Sarrasine* where castration is linked to power and activity and castration to passivity. Inscribed atop gender divisions, but not aligned with them, the question of castration appears to enable homosexualities by aligning females with the position of noncastration (lesbians), and males with castration (being instead of having—male homosexuality). But in *Sarrasine* the question of gender whose answer constitutes the "knowledge" and mastery of the narrative is answered by the revelation of a castrato who appears publicly as a "female" singer; castration is what must be revealed and its revelation explains the (perhaps)

ironic devolution of the castrato's wealth through the family who enjoys it. For this reason, castration is in a sense the operative term. See *S/Z*, 35–36.

While *Sarrasine* reveals a phallic drama of desire disappointed when its object neither is nor has the phallus, castration is often a less overt category than the phallus, whose fantasy of wholeness functions as one signifier of narrative desire, enabled by castration and lack in the first place but working to cover lack over.

11. Henri F. Ellenberger, *The Discovery of the Unconscious*, 297; and David F. Greenberg, *The Construction of Homosexuality*, 380–381.

12. Ellenberger, 299–300.

13. Ibid., 302.

14. See Freud's "Three Essays" for the developmental, familial sexual story.

15. This is the trajectory Freud traces in his last lesbian case history, "Psychogenesis of a Case of Homosexuality in a Woman."

16. Freud more often connects narcissism and male homosexuality. See "On Narcissism." In "Psychogenesis," he acknowledges the distinction between biological sex and gender.

17. See particularly "Psycho-analytic Notes;" and "A Case of Paranoia."

18. This is true even if mother isn't mother, but a surrogate womb. Mother becomes the egg donor necessitating an emphasis on mothering as a quality rather than a biological relation. Even so, the wars fought to regain custody of children given up for adoption are all battles between biology and other narratives of parenting. These have proliferated as biology has recently taken the upper hand.

4. The Second Coming

1. The reasons for contemporary cultural visibility of the lesbian are complex, linked I believe, to a gradual loss of symbolic stability. This is not to say that the lesbian is the harbinger of the unstable but that the decay of the paternal metaphor enables the coexistence of more multiples that reflect a specifically reproductive anxiety in myriad forms. This includes simulation. See my *Reproductions of Reproductions*.

2. This is true of the appearance of a transient lesbian character on *St. Elsewhere* where she appeared, positively portrayed as a doctor, to spend some time as a guest in the apartment of the token woman surgeon whose crisis over her guest's sexuality was the subject of one episode. In *L. A. Law* the lesbian (really bisexual) D. J. Lamb, depicted as a complete legal maverick from her unorthodox procedures to her accent, comes on to one of the show's main female junior lawyers, precipitating a crisis said to be the reason the junior lawyer left the show. Lamb's sojourn in MacKenzie, Brackman was also quite brief. In the 1994 fall entry sitcom *Friends*, a newly divorced main male character's ex-wife is a lesbian who, it turns out, is pregnant with his child but is having it with her lesbian lover.

3. In the introduction to their collection, *The Coming Out Stories*, Julia Penelope Stanley and Susan J. Wolfe claim that coming out stories "are the foundation of our

lives as lesbians, as real to ourselves; as such, our sharing of them defines us as participants in Lesbian culture, as members of a community" (xxi).

4. See, for example, Hall Carpenter Archives Lesbian Oral History Group, *Inventing Ourselves*; Gilbert Herdt, " 'Coming Out' as a Rite of Passage"; and Bonnie Zimmerman, "The Politics of Transliteration."

5. Vladimir Propp, *Morphology of the Folktale*.

6. The quintessentially narrative nature of this entire visibility/identity project is reflected even in the narrative that constitutes *What A Lesbian Looks Like*, where the section on coming out stories ("Becoming") comes in the middle of the book's very traditional heteronarrative shape, following "Beginnings" and "Kin" and preceding the sections that rush toward synthesis titled (in order), "Out," "Mind and Body," "Together," "Power," "Community."

7. The *Roseanne* show starring comedienne Roseanne (Barr) (Arnold) is a long-running, highly popular television sitcom whose apparent irreverence about family and parents translates into an acute valuation of the specifically American family as not too formal, nor too serious, but loving, stable, and able to get the job done. Its popularity bespeaks both its realist irreverence (what family is what it's supposed to be) and its very real valuation of the family. Its ideological value lies in its apparent critique of ideology while replacing this ideology with another, more real ideology.

8. See Bernhardt's "Not Just Another Pretty Face," *Playboy* (September 1992).

9. The 1994–95 *Roseanne* season was fixated on D. J.'s puberty, including shows on unwelcome erections and masturbation. The show's shift to the problems of male adolescence accompanies its focus on literal reproduction and financial security. This moment follows several years of financial failure and insecurity associated with the presence of adolescent daughters. The replacement of the show's girls with a bevy of boys (the pseudo-son David, D. J., and Jackie's new baby, Andrew) symbolizes a shift into prosperity.

10. Lacan's notion of the Law-of-the-Name-of-the-Father refers to the oedipal structure, to "the symbolic effect of his dividing presence" as Ellie Ragland-Sullivan describes it, "spelling prohibition, separation, difference, and individuation" (55, 279).

11. The figure of the lesbian vampire fascinates both audiences and critics. Several excellent studies of the phenomenon of lesbian vampires are available, including Bonnie Zimmerman, "Daughters of Darkness"; Andrea Weiss, *Vampires and Violets*; and Barbara Creed, *The Monstrous Feminine*. All of these analyses illustrate the cultural felicity of the combination of lesbian and vampire as satisfying stereotypes while offering some threat to patriarchy through aggressive sexuality, boundary crossing, or female empowerment.

12. When this portion of the book was presented as a paper, several members of the audience protested that the lesbian writer was in fact bisexual and that the film evinced a fear of bisexuality linked to a contagion model. While I think that the film works in that way on one level, it is the specifically lesbian identity of the murderers that links them together. If every woman who had a relation with a man was

bisexual, there would be few lesbians. In this context, bisexuality itself, especially as an insistent application of literal definitional orthodoxy, functions as a cover for lesbophobia and reveals a need to reinsert the phallus where one is feared not to exist. Those making the objection were all males.

13. See especially Bonnie Zimmerman's description of the myriad lesbian fiction production in *The Safe Sea of Women*.

14. Marilyn Frye would question my reading of any of these passages as lesbian sex, since in a move that echoes Wittig, Frye offers a definitional gambit in "Lesbian 'Sex.' " For Frye, " 'sex' is an inappropriate term for what lesbians do," as if changing the name would solve the whole problem; but Frye's challenge brings the same issue of sexual ideology to the fore (109).

15. This is as opposed to the homosexual male character whose phallus/penis overload renders him comic and generally either heterosexual parody or victim.

16. Julia Penelope Stanley and Susan J. Wolfe state that lesbian writing is by nature experimental in "Toward a Feminist Aesthetic."

17. Elaine Marks, "Lesbian Intertextuality"; Judith Butler, *Gender Trouble*; and Teresa de Lauretis, *Alice Doesn't*.

18. Paradoxically, a similar exploitation of the middle is employed by very mainstream narratives (or narratives for the mainstream such as garish 1950s novels exposing the truth of seamy lesbian life) that illustrate the lesbian's menace to society by simply emphasizing a heterosexual moral imperative via the narrative disposition of lesbian characters as mediate, confused, immature, adolescent, unfulfilled, etc.

19. Laura Doan's anthology, *The Lesbian Postmodern* plays out this parallel and sometimes confused identification between lesbian and postmodern.

20. Namascar Shaktini, "Displacing the Phallic Subject"; Marilyn Farwell, "Toward a Definition of the Lesbian Literary Imagination"; Diane Griffith Crowder, "Amazons and Mothers?" 127. Portions of my argument about Wittig appear in "Lesbians and Lyotard: Legitimation and the Politics of the Name" in *The Lesbian Postmodern*, ed. Laura Doan.

21. In "Heterosexual Plots and Lesbian Subtexts," Marilyn Farwell characterizes Wittig's work as privileging the lesbian "as the place of new alterity." "Thus," Farwell claims, "they [Wittig and Luce Irigaray] provide a basis for my development of the idea of a lesbian narrative space as a disruptive space of sameness as opposed to difference which has structured most Western narratives" (93).

22. In *The Dismemberment of Orpheus*, Hassan lists a series of traits that characterize the postmodern.

23. In "Lifting Belly Is a Language," Penelope Engelbrecht, a most fervent advocate of the lesbian *as* postmodern finally must decide that Wittig is not really completely postmodern since, as Engelbrecht observes, Wittig's "concentration on essence limits her postmodern strategy" (96).

24. This confusion is particularly the case in the work of Julia Kristeva. See "Stabat Mater."

25. Teaching this novel in a class on Women in Literature, I discovered that the vast majority of the class did not read it past the first few pages and in fact were

actively hostile to it, angry particularly about having had to purchase the book. Despite the probable homophobia associated with their dislike, the narrative (or lack thereof) angered them more, since they had already read more mainstream narratives with lesbian content and had not complained too much. The class's self-identified lesbians persevered, since *The Lesbian Body* seemed to be addressed to them, but were ambivalent about it. The book's best reader was a forty-two-year-old married male retired marine data-processing expert who not only loved the book but wrote about it eloquently. In this sense, perhaps its narrative challenge works on a limited scale.

26. Bertha Harris, "What We Mean to Say." Harris emphasizes the monstrous quality of the lesbian, suggesting even that *Jaws* is a lesbian narrative.

27. Elizabeth Meese, *(Sem)Erotics*, 55.

28. Donna Gerstenberger, "The Radical Narrative of Djuna Barnes's *Nightwood*," 130. Frann Michel, in "Displacing Castration," also argues that "*Nightwood* exploits rather than actively disrupts masculine-oriented practices of linear narrative and representation" 39. See also other analyses of how *Nightwood* breaks down gendered oppositions in Carolyn Allen, "Writing Toward *Nightwood*."

29. Characterizing the novel's method as "metaphoric displacement," Alan Singer explores the "catachrestic" nature of Dr. O'Connor's narration. "The Horse Who Knew Too Much," 73.

5. Come As You Are

1. Discussions of outing as a political practice first occurred in 1990 magazines including David Gelman, Lydia Denworth and Nadine Joseph, " 'Outing': An Assault on Sexual Privacy," *Newsweek* (April 30, 1990): 66; Lindsy Van Gelder, "Straight or Gay, Stick to the Facts," *CJR* (November/December 1990): 52–53; Jeanie Kasindorf, "Mr. Out," *New York Magazine* (May 14, 1990): 85–94; Victoria Brownworth, "Campus Queer Theory," *Outweek* (May 16, 1990); Richard Goldstein, "The Art of Outing," *The Village Voice* (May 1, 1990). For a more thoughtful treatment of the phenomenon, see Larry Gross, "The Contested Closet."

2. For an extensive discussion of this asymmetry, see Eve Sedgwick, *Epistemology of the Closet*.

3. This also participates in a market logic by which the sustained appearance of any character appears to have a cultural imprimatur, since commercial interests will not support socially "objectionable" material. Popular culture lesbian visibility first seems to challenge the system of marketers and pollsters, then, if sustained, seems a form of acceptance. The same logic also explains the reverse: lesbians do not appear often in popular culture because right-wing pressure groups make commercial interests unwilling to support them. Unfortunately the only sustained public narrative of an openly lesbian protagonist is the tennis career of Martina Navratilova whose court expertise and hence presence on the tour made her a public figure whether sponsors liked it or not. (And Avon

didn't.) In this context her open acknowledgment of lesbian sexuality was a calculated, but brave risk.

4. Zimmerman, *The Safe Sea of Women*, 7.

5. While discussing the relations between the postmodern and lesbian, some contributors to *The Lesbian Postmodern* look for or play upon fairly traditional "lesbian" identifications even as they appear to be suggesting identificatory instability or particularly subversions of commodity culture. See especially Erica Rand, "We Girls Can Do Anything"; Terry Brown, "The Butch Femme Fatale"; and Jean Walton, "Sandra Bernhard."

6. For a fuller analysis of Freud's competitive stance, see Cynthia Chase, "Desire and Identification."

7. For further commentary on the position of identification in relation to narcissism see Teresa de Lauretis, *The Practice of Love* and Diana Fuss, "Freud's Fallen Women."

8. For an account of identification's repression of the homosexual, see Judith Butler, *Bodies That Matter*.

9. The section referring to infantile oral assimilation was added in 1915.

10. See for example, Jean Walton, "Sandra Bernhard" in *The Lesbian Postmodern*.

11. Judith Butler, *Gender Trouble*, 127.

12. Shane Phelan, *Identity Politics*, 156.

13. Michel Foucault, "Nietzsche, Genealogy, History." 157–158.

14. In *The Political Unconscious*, Fredric Jameson suggests the coexistence of multiple, coexisting narrative possibilities that seem to offer a way out of the heteronarrative lock. The problem is that the coexisting narrative possibilities are rarely recognized as such, or are only recognized as that against which true narrative battles.

Achebe, Chinua. *Things Fall Apart*. Greenwich, Conn.: Fawcett, 1959.

Acker, Kathy. *Portrait of an Eye: Three Novels*. New York: Pantheon, 1992.

All of Me. Dir. Carl Reiner, with Steve Martin, Lily Tomlin, and Victoria Tennant. 1984.

Allen, Carolyn. "Writing Toward *Nightwood*: Djuna Barnes' Seduction Stories." In Mary Lynn Broe, ed., *Silence and Power: A Reevaluation of Djuna Barnes*, 54–65. Carbondale: Southern Illinois University Press, 1991.

Althusser, Louis. "Ideology and Ideological State Apparatuses (Notes Toward an Investigation)." In Ben Brewster, trans. and ed., *Lenin and Philosophy and Other Essays*, 121–173. London: NLB, 1971.

Aristotle. *Rhetoric and Poetics*, trans. Ingram Bywater. New York: The Modern Library, 1954.

Barnes, Djuna. *Nightwood*. New York: New Directions, 1937.

Barthes, Roland. "Myth Today." In Annette Lavers, trans., *Mythologies*, 109–159. New York: The Noonday Press, 1972.

——. *S/Z*, trans. Richard Miller. New York: Hill and Wang, 1974.

——. *The Pleasure of the Text*, trans. Richard Miller. New York: Hill and Wang, 1975.

——. *Image, Music, Text*, trans. and ed. Stephen Heath. New York: Hill and Wang, 1977.

——. "Introduction to the Structural Analysis of Narratives." In Stephen Heath, trans. and ed., *Image, Music, Text*, 79–124. New York: Hill and Wang, 1977.

Basic Instinct. Dir. Paul Verhoeven, with Michael Douglas and Sharon Stone. 1992.

Bataille, Georges. *Erotism: Death and Sensuality*, trans. Mary Dalwood. San Francisco: City Lights Books, 1986.

——. *Story of the Eye*, trans. Joachim Neugroschel. San Francisco: City Lights Books, 1987.

Baudrillard, Jean. *Simulations*, trans. Paul Foss, Paul Patton, and Philip Beitchman. New York: Semiotext(e), 1983.

——. "Consumer Society," trans. Jacques Mourrain. In Mark Poster, ed., *Jean Baudrillard: Selected Writings*, 29–56. Stanford: Stanford University Press, 1988.

——. "Symbolic Exchange and Death." Translated by Charles Levin. In Mark Poster, ed., *Selected Writings*, 119–148. Stanford: Stanford University Press, 1988.

Beckett, Samuel. *Endgame*. New York: Grove Press, 1958.

Benjamin, Walter. *Illuminations*, trans. Harry Zohn. New York: Schocken Books, 1969.

Bernhard, Sandra. "Not Just Another Pretty Face," *Playboy* (September 1992): 70–76.

Berthoud, J.-A. "Narrative and Ideology: A Critique of Fredric Jameson's *The Political Unconscious*." In Jeremy Hawthorn, ed., *Narrative: From Malory to Motion Pictures*, 100–115. London: Arnold, 1985.

Booth, Wayne. *The Rhetoric of Fiction*. Chicago: University of Chicago Press, 1961.

Bordwell, David and Kristin Thompson. *Film Art: An Introduction*. New York: McGraw-Hill, 1990.

Brooks, Peter. "Freud's Masterplot." In Shoshana Felman, ed., *Literature and Psychoanalysis: The Question of Reading Otherwise*, 280–300. Baltimore: Johns Hopkins University Press, 1982.

Brossard, Nicole. *Picture Theory*, trans. Barbara Godard. New York: Roof Books, 1990.

Brownworth, Victoria. "Campus Queer Theory," *Outweek* (May 16, 1990).

Butler, Judith. *Bodies That Matter*. New York and London: Routledge, 1993.

——. *Gender Trouble*. New York: Routledge, 1990.

Chase, Cynthia. "Desire and Identification in Lacan and Kristeva." In Richard Feldstein and Judith Roof, eds, *Feminism and Psychoanalysis*, 65–83. Ithaca, N.Y.: Cornell University Press, 1989.

Colette. "The Secret Woman." In Susan Cahill, ed., *Women in Fiction*, 48–41. New York: New American Library, 1975.

——. *Claudine Married*, trans. Antonia White. In *The Complete Claudine*, 365–519. New York: Farrar, Strauss and Giroux, 1981.

Creed, Barbara. *The Monstrous Feminine: Film, Feminism, Psychoanalysis*. London and New York: Routledge, 1993.

Crowder, Diane Griffith. "Amazons and Mothers? Monique Wittig, Hélène Cixous, and Theories of Women's Writing." *Contemporary Literature* 24, no. 2 (1983): 117–144.

Daughters of Darkness. Dir. Harry Kumel, with Delphine Seyrig, Daniele Ouimet, and John Karlen. 1971.

de Lauretis, Teresa. *Alice Doesn't: Feminism, Semiotics, Cinema.* Bloomington: Indiana University Press, 1984.

———. *Technologies of Gender.* Bloomington: Indiana University Press, 1987.

———. *The Practice of Love: Lesbian Sexuality and Perverse Desire.* Bloomington, Indiana University Press, 1994.

DeLillo, Don. *Running Dog.* New York: Vintage, 1989.

Derrida, Jacques. "The Purveyor of Truth." *Yale French Studies* 52 (1975): 31–113.

Doan, Laura, ed. *The Lesbian Postmodern.* New York: Columbia University Press, 1994.

Doane, Mary Ann. "Commentary: Post-Utopian Difference." In Elizabeth Weed, ed., *Coming to Terms: Feminism, Theory, Politics,* 70–78. New York: Routledge, 1989.

Dollimore, Jonathan. *Sexual Dissidence: Augustine to Wilde, Freud to Foucault.* Oxford: Clarendon Press, 1991.

Eagleton, Terry. *Literary Theory: An Introduction.* Minneapolis: University of Minnesota Press, 1983.

———. ed. *Ideology.* New York: Longman, 1994.

Ellenberger, Henri F. *The Discovery of the Unconscious: The History and Evolution of Dynamic Psychiatry.* New York: Basic Books, 1970.

Engelbrecht, Penelope. "Lifting Belly Is a Language: The Postmodern Lesbian Subject." *Feminist Studies* 16, no. 1 (Spring 1990): 85–114.

Farwell, Marilyn. "Toward a Definition of the Lesbian Literary Imagination." *Signs* 14 (1988): 100–118.

———. "Heterosexual Plots and Lesbian Subtexts: Toward a Theory of Lesbian Narrative Space." In Karla Jay and Joanne Glasgow, eds., *Lesbian Texts and Contexts: Radical Revisions,* 91–103. New York: New York University Press, 1990.

Felman, Shoshana. "Beyond Oedipus: The Specimen Story of Psychoanalysis." In Robert Con Davis, ed., *Lacan and Narration: The Psychoanalytic Difference in Narrative Theory,* 1021–1053. Baltimore: Johns Hopkins University Press, 1983.

Forrest, Katherine and Barbara Grier, eds. *The Erotic Naiad.* Naiad Press, 1992.

Foucault, Michel. "Nietzsche, Genealogy, History." In Donald F. Bouchard ed., *Language, Counter-Memory, Practice: Selected Essays and Interview* 139–164. Ithaca, N.Y.: Cornell University Press, 1977.

———. *The History of Sexuality,* vol. 1, trans. Robert Hurley. New York: Vintage, 1978.

Frank, Lisa and Paul Smith, eds. *Madonnarama: Essays on Sex and Popular Culture.* Pittsburgh: Cleis Press, 1993.

Freud, Sigmund. 1900. *The Interpretation of Dreams.* In *Standard Edition,* vols. 4 and 5.

———. 1905 "Fragment of an Analysis of a Case of Hysteria." In *Standard Edition* 7:3–122.

———. 1905. "Three Essays on the Theory of Sexuality." In *Standard Edition* 7:125–246.

———. 1907. "Obsessive Actions and Religious Practices." In *Standard Edition* 9:117–127.

———. 1911. "Psycho-analytic Notes on an Autobiographical Account of a Case of Paranoia." In *Standard Edition* 12:1–82.

———. 1914–16. "A Case of Paranoia Running Counter to the Psychoanalytic Theory of the Disease." In *Standard Edition* 14:263–272.

———. 1914–16. "On Narcissism: An Introduction." In *Standard Edition* 17:175–204.

———. 1917. *Mourning and Melancholia*. In *Standard Edition*, 14: 239–258.

———. 1920–22. "Psychogenesis of a Case of Homosexuality in a Woman." In *Standard Edition* 18: 143–170.

———. 1921. *Group Psychology*. In *Standard Edition* 18: 65–142.

———. *Beyond the Pleasure Principle*, trans. and ed. James Strachey. New York: Norton, 1961.

———. *The Complete Letters of Sigmund Freud to Wilhelm Fliess, 1887-1904*, trans. and ed. Jeffrey Masson. Cambridge: Harvard University Press, 1985.

Frye, Northrup. *Anatomy of Criticism*. Princeton: Princeton University Press, 1957.

Frye, Marilyn. "Lesbian 'Sex.' " In *Willful Virgin: Essays in Feminism*, 109–119. Freedom, Calif.: The Crossing Press, 1992.

Fuss, Diana. "Freud's Fallen Women: Identification, Desire, and 'A Case of Homosexuality in a Woman.' " In Michael Warner, ed., *Fear of a Queer Planet: Queer Politics and Social Theory*, 42–68. Minneapolis: University of Minnesota Press, 1993.

Gallop, Jane. *Reading Lacan*. Ithaca, N.Y.: Cornell University Press, 1985.

Gelman, David, Lydia Denworth, and Nadine Joseph. " 'Outing': An Assault on Sexual Privacy." *Newsweek* (April 30, 1990): 66.

Genette, Gérard. *Narrative Discourse: An Essay in Method*, trans. Jane E. Lewin. Ithaca: Cornell University Press, 1980.

Gerstenberger, Donna. "The Radical Narrative of Djuna Barnes's *Nightwood*." In Ellen Friedman and Miriam Fuchs, eds., *Breaking the Sequence: Women's Experimental Fiction*, 129–139. Princeton: Princeton University Press, 1989.

Gilman, Sander L. *Difference and Pathology: Stereotypes of Sexuality, Race, and Madness*. Ithaca, N.Y.: Cornell University Press, 1985.

Goldstein, Richard. "The Art of Outing." *The Village Voice*, May 1, 1990.

Greenberg, David F. *The Construction of Homosexuality*. Chicago: University of Chicago Press, 1988.

Greimas, Algirdas J. *On Meaning: Selected Writings in Semiotic Theory*, trans. Paul J. Perron and Frank H. Collins. Minneapolis: University of Minnesota Press, 1987.

Gross, Larry. "The Contested Closet: The Ethics and Politics of Outing." *Critical Studies in Mass Communication* 8 (1991): 352–388.

Hall Carpenter Archives Lesbian Oral History Group. *Inventing Ourselves: Lesbian Life Stories*. London: Routledge, 1989.

Halperin, David. *One Hundred Years of Homosexuality*. New York: Routledge, 1990.

Harris, Bertha. "What We Mean to Say: Notes Toward Defining the Nature of Lesbian Literature." *Heresies* 3 (Fall 1977): 5–9.

Hassan, Ihab. *The Dismemberment of Orpheus: Toward a Postmodern Literature*. New York: Oxford University Press, 1971.

Heath, Stephen. *The Sexual Fix*. New York: Schocken, 1982.

Herdt, Gilbert. " 'Coming Out' as a Rite of Passage: A Chicago Study." In Gilbert Herdt, ed., *Gay Culture in America: Essays from the Field*, 29–67. Boston: Beacon, 1991.

Irigaray, Luce. "When Our Lips Speak Together." In Catherine Porter, trans., *This Sex Which Is Not One*, 205–218. Ithaca: Cornell University Press, 1985.

Jameson, Fredric. *The Political Unconscious: Narrative as a Socially Symbolic Act*. Ithaca, N.Y.: Cornell University Press, 1981.

——. "Pleasure: A Political Issue." In *The Ideologies of Theory: Essays 1971–1986*, vol. 2. Minneapolis, University of Minnesota Press, 1989.

Kasindorf, Jeanie. "Mr. Out." *New York Magazine* (May 14, 1990): 85–94.

Kerby, Anthony. *Narrative and the Self*. Bloomington: Indiana University Press, 1991.

Kristeva, Julia. "Stabat Mater." In *Tales of Love*, trans. Léon Roudiez, 234–263. New York: Columbia University Press, 1987.

——. *In the Beginning Was Love: Psychoanalysis and Faith*, trans. Arthur Goldhammer. New York: Columbia University Press, 1987.

Lacan, Jacques. "The Signification of the Phallus." In Alan Sheridan, trans., *Ecrits: A Selection*, 281–291. New York: Norton, 1981.

——. "Guiding Remarks for a Congress on Feminine Sexuality." In Juliet Mitchell and Jacqueline Rose, eds., Jacqueline Rose, trans., *Feminine Sexuality*, 86–98. New York: Norton, 1985.

——. *The Seminar of Jacques Lacan: Book 2*, ed. Jacques-Alain Miller, trans. Sylvana Tomaselli. New York: Norton, 1991.

Lacoue-Labarthe, Philippe. *Typography: Mimesis, Philosophy, Politics*. Cambridge: Harvard University Press, 1989.

Leitch, Thomas M. *What Stories Are: Narrative Theory and Interpretation*. University Park: Pennsylvania State Press, 1986.

Lévi-Strauss, Claude. "The Structural Study of Myth." In Claire Jacobson and Brooke Grundfest Schoepf, trans., *Structural Anthropology*, 206–231. New York: Basic Books, 1963.

Lyotard, Jean-François. *Libidinal Economy*, trans. Iain Hamilton Grant. Bloomington: Indiana University Press, 1993.

——. *The Postmodern Condition: A Report on Knowledge*, trans. Geoff Bennington and Brian Massumi. Minneapolis: University of Minnesota Press, 1989.

Manhattan. 1979. Woody Allen, with Woody Allen, Diane Keaton, Mariel Hemingway, and Meryl Streep. 1979.

Mannoni, Octave. *Clefs pour l'imaginaire ou l'autre scène*. Paris: Editions du Seuil, 1969.

Marcus, Steven. "Freud and Dora: Story, History, Case History." In Charles Bernheimer and Claire Kahane, eds., *In Dora's Case: Freud—Hysteria—Feminism*, 56–91. New York: Columbia University Press, 1985.

Marks, Elaine. "Lesbian Intertextuality." In Elaine Marks and George Stambolian, eds., *Homosexualities and French Literature*, 353–377. Ithaca: Cornell University Press, 1979.

Martin, Wallace. *Recent Theories of Narrative*. Ithaca: Cornell University Press, 1986.

Maugham, W. Somerset. *The Razor's Edge*. Garden City, N.Y.: Country Life Press, 1944.

Meese, Elizabeth. *(Sem)Erotics: Theorizing Lesbian:Writing*. New York: New York University Press, 1992.

Michel, Frann. "Displacing Castration: *Nightwood, Ladies Almanack*, and Feminine Writing." *Contemporary Literature* 30, vol. 1 (1989): 33–58.

Miller, D. A. *Bringing Out Roland Barthes*. Berkeley: University of California Press, 1992.

Miller, Henry. *Tropic of Cancer*. New York: Grove Weidenfeld, 1961.

Morrison, Paul. "End Pleasure." *Gay and Lesbian Quarterly* I (1993): 53–78.

Mowry, Melissa. "(Re)Productive Histories: Epistolary Fiction and the Origins of the English Novel." Unpublished dissertation, University of Delaware, 1993.

Mulvey, Laura. "Visual Pleasure and Narrative Cinema." *Screen* 16 (1975): 6–18.

Nabokov, Vladimir. *Lolita*. New York: Vintage, 1958.

National Lesbian and Gay Survey. *What A Lesbian Looks Like: Writings by Lesbians on Their Lives and Lifestyles*. London: Routledge, 1992.

Phelan, Shane. *Identity Politics: Lesbian Feminism and the Limits of Community*. Philadelphia: Temple University Press, 1989.

Plato. *Euthyphro, Apology, Crito, and Symposium*, trans. Benjamin Jowett. Chicago: Henry Regnery, 1967.

Polan, Dana. "Brief Encounters: Mass Culture and the Evacuation of Sense." In Tania Modleski, ed., *Studies in Entertainment: Critical Approaches to Mass Culture*, 167–187. Bloomington: Indiana University Press, 1986.

Prince, Gerald. *Narratology: The Form and Functioning of Narrative*. Berlin: Mouton, 1982.

Propp, Vladimir. *Morphology of the Folktale*, 2d ed., trans. Laurence Scott. Austin: University of Texas Press, 1968.

Radicalesbians. "The Woman-Identified Woman." In Karla Jay and Allen Young, eds., *Out of the Closets: Voices of Gay Liberation*, 172–177. New York: New York University Press, 1992.

Ragland-Sullivan, Ellie. *Jacques Lacan and the Philosophy of Psychoanalysis*. Urbana: University of Illinois Press, 1986.

Riviere, Joan. "Womanliness as a Masquerade." In Victor Burgin, James Donald, and Cora Kaplan, eds., *Formations of Fantasy*, 35–44. London: Methuen, 1986.

Roof, Judith. *A Lure of Knowledge: Lesbian Sexuality and Theory*. New York: Columbia University Press, 1991.

——. *Reproductions of Reproduction: Imaging Symbolic Change*. New York: Routledge, 1996.

Schafer, Roy. "Narration in the Psychoanalytic Dialogue." In W. J. T. Mitchell, ed., *On Narrative*, 25–49. Chicago: University of Chicago Press, 1981.

Scholes, Robert. *Fabulation and Metafiction*. Urbana: University of Illinois Press, 1979.

Scholes, Robert and Robert Kellogg. *The Nature of Narrative.* New York: Oxford University Press, 1966.

Sedgwick, Eve Kosofsky. *Epistemology of the Closet.* Berkeley: University of California Press, 1990.

Shaktini, Namascar. "Displacing the Phallic Subject: Wittig's Lesbian Writing." *Signs* 8, no. 1 (Autumn 1982): 29–44.

Singer, Alan. "The Horse Who Knew Too Much: Metaphor and the Narrative of Discontinuity in *Nightwood.*" *Contemporary Literature* 25, no. 1 (1984): 66–87.

Sobule, Jill. "I Kissed a Girl." Dir. Morgan Lawley. Lava Records/The Atlantic Group, 1995.

Sophocles. *Oedipus Tyrannus*, trans. Luci Berkowitz and Theodore F. Brunner. New York: Norton, 1970.

Stanley, Julia Penelope and Susan Wolfe. "Toward a Feminist Aesthetic." *Chrysalis: A Magazine of Women's Culture* 6 (1978): 57–71.

—, eds. *The Coming Out Stories.* Watertown, Mass.: Persephone Press, 1980.

Stewart, Susan. *Crimes of Writing: Problems in the Containment of Representation.* New York: Oxford University Press, 1991.

Switch. Dir. Blake Edwards, with Ellen Barkin, Jimmy Smits, and Jo Beth Williams. 1991.

The Hunger. Dir. Tony Scott, with Catherine Deneuve, David Bowie, and Susan Sarandon. 1983.

Todorov, Tsvetan. *The Poetics of Prose*, trans. Richard Howard. Ithaca, N.Y.: Cornell University Press, 1977.

Van Gelder, Lindsy. "Straight or Gay, Stick to the Facts." *CJR* (November/December 1990): 52–53.

Victor/Victoria. Dir. Blake Edwards, with Julie Andrews, James Garner, Robert Preston, Alex Karras, and Mary Ann Mobley. 1982.

Walton, Jean. "Sandra Bernhard: Lesbian Postmodern or Modern Postlesbian?" In Laura Doan, ed. *The Lesbian Postmodern*, 244–261.

Warner, Michael. "Homo-Narcissism; or, Heterosexuality." In Joseph Boone and Michael Cadden, eds., *Engendering Men*, 190–206. New York: Routledge, 1990.

Weiss, Andrea. *Vampires and Violets.* New York: Penguin, 1992.

Wellek, René and Austin Warren. *Theory of Literature.* New rev. ed. New York: Harcourt, Brace, Jovanovich, 1977.

White, Hayden. "The Value of Narrativity in the Representation of Reality." In W. J. T. Mitchell, ed., *On Narrative*, 1–23. Chicago: Chicago University Press, 1981.

Wings, Mary. *She Came Too Late.* London: The Women's Press, 1986.

Wittig, Monique. *The Lesbian Body*, trans. David Le Vay. New York: Avon, 1975.

——. "The Straight Mind." *Feminist Issues* 1, no. 1 (1980): 103–111.

Yeats, W. B. "The Second Coming." In Warren Taylor and Donald Hall, eds., *Poetry in English*, 503. New York: Macmillan, 1963.

Zimmerman, Bonnie. "Daughters of Darkness: the Lesbian Vampires on Film." In Barry Keith Grant, ed., *Planks of Reason: Essays on the Horror Film*, 153–163. Metuchen, N.J.: Scarecrow, 1984.

――. "The Politics of Transliteration: Lesbian Personal Narratives." *Signs* 9, no. 4 (1984): 663–682.

――. *The Safe Sea of Women: Lesbian Fiction 1969–1989.* Boston: Beacon, 1990.

Žižek, Slavoj. *For They Know Not What They Do: Enjoyment as a Political Factor.* London: Verso, 1991.

Zola, Emile. *Nana*, trans. George Holden. New York: Viking Penguin, 1985.

INDEX